PROBLEMS OF PEACE

THIRD SERIES

PROBLEMS OF PEACE
THIRD SERIES

LECTURES DELIVERED AT
THE GENEVA INSTITUTE OF
INTERNATIONAL RELATIONS
August 1928

Essay Index Reprint Series

BOOKS FOR LIBRARIES PRESS
FREEPORT, NEW YORK

Third Series First Published 1929
Reprinted 1968

LIBRARY OF CONGRESS CATALOG CARD NUMBER:
68-57317

INTRODUCTION

THE present volume is the third of the series, *Problems of Peace*. It contains the lectures delivered at the fifth meeting of the Geneva Institute of International Relations.

The Institute came into being as the result of an attempt to co-ordinate the organization of certain British and American summer schools held in Geneva for the purpose of securing first-hand information about the League and the International Labour Organization.

In the beginning the purpose of these summer schools was simply to learn by direct observation and by contact with the permanent officials the structure and actual working of the new international organizations. But as the League became better known it became necessary to make some special provision for those who were already familiar with the general facts concerning it and whose need was an opportunity for a more critical examination of its problems. The Institute, organized in co-operation with the British League of Nations Union and with the League of Nations Non-Partisan Association of the United States, was accordingly created, and its programme was gradually widened to include not only the discussion of questions directly affecting the League but all aspects of international affairs which might influence the League or be influenced by it. The Institute now provides, therefore, a meeting-ground for officials of the League, who have a unique experience of its working from the inside, and recognized authorities on international questions who can bring a contribution of comment and criticism from the outside. The attendance at the meetings of the Institute has been maintained at an average of two hundred and fifty, which in itself is a sufficient proof that it meets a real need.

After two experimental meetings it was thought that the proceedings of the Institute might usefully be made available for students of international affairs who might be unable to attend at Geneva and the publication of *Problems of Peace* was begun in 1927 and has been continued since.

The previous volumes have been received with almost universally favourable comment. Only one criticism seems to call for a word of explanation. The complaint was made that while most of the lectures were excellent, and their authors of undeniable authority, there were too many of them, and not enough of any one. Such a criticism is almost a compliment, and might indeed be taken as such did it not suggest an entire misconception of the purpose of the volume. The volume is a collection of lectures: each deals with a different subject: each is by a different author. There may be lacunae, there may be overlapping, and there may be views expressed by one author which are in contradiction with those expressed by another. The volume is admittedly and of necessity a patchwork. It is hardly fair to complain that it is not one single piece of material. And if it were it would not be a substitute for what it is, still less an improved substitute. It is eminently desirable that, say, Sir Arthur Salter, or Professor Zimmern should write a complete text-book on international problems, and it is to be hoped that some day they will. But it is not to be anticipated that they could rewrite their text-books every year. *Problems of Peace* does not pretend to be or to replace a text-book. But it does do what a text-book cannot. It provides a kind of running commentary year by year. It is a kind of annual *mise au point*, not from one point of view but from many, and as such it may claim to be a useful adjunct to the numerous text-books which it completes but with which it does not aspire to compete.

The present volume follows in general the scheme of its predecessors and calls for little special comment. The appendix containing a summary of certain of the discussions has been omitted. Interesting as the points raised in discussion frequently were, it was felt that the treatment which could be afforded them was necessarily inadequate, and that it was better to allow the lecturer to incorporate them in the manuscript submitted for publication if he considered it desirable to do so, or to note them for fuller treatment in the programme of a subsequent session. A fuller table of contents has been given so as to enable readers to gather beforehand the general lines on which each author has treated his subject and to facilitate subsequent reference.

*   *   *

The Institute wishes to tender its thanks to the Under-Secretary-General of the League, Herr Dufour Feronce, and to the Director of the International Labour Office, Mr. Albert Thomas, who welcomed its members to the Secretariat of the League and the International Labour Office respectively, to the speakers, and to Dr. Delisle Burns, Dr. Sherwood Eddy, Mr. Halcombe, Mr. Duncan Hall, Professor Manley Hudson, Professor Hull, Mr. Huston, Mr. Whelan, and Mr. Zilliacus, who presided over its different sittings with knowledge and distinction.

*   *   *

Only a few weeks before the opening of its meeting the Institute suffered a severe loss by the sudden and untimely death of Mr. Sherman.

Mr. Sherman was Secretary of the Educational Committee of the League of Nations Union and was one of the most active organizers of the earlier meetings of the Institute.

Several of the speakers who had been associated with him in that work, in the course of their addresses spoke in terms of high appreciation of the zeal and energy he displayed in promoting the cause of international understanding. His contribution to that effort will long be remembered by those with whom he collaborated in the Institute, and they wish to take this opportunity of paying a tribute to his memory and of expressing their sincere sympathy with his relatives.

THE EDITOR.

Particulars of the Meeting of the Geneva Institute of International Relations for 1929 can be obtained from—

The Secretary, League of Nations Union, 15 Grosvenor Crescent, London, S.W. 1.

The Secretary, League of Nations Non-Partisan Association, 6 East 39th Street, New York.

The Secretary, American Committee, International Club, Geneva.

CONTENTS

Contents

SECTION III
SOME SPECIAL PROBLEMS

Contents

SECTION IV

THE GENERAL PROBLEM

APPENDIX

SECTION I

THE PROBLEM OF THE FUTURE

CHAPTER I

THE FUTURE OF THE LEAGUE OF NATIONS

Professor W. E. RAPPARD:

THE League of Nations has a very short past, but, we hope and believe, a very long future. It is in fact a problem of the future.

In the course of its short past, it has already accomplished many useful things, or, to speak more accurately, it has been instrumental in the accomplishment of many useful things. But, born of the great war, it was intended primarily to spare humanity the repetition of that tragic catastrophe. This end it has not yet attained. It is safe to assume that, League or no League, the world would not, by 1929, have witnessed a renewal of the horrors of 1914–18. Therefore we are justified in declaring that the future of the League of Nations is its real problem. It has yet to stand its supreme test, and no one can assert with certainty when, how, or whether it will stand that test.

It is with the League as an object of scientific inquiry that we are, as students, here concerned. But can the future of the League be considered scientifically? No and Yes.

No. The past alone is knowable, the past and those necessary relations between logical concepts which we deem to be beyond the categories of time and space and which may or may not be independent of the human mind. The future of the League is neither the past nor a logical relationship. It is therefore, as the future itself, unknown and scientifically unknowable.

We hold, however, that it is none the less worthy of our attention and that it is even susceptible of being considered scientifically, if by that we mean considered without bias or prejudice, without fear or favour, without extolling or condemning, but with the sole purpose of discovering the probable truth. Certainty is of course out of the question. Astronomers, as most other natural scientists, are in the fortunate position of dealing with relatively simple phenomena. They can confidently outline the future merely by prolonging beyond the present the curves of the evolution of the past. Such a course is doubtless also open to those who are engaged in the social sciences. It is by the same methods, for instance, that statisticians estimate the probable birth and death rates of the future. As the phenomena they are considering are, however, much more complex, their confidence in their estimates is correspondingly weaker or at least far less justified.

Now, of all social facts, few are more complex than those dealt with in the new science of international relations. Even if we admit, as we must for the purposes not of our action but of our present inquiry, that a stern determinism presides over the evolution of international affairs, our forecasts concerning them will be highly conjectural. The only basis on which we can found any forecasts at all is our knowledge of the past and present and our understanding of human nature. And that knowledge and that understanding are themselves so imperfect and so fragmentary, that the superstructure of our prophecies must necessarily be but frail and tentative. Only the absolutely ignorant can speak with absolute assurance of the future of such an institution as the

League of Nations. This does not imply, of course, that to speak of it with caution as we shall feel bound to do, is to prove one's knowledge of its past and present. It is merely an indication of one's consciousness of the intricacies and uncertainties of the problem.

The League of Nations, as it was originally intended to be by its principal founders and as it has tended to become in the first years of its existence, we have sought to outline elsewhere.[1] Our present task is to prolong into the future the lines of previous development. But this is by no means a simple mechanical operation. The lines of previous development, as they appear to the careful student, are neither straight lines nor even simple curves. Moreover, it is obvious that in certain cases this previous development has run its full course and that the future cannot therefore be a mere continuation of the past.

After these brief preliminary observations, intended to show the difficulties of our task and the method we shall adopt in striving to overcome them, let us now embark on our very hazardous journey towards our most uncertain goal.

We shall consider the probable future, first of the structure, then of the functions of the League.

i. *Membership.*

As has been repeatedly stated before, but as is still too little recognized, the most important element in the League's structure is the material used by its architects, that is the

---

[1] See my articles on 'The League of Nations as an Historical Fact' and on 'The Evolution of the League of Nations' in *Problems of Peace*, 1st and 2nd series, London, 1927 and 1928.

States which compose it. The stuff of which the League is made is its membership.

When the first Assembly met in Geneva, in November 1920, 42 States belonged to it as original members. To-day, 14 new members having been admitted and 2 having withdrawn, the total membership is 54.

Of the 42 original members, 16, that is 38·1 per cent., were European States and 29, that is 69 per cent., were victors in the world war. Of the 54 present members, 27, that is exactly half, are European States, and 28, that is 51·9 per cent., were victors of the war.

The three main tendencies which can thus be clearly recognized in the evolution of the membership of the League are: first, its general, very appreciable increase in size; second, its Europeanization; and third, what we may call, for lack of a simpler term, its debellicization, that is, the disappearance of distinctions due to the war.

Are these tendencies likely to persist in the future?

That the membership of the League will further increase is not only our ardent hope, but also a reasonable expectation. This is not the place to explain fully why it is our ardent hope. Suffice it to say that, so long as the League is not practically universal, so long especially as it is deprived of the co-operation of the United States of America and of Russia, it cannot be expected satisfactorily to accomplish its main purpose of effectively maintaining the peace of the world. Not only could it not prevent war beyond its own boundaries, but it is to be feared that, in a crisis, it would not command the complete loyalty of its members. Would they not be very reluctant to co-operate in the measure provided for in Article 16 of the Covenant against an aggressor, as long as they might thereby be brought into conflict with some powerful non-member State, insistent on its trading rights as a neutral? This fear, which the coming into force of the Kellogg Pact will doubtless do much to allay, has hitherto paralysed the League in the elaboration of its machinery for the prevention of war and in the application of its disarmament programme.

Whatever our hopes and fears on this vital matter, the universalization of the League is a process which, I believe, may reasonably be expected to continue. The social and moral forces which created an organization for international co-operation and peace are steadily at work on the whole surface of the globe. From year to year they are bringing the nations into closer economic interdependence and making them more conscious of their real solidarity. Nothing could show this more clearly than the position of the great powers which still hold aloof from the League and their changing attitude towards it.

Russia, partially isolated from the rest of the world, is vainly struggling against misery, starvation, and internal dissension. After reviling and ridiculing the League in the most caustic terms, it has gradually come to accept invitations to Geneva and to offer and even to solicit co-operation in very clear language.

At the other extreme of the economic ladder, the United States is developing its foreign trade by leaps and bounds, a development largely financed by its own foreign loans and sedulously fostered by its own Government. In spite, or rather on account of, the exceptional wealth of its natural resources and the technical ingenuity of its people, it is becoming more and more closely linked up with the rest of the world. It is accordingly co-operating with the League with increasing interest and continuity. The very administration which, for reasons which we have not to consider here, was and still is most opposed to signing the Covenant, and most eager to avoid foreign commitments and entanglements, has done more perhaps than any of its predecessors to make of the United States a world power, that is a power in and with the rest of the world. Is it surprising therefore that proposals for disarmament and for the outlawing of war should come so persistently from Washington? And would it not be surprising if the general trend of events did not sooner or later bring about a complete reconciliation between that capital and Geneva? That strikes me as being so much in the line of natural and almost necessary evolution, that it takes more historical imagination than I possess to conceive of a League of Nations, say fifty years hence, of which the United States should not be a full-fledged member.

That is, I submit, a rational and not a sentimental view of the future. Sentiment may impede or precipitate a natural process. So far it has retarded rather than hastened it in the United States. But reason and enlightened self-interest are bound, in the end, to prevail. That is why we expect the gradual universalization of the League as confidently as we hope for it eagerly.

In the second place, we have noted what we have called a Europeanization of the League in the course of the last nine years. This tendency can no longer exist for the simple reason that all the European States with the exception of Russia and Turkey—and are they truly exceptions?—have already acceded to the Covenant.

The League idea took root first and deepest in the soil of Europe, that is of the continent which has the greatest density both of population and of so-called independent sovereign States. It is here that the need for an international co-ordinating agency is greatest. But the density of population is everywhere increasing and the density of States, that is, their number on a given area, seems likely to increase also rather than to diminish, if we interpret correctly the course of events in China, Russia, and in colonial regions.

We therefore look forward to a demographic and political structure of the non-European world which, again say fifty years hence, will more closely resemble the Europe of 1928 than it does to-day. That is why we expect the League idea to spread from the continent, where the need for international co-operation was most pressing and where it first became effective, to those where similar conditions will gradually arise.

As for the third tendency noted in the past evolution of the membership of the League which we have termed its debellicization, it has likewise run its natural course. The League was founded by the victors of the great war, but, for reasons which seem strange only at first sight, it has on the whole had more attractions for the neutral and for the defeated nations than for its founders.

At Paris in 1919, it was decided that with six of their victorious allies, the United States, and Brazil should govern the League of Nations, which thirteen neutral States were invited to join, but from which Germany, Austria, Hungary, and Bulgaria were to be, at least temporarily, excluded. To-day, while all the neutrals and those excluded have joined, the United States have remained aloof and Brazil has seceded.

As all law, the Covenant of the League of Nations may seem superfluous and sometimes even objectionable to the strong, who may be tempted to disregard the rights of the weak. But, as all law also, the Covenant is a very useful safeguard for the weak, who have no other effective protection against the encroachments of the strong. That is why the third tendency we have noted in the past evolution of the League's membership is less strange than it might seem at first glance. But as it has reached its natural end, there is no more to be said about it here. It is true that, outside the limits of the Ottoman Empire, Turkey was commonly counted among the defeated Powers in 1918, but as that certainly is no longer the case to-day there are no more any vanquished former foes to admit into the League. The roles will therefore have to be reversed in the future.

ii. *The Council.*

After the membership of the League, the most important, or at least the most conspicuous feature of its structure is the Council.

As Lord Robert Cecil originally conceived the Council, it was to be a body consisting of the representatives of the five principal allied and associated Powers, while delegates from other States were to be invited to attend its sessions when some matter of special importance to them was to be considered. From this original conception, the Council of the League as it exists to-day, after all the debates to which its structure has given rise in Paris and Geneva, differs in the following respects:

1. It has fourteen members instead of five.

2. A representative of Germany has taken the place of the absent American, as one of the five permanent members.

3. Of the fourteen members, nine are elected by the Assembly as representatives of other than great Powers.

4. There are three categories of members instead of only one, or, to be quite accurate, four instead of two. Besides the five permanent and the occasional, there are nine elected

members, of whom three may be and six may not be re-elected after every term of service.

The Cecilian Council, like the Supreme Council of the League Conference, was to be a small homogeneous body. The present Council is a large, heterogeneous committee of members who differ very considerably from one another in respect both of the political importance of the States they represent and of the tenure of their office.

Is it to be expected that this double process of expansion and differentiation will continue? The question is one of great and perhaps of increasing importance for the efficiency and possibly even for the very life of the League. In attempting to answer it, every one will naturally consult his hopes and fears, as it would be as unreasonable to expect the League indefinitely to pursue a course contradictory to its true interests as to expect it to abandon a course deemed wise and profitable.

Personally, I look upon the evolution of the last years in this respect with grave misgivings and I am therefore led to anticipate a reversal of policy. But I fully recognize both the force and the permanent character of the factors which have shaped that evolution.

The Council was never, except perhaps in 1919, enlarged because a larger Council was in itself held to be superior to a smaller one. During the discussions at the Peace Conference, where the unrepresented Powers demanded and obtained first two and then four seats, in 1922, when two further seats were created for them, as well as in 1926, when they were granted nine seats in all, their victories, especially the latter ones, were due to the fear of the possible consequences of a refusal much more than to the recognition of the inherent justice of their cause. To refuse the proposed enlargement of the Council was in every case to bring about a crisis by provoking immediate resignations or at least threats of resignations. To accept it in spite of its obvious disadvantages was, if not to avoid the crisis, at least to defer it and perhaps to extenuate its evil consequences.

That the Council is to-day larger than is good for its own efficiency and prestige, larger than is good for the dignity of the smaller States represented on it by practically excluding them from its inner deliberations, larger than is good for the authority of the Assembly, and larger than is good for the harmonious working of the League machine as a whole is a fact which many, if not most, careful students of international affairs will admit. That a still further enlargement would be wellnigh disastrous, strikes me as very probable, but with the present structure of the Council it is difficult to see how a further enlargement of at least its semi-permanent membership is to be avoided.

Three semi-permanent seats were instituted to satisfy Poland, Spain, and Brazil. Poland accepted the offer because she realized that she could not fairly aspire to more and because she could not convincingly threaten to leave the League unless offered more. Spain and Brazil seceded from the League because they were not content with the concession and because their Governments thought that they could get on without the League. Spain, happily but illogically, withdrew her resignation; Brazil, unfortunately but more consistently, has maintained hers.

In the coming Assembly, Spain will doubtless be elected to one of the two vacant non-permanent seats on the Council. Can Argentine be content with less than what Brazil deemed insufficient for her dignity? Can China, if the Nationalist Government consolidates its position? Could

Turkey, if she decided to join the League? To say nothing of the United States and of Russia, which would of course demand and obtain permanent seats.

Now, if the present Council remained unaltered and if, as we hope and trust, all the above-mentioned States remain in the League, re-enter, or enter it, there would be thirteen candidates for permanent and semi-permanent seats and only eight such seats available. If the number of permanent seats were increased by two to make room for the United States and Russia and if the number of semi-permanent seats were increased from three to six in order to placate Poland, Spain, Brazil, Argentine, China, and Turkey, the Council would have nineteen instead of the present fourteen ordinary members. Would that not be an almost impossible state of affairs?

Not only would such a Council in itself be a most unwieldy body in which the great Powers would still more than to-day constitute a closed inner circle, but the very existence of such a body, in which a third of the League would be represented, would tend to dwarf the Assembly and to arouse the most justified discontent among the remaining two-thirds.

In view of these facts and tendencies, is it possible to view the future of the Council without concern? A complete reorganization will doubtless prove inevitable. What that reorganization will be, no one can foresee. The safest or the least dangerous change would seem to lie in the abolition of the institution of the non-elective seats, which has been at the root of most of the past difficulties. An elected Council of fourteen members, of which half, that is, a number corresponding to that of the traditional great Powers, would be continuously re-eligible, might prove the least unsatisfactory of all possible solutions.

Another conceivable way out of the present situation would be to allow the past evolution to continue its course and then to legalize the existence of the above-mentioned inner circle. When in time the Council would have reached the total membership of nineteen, a new body on which the seven great Powers would alone be represented would be set up as an executive committee. The importance of the present Council would then of course be very much diminished, but its existence might still be necessary to satisfy the ambition of such States as those which, while not being great Powers, are apparently not content to be classed with the small ones.

But these super-hypotheses, built upon other hypotheses, all of which concern the future and none of which are therefore certain, are of course mere speculation. The only certain fact is that some change will be necessary if the League is not to founder on the rock of this structural difficulty.

This difficulty itself arises from the fundamental discrepancy between the fiction of the legal equality and the reality of the effective inequality of States. As long as States cling to the right of full sovereignty, they will naturally all claim full equality. But the principle of complete equality applied in a League of most unequal members must necessarily paralyse it. The difficulty is therefore real and deep-rooted. But that it is not insuperable is shown by the analogy of political democracy.

Political democracy also is confronted with the similar problem of reconciling the principle of the equal rights of man with the fundamental inequality of men and the necessity of leadership. The solution has been found in the practice of universal suffrage and of elections. Universal suffrage is the tribute paid to the principle of human equality, while elections are the methods of choosing the necessary leaders and therefore the recognition of the fact of inequality. Is it not probable that international society will follow in its evolution the same paths as those which have led advanced civil society to the solution of democracy?

This solution has so far been adopted only in part in the League of Nations, although it is doubtless favoured by most of its members. Some of the great Powers are insistent on their right of permanent non-elective representation on the Council, and the League can of course not spare the great Powers. If and when, however, the League, having become universal, will have lost its fear of secessions, the main obstacle in the way of a purely elected Council will have been removed.

As we have observed elsewhere and as the following table will confirm, the Council has more and more tended to become a periodic conference of the foreign ministers of the European States represented thereon.

Year.	Number of Council sessions.	Number of States represented.	Number of prime and foreign ministers among Council members.	Proportion of prime and foreign ministers to number of Council members.
1920	11	8	5	5·7 per cent.
1921	4	8	0	0·0 ,,
1922	7	8	0	0·0 ,,
1923	5	10	1	2·0 ,,
1924	5	10	7	14·0 ,,
1925	5	10	16	32·0 ,,
1926	6	10 and 14	27	39·6 ,,
1927	5	14	35	50·0 ,,
1928	2	14	12	42·9 ,,

We believe that this very happy tendency will continue in future. If the stabilization of world conditions permit and if, in order to assure the regular attendance of foreign ministers at the Council meetings, it should be found necessary to reduce the number of sessions as is proposed, such a reduction from four to three, although unwelcome in itself, would doubtless be the lesser of two evils. But, unless there really should be no important business on hand at a Council meeting, which has as yet never been the case, it is difficult to imagine what more vital duty there could be for a foreign minister than to spend a few days every three months in Geneva in personal consultation with his principal colleagues from other countries.

iii. *The Assembly.*

The Council has, on the whole, since the beginning of its existence followed a regular line of development. It already has its traditions. The same is not true to a like extent of the Assembly.

The Assembly, in its annual sessions, has had its ups and downs irregularly since 1920. It has been dramatic or uneventful, well or indifferently attended, constructive and energetic or timid, according to external circumstances more than to any regular tendency. It is therefore particularly difficult to forecast its future.

As the League grows in membership and in real influence, it is to be expected that its annual conferences will also grow in importance and will more and more attract the leading statesmen of the world. There are already some indications of this latter tendency, as the table on page 15 shows:

Whether the lack of effective leadership which has characterized the last three Assemblies more than those preceding, will persist or not, remains to be seen. It depends among other things on that most imprevisible element in human affairs: personalities. But it depends also on the character which the Assembly will ultimately adopt.

Year.	Number of States represented.	Number of prime and foreign ministers among delegates.	Proportion of prime or foreign ministers to number of delegations.
1920	47	6	12·8 per cent.
1921	52	8	15·4 ,,
1922	51	9	17·6 ,,
1923	50	6	12·0 ,,
1924	51	22	43·1 ,,
1925	50	17	34·0 ,,
1926 (extr. Ass.)	47	16	34·0 ,,
1926	50	18	36·0 ,,
1927	49	22	44·9 ,,

So far, it has seemed to hesitate between two possibilities. Is it to be merely a periodic conference of diplomatic plenipotentiaries, as it has perhaps rather tended to become, or is it gradually to develop into an international parliament, as would seem, in the long run, to be more probable?

In the first case, for obvious reasons, leadership could hardly be expected to assert itself. In the second, if all goes well with the League and if the consciousness of international solidarity increases in coming years, one could anticipate the gradual emergence of something like political parties in the Assembly. Such groups, based heretofore on purely national or regional considerations, might little by little come to pivot more on those economic interests and social ideals which are at the base of all national politics.

That such an evolution will eventually take place seems highly probable, but when it will set in and how rapid it will be, no one can say.

The character of the Assembly will always be a function of the League itself. As long as the League remains a very loose confederation of fully sovereign and independent States, the Assembly will remain a diet of plenipotentiaries strictly bound by official instructions. Only if and when the League becomes something more and the interdependence of its members takes precedence over their independence will the Assembly become more parliamentary in its spirit and more mindful of and responsive to the public opinion of the world.

iv. *The Secretariat.*

The most novel and distinctive organ of the League is its permanent international Secretariat. Every time that, since the Middle Ages, the great Powers of the day met in concert, they constituted something analogous to the Council and every time that, in the course of the last century, a large number of States were summoned to attend a diplomatic conference, they formed something akin to the Assembly. But, prior to the birth of the League of Nations, there was nowhere to be found a general and common administrative body, such as has always and everywhere proved necessary whenever and wherever independent States joined to found a confederation.

The Secretariat of the League, as an international administrative body, could conceivably adopt either of two forms. It could be made up of officials paid out of a common treasury and released from all bonds of loyalty to their respective Governments. Or it could be constituted by national delegations salaried and instructed by their respective Governments to co-operate towards common ends.

The present Secretariat of the League is, or rather has come to be in the course of the last years, of a somewhat hybrid nature. Its members are appointed and instructed by the Secretary-General, himself selected by the Peace Conference to be purely an official of the League, and their choice is subject to the ratification of the Council as a whole. They receive their very adequate remuneration out of the treasury of the League and they are not, except possibly in a few individual cases, in any way subsidized by their respective Governments. They are, in fact, formally debarred from accepting any 'special marks of distinction or favour, either from their own or any other country', to quote from a report adopted by the Council on 19 May 1920 which has never been altered or revoked. In all these respects, the Secretariat is a body which owes its sole allegiance to the international institution as a whole. It can therefore fairly be said that the Council, in laying its foundations, intended to adopt the first of the two conceptions defined above.

As a matter of fact, however, various unmistakable symptoms show that a gradual evolution is tending towards the realization of the second conception. The Governments of various States, members of the League, are taking an increasing interest in the selection as League officials of their own nationals. Not only do they tend to insist on being represented by them in an adequate proportion of numbers and rank, but also they tend to favour the selection of individuals chosen from the lists of their own diplomatic services. Rumours have been abroad of high officials informed of their appointments to Geneva by their own Governments and ordered by them to the League from the diplomatic post they were holding as to another. Rumours have been abroad also of diplomatic titles and indemnities retained by or even conferred upon League officials during their period of service at Geneva. But even if we disregard such well-accredited rumours, a close examination of the personal composition of the Secretariat will readily reveal its increasingly national and diplomatic character. That, under these circumstances, it should not also tend to become increasingly national in its methods and in its spirit would indeed be surprising.

We are not here concerned with the justification or condemnation of this evolution, which has been recently discussed notably in the British and in the Italian press, but with its explanation and probable future. It is primarily due, as we noted last year, to the increasing importance which the League in general and which the Secretariat in particular has been gaining in the estimation of the States, its members, and of their Governments, its real masters. It is also due to the fact that the League has come to be looked upon generally more as a useful instrument of peaceful co-operation than as an impartial and therefore authoritative and successful arbitrator in international disputes.

If this is a sound explanation of the past, what may we conclude from it in view of the future?

That the League will continue to grow in the estimation of national Governments and that, for this reason, they will become more and more interested in the personal and professional composition of the Secretariat would seem highly probable. But that the co-operative and technical functions of the League will increasingly tend to overshadow its action as a mediator and as a judge of conflicts is at least doubtful. Should the League become stronger by becoming more universal in its membership and by succeeding in more closely integrating its component parts, its action in the latter capacity would doubtless become more important and more effective. The need for a more impartial and less national Secretariat would then very probably also be more generally felt and the pressure of particular Governments in the matter of appointments might be expected, if not to relax, at least to be more successfully resisted by the Secretary-General as representing the interests of the whole.

When examining presently the functions of the League, we shall be led to anticipate such an evolution, but only for a more or less distant future. Our conclusions as regards the probable development of the Secretariat are therefore: first, that the tendency away from its original purely international conception will probably continue for a time, but that, second, as the League grows stronger *vis-à-vis* its constituent States, there will eventually be a return to this bolder and more fruitful conception.

In the League as in all other political organisms, nothing is less wholesome than a recognized discrepancy between the law and the facts, because nothing is more demoralizing than the hypocrisy and lack of straightforwardness to which such a discrepancy inevitably leads. If therefore, as concerns the Secretariat, the facts of 1928 cannot be made to conform to the law of 1920, we should prefer a restatement of the law to a continued violation of its spirit.

v. *The Technical Organizations.*

The multiplication and diversification of the consultative technical commissions of the League constitute perhaps the most striking and least expected phase of its past evolution. As instruments for the transaction of international affairs or rather for the preparation of such transaction they have proved both convenient and extremely effective. Most of these commissions have been set up by the Council at the suggestion of the Assembly for the study of problems of generally appreciated, international interest. As such problems are bound to arise with every further step in the closer development of international relations, one may expect the total amount of work of the consultative bodies to continue to increase. Moreover, as the co-operation in technical matters of States not yet full-fledged members of the League will probably also increase until they decide to join, the autonomy of technical organizations within or beside the League will probably be more and more generally admitted.

The probable further multiplication of the advisory commissions does not mean that all of those which have heretofore justified their existence by useful results, nor especially that those which have failed to produce such results, will or should necessarily continue to exist. Some tasks, such as several of those arising out of the unsettled state of post-war Europe, have been or will soon be accomplished. There is a natural tendency of organs to outlive the functions they were created to exercise, as there is also in some quarters a disposition to suggest imaginary functions which might justify the creation of new organs. Both this tendency and this disposition should, I believe, be firmly resisted in the true interests of the League, as nothing lends more force to the always latent opposition against all its activities, which prevails among certain influential national bureaucrats, than the feeling that countless commissions and sub-committees were being maintained or established for their own sake. The number of new important tasks continually arising will, I believe, prove quite sufficient to assure the normal development of the consultative organs of the League, which an excessive zeal on the part of their friends might impede more than favour.

All that has been said concerning the technical organizations of the League would seem to apply also to the International Labour Organization, which is but the greatest and most independent one among them.

The discussion concerning the probable and desirable future of the autonomous organizations of the League has in the course of the last year become particularly acute on the occasion of Brazil's seceding from the League, while wishing to remain a member of the Labour Organization. The legal question involved turns on the interpretation of Article 387, § 2, of the Treaty of Versailles, which reads as follows:

'The original members of the League of Nations shall be the original members of this Organization, and hereafter membership of the League of Nations shall carry with it membership of the said Organization.'

Inasmuch as Germany was invited to become a member of the Labour Organization before she joined the League, it was argued that Brazil could remain a member of that Organization after leaving the League. The analogy of the two cases has been disputed in view of the wording of the clause above-quoted. As a legal issue it strikes me as quite debatable.

It is perhaps less debatable when judged from the political point of view. Those favourable to the position adopted by Brazil argue that, from the point of view of international co-operation and peace, such a quasi-membership as that which she has retained, is better than none. They add further that Brazil, as Germany before her, may be pointing the way to a closer co-operation with the League, for the benefit of other non-member States. On the other hand, the fear has been expressed that, by tolerating Brazil's present position, one may endanger the complete loyalty of other members of the League, who might be tempted to secede as Brazil has done, if they were not retained by the fear of being forced out of the Labour Organization.

Although the question is not a simple one, it would on the whole seem probable that nothing will be undertaken to

question the legitimacy of Brazil's present position and undesirable that anything should be. Doubtless that position
is in itself much less satisfactory than that of a State completely loyal to the League. But the danger of anything re-
sembling an attempt to oust Brazil from the Labour Organization would seem much greater than that which her example
may constitute for any of the present members of the League.
And the advantages of allowing for gradual co-operation with
and accession to the League would seem decisively to out-
weigh the perils involved.

vi. *The Court.*

Of the past and future evolution of the Permanent Court
of International Justice I can here say but a word. The
number of cases examined by the Court is larger than was
anticipated by its founders and seems likely to continue to
increase. Of these cases, a larger proportion than was originally anticipated are submitted to it in its advisory and not in
its judicial capacity. It seems probable also that this proportion will not grow less in the immediate future.

But, whereas the total labours of the Court may be expected to increase almost indefinitely, its consultative activities will, I foresee, eventually be reduced, as the League
grows stronger and as judicial settlement comes to be looked
upon as the normal method of solving legal international
problems.

The progress of arbitration as an ideal in the broad sense
of the term has been so rapid since the war, that it does not
seem over-optimistic to believe that the time will soon come
when the refusal by any Government to lay any justiciable
case before an international tribunal will be looked upon as
an international scandal. Several most deplorable incidents

of the past year, it is true, show that this time is not yet quite at hand, but many encouraging symptoms, of which the Kellogg Pact is not the least, lead one to believe that it is no longer very far distant. When it comes, the position of the Hague Court and of its members should be much enhanced, as their labours will be much increased. They will be increased not only by a more frequent recourse to arbitration in general, but by a more frequent recourse to the Court in particular, as a result of the increasing number of international conventions and arbitration treaties which provide for it.

Having thus briefly outlined the probable future of the organs of the League, let us now consider the probable future of its functions.

If we seek to classify the varied activities of the League according to their main purpose, we shall recognize that they may all be brought under one of the three following headings: execution of the peace agreements, promotion of international co-operation, and prevention of war.

This classification, which I have already adopted in previous publications, while considering the origin and past evolution of the League, may also serve here when considering its future. Ever since its birth, the League has been engaged in the fulfilment of these three distinct sets of duties. But, curiously enough, it would seem as if it had at first devoted itself to them in the inverse ratio of their real and permanent importance.

vii. *The Execution of the Peace Treaties.*

The execution of the treaties of peace, in which the Covenant is embodied, was for the League an ungrateful, but none the less an urgent and a useful task. It was an ungrateful task because it was bound to force the League out of the position of serene impartiality which it should occupy in the estimation of the world for the successful performance of its main duties. This was due to the nature of the peace treaties themselves and to the primitive composition of the League.

It is an unfortunate but obviously inevitable fact that treaties of peace should always have to be made on the morrow of wars. Thus the legal status of the future in international affairs is always established under singularly unfavourable circumstances. No task is more difficult, none requires more certain knowledge and more clearsighted and dispassionate disinterestedness than the redrafting of the political map of the world. It is therefore not to be expected that all-powerful victors, especially when animated by feelings of exasperation and vengeance towards their enemies, whom defeat has condemned to complete impotence, should ever succeed in such an undertaking.

When we consider the circumstances under which the peace settlements of 1919 were arrived at, we are far less surprised that they should fail to satisfy completely our sense of fairness and justice than that they should not offend against it more grievously than they do. The relative moderation of the peace terms was due in a very large measure to the influence of the American peace delegation. When the League set out to execute the treaties, as its founders obliged it to do, the restraining influence of America was unfortunately no longer active. On no single point was the absence of the United States from Geneva more clearly felt and more deplorable than in the decisions reached by the League in the execution of the peace treaties during the first years of its existence.

As time goes on, the importance of this first duty of the League is gradually diminishing. Moreover, as the vindictive feelings inspired by the war died out and as the League itself became more universal, the action of the Council has tended to become fairer and wiser. This evolution is clearly demonstrated for instance by the gradual change in the composition of the Saar Government Commission which, from a purely French tool as it was constituted in 1920, has become truly an international body.

There is every reason to expect both these tendencies to continue in the future. Some of the duties imposed on the League regarding the execution of the peace agreements have been performed once for all. An example is the recognition of the results of the pseudo-plebiscite of the former German districts of Eupen and Malmédy, according to Article 34 of the Treaty of Versailles. Others, such as those relating to the administration of the Saar basin and the settlement of the Upper Silesian question, are essentially of a temporary nature. The time is not far distant when they will entirely disappear from the agenda of League sessions.

There will remain, it is true, other obligations arising out of the peace settlement, such as the guardianship of the rights of minorities and the supervision of the administration of mandated territories, which are of a permanent nature or at least of an indefinite duration. It is probable, however, that these obligations will more and more come to be looked upon as being of a general political and administrative character and that their historical origin will exercise less and less influence on the spirit in which they are carried out.

viii. *International Co-operation.*

The promotion of international co-operation by the League has heretofore been its most important achievement. Two main causes have led it to develop its activities in this field.

First, the universally felt need for a general co-ordinating agency of such co-operation, and, second, its relative inability to solve by other means its main problems relating to the prevention of war.

The first of these two causes may be held to be a permanent factor of further evolution and one whose importance will not cease to grow in a constantly shrinking world. As long as economic and cultural relations of all sorts continue to become more and more intimate between politically independent nations, the League's co-operative function may be expected to develop in variety and to increase in importance. The only probable limit to such an evolution would seem to be the fusion or closer federation of hitherto independent States. The day may come ultimately when the social interdependence of the political units which constitute the League will have become such as to call for more than mere voluntary co-operation between them. Then, but only then, the League will become a real super-State. Not content with facilitating and encouraging co-ordination of the activities of its members as it is to-day, it will then compulsorily legislate for them all. Such has been the historical evolution of all successful political federations and such may be the ultimate future of the League of Nations.

But, as that evolution is of necessity very long and very gradual, it may be premature even to foresee its results. And as it is both extremely beneficent for all, if wisely and cautiously guided, and most terrifying in the eyes of our conservative contemporaries, it may be even undesirable to allude to it, lest a violent reaction be staged against its very beginnings. These timid beginnings, however, I perceive in the co-operative functions of the League as it is to-day and with which the leading candidate for the presidency of a great State not yet member of the League has just declared that he and his party are most eager to associate themselves.

Wars of the past have often been generated by just such forms of international friction as the League, through its promotion of peaceful co-operation, is seeking to eliminate or at least to diminish. There is therefore a very real and close connexion between its second function and that which I would now refer to in the third place as the prevention of war.

ix. *The Prevention of War.*

By prevention of war, as distinct from although related to international co-operation, I mean that function which, in the intention of the founders of the League, was to be its main *raison d'être*, that for which thousands and ten thousands of men died on the battlefields of Europe from 1914 to 1918.

It was not only in order to impose a victorious peace on their enemies that they fought and died, nor in order that new methods of international co-operation be devised and applied throughout the world. It was essentially to kill war that they laid down their lives, to kill war through the creation of a league of pacific nations that would and could enforce and maintain universal peace on the basis of justice.

That league—it may seem brutal, but it is not unnecessary to declare it frankly—does not exist to-day. Its foundations were laid in 1919 and attempts to build it up have been made and pursued ever since. But, for various reasons, chief of which in my opinion is the recalcitrant aloofness of the nation whose leader had done most to keep the pledges given to those who died to end war, the structure stands uncompleted to-day. To declare that the victims of the world war had died in vain would be not only inhuman, but wrong. On the other hand, to say that their purpose had been achieved and that we, the survivors, had but complacently to reap the harvest of their sacrifice would be no less cruel and mistaken.

No. That harvest will not be ripe until wars will have been universally and truly outlawed. Outlawed not only in the words of politicians and in the phrases of diplomats, but in the hearts of men, in the will of statesmen, and in the positive institutions of the society of nations. For that purpose, great progress, much greater progress than has been realized heretofore, has to be made and, I believe, will be made in three main directions.

First, all nations will have to adopt as fundamental law among themselves the absolute rule that all conflicts of whatever origin or nature must, in the last resort, be submitted to and settled by an impartial authority according to generally recognized principles. Secondly, all nations will have to pledge themselves to uphold that authority by carrying out its decisions and by uniting their forces against any who would defy it. Finally, thirdly, as a consequence of such measures and as a symptom of the new security thus created, much more than as a contributing cause, all nations will have to reduce their national armaments to a point consistent with the exigencies of international order.

Towards such goals the world must tend if civilization is to survive. That it is tending in their direction, even if slowly and with discouraging relapses, is, I believe, a fact. And that it will continue to tend towards them is a reasonable, although not of course a certain, expectation.

The progress made towards the first of these three goals, that is the progress in the technique of the peaceful settlement of disputes or arbitration in the very broadest sense of that term, has already been appreciable. In many respects, and in most countries, it has been greater in the course of the last ten years than in the whole previous course of the history. That is, in my opinion, the greatest achievement for peace, not only of the League but of contemporaneous statesmanship in general. The elaboration and general acceptance of the principles which should guide the conduct of nations in their relations with each other will, however, have to proceed much further before arbitration can be expected to provide a means of settling the most difficult and dangerous international conflicts.

The progress made towards the second goal, that of international security based on active international solidarity is still little more than verbal. This is not in the least surprising, as it can hardly be pursued with any great measure of success, until the first goal is already attained. This progress was foreboded and prepared in the Covenant of the League of 1919, but impeded rather than favoured by subsequent developments, at least until Locarno. All nations, except a very few who seem to believe that they will always, under all circumstances, be able to do without the aid of others, have clamoured for the organization of their own security through international support. But none, and the most powerful least of all, have as yet consented to place their resources unreservedly at the disposal of the international community to generate that security, without which peace will always be uncertain and disarmament impracticable and, in some cases, perhaps even dangerous.

It is very natural therefore that the third and final goal, that of national disarmament, is still almost completely hidden from the view of our generation. To be sure, reductions there have been here and there, due either to the will of the victors in the war or to reasons of finance and military technique. But among those nations who have not been disarmed in spite of themselves, where is one whose statesmen to-day really count less on their own forces for their own security than they did in 1914?

x. *Conclusion.*

That, in spite of all disquieting symptoms, the world and the League of Nations are on the whole moving in the right direction is, I repeat, a fact, in my opinion. That they will continue so to move, I repeat also, seems probable. But that such progress is certain, I do not believe. And that it can be automatic, I absolutely deny.

That progress depends essentially on the will of mankind. Not on its goodwill only, which may always be counted on up to a certain point, but which is always insufficient by itself to maintain peace, as all past history shows. It depends on the will of mankind, that is, in the last analysis, on the firm and enlightened determination of all leaders of opinion who, in this democratic age, are the real leaders of nations. It depends on their will and determination never, under any circumstances, to claim for their country rights and privileges which they would deny others, never to appeal to force but always to reason and fairness only, in pursuit of their own policies, never to preach aloofness and always to recommend co-operation, when aloofness means the toleration of violence and injustice and when co-operation alone can ensure the peace of the world.

SECTION II

SOME PROBLEMS OF THE PRESENT

CHAPTER II

THE WORKING OF THE LEAGUE COUNCIL

M. MANTOUX:

THIS title 'The Working of the League Council' might be used for different chapters of one story. It might mean a description of the Council procedure, or an account of the general activities of the Council, or only of its doings in any particular year, which in many ways would amount to the same as a description of its procedure. The document I would recommend any one interested in the subject to read is the Annual Report to the Assembly on the work of the Council and the Secretariat. That report supplies general information on the work done not only by the Council and the Secretariat, but also by all the Commissions or other bodies working throughout the year under the Council's or the Assembly's directions. No other official document can supply such a bird's eye view of the League, and each section of the Secretariat pays a special attention to its drafting. All its parts do not seem to be equally clear when read for the first time, because some of them refer to other publications; but it provides an admirable key with which to open the door to the League's documents and activities generally.

i. *The Composition of the Council.*

The Council is an essential part of the machinery of the League. Constitutionally it is somewhat difficult to see how the duties and rights of the Council differ from those of the Assembly. While all the States Members of the League are represented in the Assembly, only a few sit on the Council, some being there by right and permanently, and others being elected. If we wished to borrow a comparison from the British constitution, we might describe the Council as a House of Lords and a House of Commons sitting together, the permanent members being the House of Lords and the elected members the House of Commons. The elected members represent, or perhaps I should say ought to represent, those who have elected them—the Assembly generally—but whether they consider in their inner conscience that they do is a question to which I am quite unable to find an answer. I suppose most of them feel that the fact they have been elected by the majority of the Assembly simply gives them the privilege of representing themselves in the Council for a number of years. Much water will have to flow under the Rhone bridges, I am afraid, before a nation which sits on the Council really thinks that its duties there are those of a representative.

The Council has many rights and duties in common with the Assembly, but if in the written documents the differences are only slight, in practice the actual working of the League constitution has created and is creating year after year material differences which now give quite a distinct appearance to the work of each of these bodies. The mere fact that the Assembly meets once a year for a few weeks only, while the Council meets several times a year—four times at present—for a week or more has, of course, far-reaching consequences. It follows from it that unless (as has sometimes happened) something important takes place during the actual session of the Assembly and can be dealt with by it, the essential duty of the Assembly is to give general directions, to examine and perhaps to criticize what has been done in the course of the year, to indicate new tasks that might be undertaken and also—and this is one of the essential tasks of the Assembly—to grant or to refuse money for the undertaking of such tasks.

The Council, meeting as it does four times a year (at least at present), deals with current affairs and with any question arising from the resolutions of the Assembly. It is naturally the body which deals with crises, because a crisis cannot be expected to happen in September, when the Assembly is meeting, and at no other time. The Council necessarily deals with current political events, the course of which cannot be exactly foreseen. That gives the Council, as compared with the Assembly, the appearance of an executive body, although there is nothing in the League Covenant which makes the Council the Executive and the Assembly the Legislative; as a matter of fact, both hold executive and legislative functions at the same time. The Council makes its own rules; it does not accept any jurisdiction, even on legal points, and is not obliged on points of competence to appeal to the Court.

These few remarks will show you how important the question of the membership of the Council can be. The fact that the Council is strong, or weak, affects the whole work of the League, and largely determines the relations between the Council and the Assembly.

This is the first point I am going to deal with, because it has attracted a good deal of attention in the last two years, and will certainly be discussed in the Assembly, though in a less exciting form, during the coming session. You will certainly remember what happened in 1926, just before Germany was admitted to the League with a permanent seat in the Council. Two nations which had been represented on the

Council from the beginning, namely Spain and Brazil, took that opportunity of claiming permanent membership, which they thought should be given to them as well as to Germany. It was considered impossible to have so many permanent seats in the Council, the main reasons being not to make the Council too independent of the Assembly, and also to draw a line between what may be called (in terms, which although certainly unpleasant for those who are excluded, are in conformity with political and historical realities) Great Powers, and Powers which, while not all of them small, are unquestionably of lesser importance.

The fundamental motive accounting for Spain's and Brazil's attitude was that of national pride. Spain thought that although she could not at present claim to rank with the wealthiest and most powerful nations in the world, her place in history and the spread of her language and civilization over a considerable part of the western continent entitled her to claim a position equal to that of any other nation, and that it was tantamount to an insult to deny her this position. Brazil's claim, on the other hand, was founded not so much on her past as on the great future which her size, resources, and recent progress lead her to expect. She also considered that, in the absence of the United States, the American continent ought to have at least one permanent seat in the Council.

You will remember that their claims were not accepted, and both Spain and Brazil declared that they would retire from the League. Brazil did what Spain would not; she prevented by her veto the admission of Germany at the March 1926 Session of the Assembly, while Spain simply abstained from voting. The result in the end was the same: both of them declared that after two years (the term prescribed by the Covenant of the League) they would leave the League altogether. This term came to an end in 1928; for Brazil in June, and for Spain in September.

What was the attitude of the Council of the League and of the interested Governments in the face of this problem? The Council of the League did everything it could to show its goodwill and to invite those two Governments to reconsider their decision and remain in or return to the League. They were sent, after the March 1928 Session of the Council, very courteous and complimentary letters saying how important it was that they, whose great services were recognized, should remain in the League. Spain accepted the invitation to remain; but Brazil did not.

The action of Spain in leaving the League after the rejection of her claim to a permanent seat in the Council was dictated by feeling, but it was also part of a policy. Spain was at that time trying to strengthen her position in the League, but at the same time to obtain an extension of her power in the direction of Tangiers. Spain had problems to solve with the French and other Governments in the Mediterranean and it has been supposed that her Government hoped either to obtain both things or to bargain one against the other. This policy, however, led to no satisfactory results. Then Spain began to negotiate. On the Tangiers question a solution was eventually arrived at, in agreement with Great Britain, France, and Italy, and the Spanish claims were sufficiently taken into account to satisfy Spanish public opinion. Then the Spanish Government felt there would be more for them to gain than to lose by coming back to the League and to the Council, where they knew their return would be welcome. The number of Members of the Council, outside the permanent members, who could be relied on in an emergency was not very great. Therefore if Spain returned to the Council she might have many opportunities to make her presence felt and her co-operation appreciated. Spain therefore accepted the invitation extended to her and said that being invited in such flattering terms, by which the importance and dignity of the country were fully recognized, she could not resist the invitation.

Spain already knew that everything would be done to give her what had been offered in 1926 but refused by her at that time as inadequate—if not a permanent seat, at any rate the nearest approach to it. The 1926 compromise, although it laid down as a basis for the elected part of the Council the principle of rotation, admitted the possibility of re-electing for another term not more than three Members. That number of three was fixed on because the framers of the resolution had in mind Spain, Poland, and Brazil. Spain and Brazil having refused to accept the compromise, Poland alone was admitted as a re-eligible member.

The Spanish Government came to realize that if they could be admitted on these terms, there would probably be many reasons for re-electing them for a certain length of time, and they might regain a position on the Council that would fully satisfy their requirements and aspirations. This was also felt by the Council, and explains why a few days ago it was announced that three of the Permanent Members of the Council—Great Britain, France, and Germany—had put forward a proposal not only to offer a re-eligible post to Spain, but to go a step further and renew in favour of Spain an arrangement which had been suggested in 1926, when it was hoped that Spain and Brazil might be retained. By that arrangement it became possible for a Member of the League to be declared re-eligible not after a three years' trial, but at the moment of its election. This was intended to be an exceptional measure, as it had been devised to solve the special difficulties of the year 1926. It is now proposed to put that temporary arrangement into force again, and it is no mystery that this is the fatted calf which will be slaughtered to celebrate the return of the prodigal son. It is probable, therefore, that Spain will not only be re-elected a Member of the Council, but will know in advance that her re-election after three years is more than a possibility.

One of the reasons why it was considered highly desirable that Spain should return to the League is that among the nations which were neutral in the recent war, Spain is the only one which is undoubtedly more than a small Power. There are problems dealt with in Geneva which from time to time call for the co-operation of a country with no direct interest in the settlement of questions arising from the peace treaties, and whose international position is such as to give weight to its suggestions.

What succeeded in the case of Spain did not succeed in the case of Brazil, whose attitude in 1926 had been much more uncompromising than that of Spain. Brazil has no vital interest involved, and the question of prestige with her is more independent of other questions. Brazil felt that part of Latin America being in the League and part out of it, she was quite free to take either position, to remain in or to go out. Brazil had also one eye on the State Department in Washington, her desire being to keep her connexion with Europe while showing her inclination in other respects to think and to act as does the Washington Government. Although the President of Brazil, whose personal views were an essential factor in the 1926 crisis, left office shortly after, and although his successor was said to hold different opinions,

the decision to part from the League has remained un-
changed.

As a matter of fact, it does not matter very much to
Brazil, as far as political problems are concerned, whether she
belongs to the League or not; but the League is not merely
a political organization; it deals through its technical organizations with many questions of considerable importance—
particularly economic questions. There the attitude of the
Brazilian Government is quite different. In the letter which
they wrote recently to express their desire to remain outside
the League they not only sent every good wish to the League,
fully realizing the great services it could render to the world,
but they added that in the technical and economic field they
would always be ready to assist the League by any means in
their power.

This means in effect that Brazil would like, while ceasing
to be a Member of the League, not to be excluded from its
technical organizations, including the International Labour
Office. The policy of the League in that respect has always
been what may be called opportunist. It was always thought
better to accept the presence even of those who came as
observers, rather than to show them the door. The problem,
however, is a little different when it is raised with regard to
a former Member who has left the League. It is a somewhat
thorny constitutional question whether a country after withdrawing from the League is to be allowed to take part in
some of its activities. Opinions on this point differ. Those
who answer in the negative think that no one should be
allowed to decline responsibility on major problems while retaining the advantage of participation in all sorts of convenient arrangements affecting material interests. If such a
privilege could be granted a good number of the present

Members of the League might wish to follow Brazil's example and cease to attend the Assembly and to support the League budget, when reserving to themselves the right of attending various Commissions and Conferences. This is the main argument against the proposal of accepting the presence of Brazilian representatives in the Labour and other technical organizations.

But there are many arguments for that proposal. Would the League prefer to lose entirely those who, although renouncing formal membership, show their interest in many of the League activities? It may be argued that such activities are not by far the least important. Would it be good policy to refuse partial co-operation for reasons of pride and principle, and may not that sort of co-operation, just because it is willingly offered, lead with the help of time to the renewal of closer relations?

The question is of particular interest as far as the International Labour Organization is concerned. That Organization, as well as the Court, are autonomous institutions. Their budget is finally approved by the Assembly, but the organization is independent from the Council and from the Secretariat of the League. They hold their own views as to the question of the participation of the various Governments in their work. The view now prevailing in the International Labour Office is that Brazil should be kept in at all costs, and that it is very fortunate that she desires to remain. The object that can be said to lie at the very foundation of the Labour Organization is to arrive at international understandings which will make it possible for progressive nations to improve the conditions of their labouring classes without endangering on that account their industrial and commercial prosperity for the benefit of countries unhampered by legislative restrictions. If any nation of importance is left out, the whole system falls to the ground, and universality is therefore essential. The Covenant provides that every Member of the League shall be a Member of the Labour Organization. This means that no country can be a Member of the League without being a Member of the Labour Organization; does it necessarily follow that a country cannot be a Member of the Labour Organization without being a Member of the League? This is the question which the Assembly probably will have to solve.

When the compromise of 1926 was arrived at, one of its provisions raised the total number of Members in the Council to fourteen—five Permanent Members, Great Britain, France, Italy, Japan, and Germany, and nine non-Permanent Members elected by the Assembly. Fourteen is a large figure for the membership of such a body as the League Council, and it was agreed to only after long discussions. The American Members of the League had expressed their desire to have no less than three representatives on the Council. On the other hand, no agreement was to be hoped for if seats were not available for the other nations which claimed permanent membership, viz. Brazil, Spain, and Poland. Three more seats were to be occupied by the other Members of the League in rotation. But nine is a large number. It is understood by a sort of gentlemen's agreement that the American Members will normally have their three seats on the Council. Brazil is out of the League and the Argentine is in a very curious position, no one being able to say whether she is in or out of the League. The accession of the Argentine to the League was never officially ratified by their Legislature, which, nevertheless, grants yearly contribution to the League budget. Brazil and the Argentine being out of the League, as well as Mexico, Chile is now the only important Latin American State in the League. Still three Members must be found to sit on the Council on behalf of Latin America and Canada. It follows that strict rotation becomes a necessity, and the presence at the Council table of representatives of small Central American States, while emphasizing the principle of equality between Members of the League, cannot be said to bring much strength to the Council.

The representation in the Council of some Central European and Eastern European Governments is followed by other consequences. They send to Geneva very competent and sometimes very remarkable men, on behalf of countries of considerable and growing importance. But those countries are involved in some of the most difficult problems with which the League has to deal, and this sometimes results in further difficulties. An example is the protracted and almost impossible question of the Hungarian optants, in which Roumania is interested. The position of the Roumanian representative no doubt is made exceedingly delicate by the fact that he belongs to the Council, whose recommendations his Government sometimes declines to accept.

The fact that fourteen nations are represented on the Council, some of them perhaps too far removed from the problems dealt with, and others too immediately interested gives an extraordinary advantage to the representatives of the few nations who hold permanent seats, and tends to encourage them in acting more high-handedly than they would otherwise do. Those with the greatest responsibilities should, no doubt, be listened to, and in many cases determine the final decision. The small nations as a matter of fact are rather too inclined to stand aside when they find that the big ones are interested in a particular question. Their timidity sometimes prevents them from doing good service in the cause of the League. In the present position of affairs three or four of the fourteen Members of the Council tend to 'run the show' on their own, but they run it, so to speak, outside the show. To them the Council meetings are convenient opportunities to meet together, but they make their arrangements between themselves sometimes before and sometimes during the debates, not in the debates themselves, and when they have reached their own conclusions they ask the others to agree. Some protests have been raised against that tendency. The meeting of a caucus round a tea-table or at lunch may be very useful, but it leaves hardly anything to say to those who have not the privilege to rank among the happy few. This is not exactly the method of open discussion contemplated when the Covenant was drafted.

ii. *The Apparent Failure of the Council.*

I should like, glancing through the Annual Report to the Assembly, to refer to a few things which the Council did this year. A clear distinction must be made between direct action of the Council, particularly on questions of political interest, and action through Committees reporting to the Council and sometimes ultimately to the Assembly. The impression left by this Report, as far as direct action of the Council is concerned, cannot be said to be altogether satisfactory.

I have referred already to the question of the Hungarian optants. It may be that any other body which might have dealt with such a question would have found itself in the same difficulty, but the fact is that the position now is much the same as it was several years ago. The Treaty of Trianon allowed Hungarian subjects living in Transylvania to retain their Hungarian nationality, and recognized their right to retain their possession of landed property in the territory which was to become part of Roumania. Shortly after an agrarian law was applied to Transylvania on similar lines to those already in force in other parts of the Kingdom, and the consequence was to deprive many of the 'optants' of their property for a nominal compensation, the Roumanian currency having dropped to a fortieth of its pre-war value. This was a general measure affecting all landowners, but the Hungarian optants who held far more property in Transylvania than the Roumanian-speaking population, complained that the law was meant to expropriate them contrary to the Treaty, and the Hungarian Government brought the case before the Council.

I will not recall the different stages of the long discussion which followed: a first stage lasted for two or three years, and led to nothing. Then the Hungarians tried to use the Mixed Arbitral Tribunals which had been set up by the Peace Treaties to deal with differences between individuals and States arising from the war or consequences of the war. They found that the Tribunal agreed to deal with the case as one of liquidation of enemy property. The Roumanian Government, which had their representative on that Tribunal, declared that the Tribunal had exceeded the limit of its competence, as it had been established to deal with individual cases of confiscation of enemy property during the war or in consequence of the war, but could take no decision the effect of which would be to cancel a general law of the Roumanian Kingdom. They refused to allow their representative to sit any more on the Tribunal, and therefore the whole procedure was stopped.

The Hungarian Government then asked the Council to appoint under the provisions of the Treaty a new member of the Tribunal to replace the Roumanian representative and to make it possible to go on with the procedure. Last year the Council proposed a compromise under which Roumania was to recognize the competence of the Tribunal, while that body accepted to act in conformity with certain principles, one of which was that it should abstain from dealing with questions arising from the enforcement of general acts of national legislation. The Hungarians rejected that recommendation, under which, they said, the Tribunal was enabled to work again, but at the same time was forbidden to deal with their case. They insisted that the Hague Court should be asked to give an advisory opinion concerning the competence of the Mixed Tribunal.

In March 1928, the Council tried another way out of the deadlock. They proposed to raise the number of the arbitrators to five, three (including the chairman) being neutrals. This time Roumania refused. Hungary has claimed over and over again that the Hague Court should be asked to give an opinion on the case, but Roumania has declared repeatedly that she will never agree to that procedure. Here, by the attitude of both Governments in turn, the action of the Council of the League has been absolutely checked.

It cannot be said that more success has been obtained in the Polish-Lithuanian dispute. It was my privilege—if that is the proper word to use—to deal as a League official with this case for about seven years, and it has given occupation to my successor ever since I left, about eighteen months ago. Last year the question came to a head, because the Lithuanians said they were threatened by the Poles and were afraid of a Polish invasion. The Poles, being annoyed by the continuation of the so-called 'state of war' perpetuated by the Lithuanian Government, and by the constant reiteration in official Lithuanian speeches and documents, that Vilna is the capital of Lithuania, were inclined to make a show of strength, or at any rate the hotheads amongst them said they felt inclined to do so, and it is not, I think, a libel against Marshal Pilsudski to say that his head is sometimes pretty hot. However, he is very shrewd, and understands a game of bluff. He let it be known that things could not continue as they were, otherwise unspecified steps would have to be taken, and the result was that both Governments were summoned to Geneva. Marshal Pilsudski and M. Voldemaras (whom I had the pleasure of meeting when dealing with this case as early as 1920) came here, and in a semi-private conversation Marshal Pilsudski asked M. Voldemaras whether it was peace or war, and M. Voldemaras answered 'Peace'. They thereupon shook hands as I had seen M. Paderewski shaking hands with this same M. Voldemaras in September 1920. It was agreed that the so-called 'state of war' between the two countries should be declared no longer to exist, and that arrangements should be made to establish more normal relations between the two countries.

It is at present more difficult to go from Vilna to Kovno, a distance of between sixty and seventy miles, than to go from Geneva to Moscow. You have to go from Vilna to Warsaw and then across the whole of Poland to East Prussia and back to Lithuania, and try to conceal the fact that you come from Poland at all. There are no postal, telegraphic, or other communications; and people who try to cross the frontier are arrested as soon as discovered by the frontier guards. Something was to be done to improve this, and a meeting was arranged at Koenigsberg, but before it took place Voldemaras declared publicly that the decision of the Council was an admission of Lithuania's rights by which the League recognized Vilna as the legitimate capital of Lithuania. This bold assertion was based on a sentence at the end of the agreement arrived at in Geneva to the effect that all questions on which the two Governments held fundamentally different views were to be left out of the intended negotiations. Voldemaras's statement did not make those negotiations easy, and no one was surprised when they failed. A second meeting led to no better results. All that can be said is that the renewal of war proper has been prevented since the autumn of 1920. But the dispute remains unsettled and a permanent menace to peace in North-Eastern Europe.

If we had more time a good many things might be said about a case which caused some sensation, in the European press, a few months ago—the case of the wagons full of machine-guns which were found on their way from Austria into Hungary, coming, apparently, from nowhere (although we know that nowhere was in Italy) being sent to no particular place (although no one would be surprised if that unknown place happened to be somewhere in Hungary). The Hungarians maintain that the destination was Poland, although it is difficult to know why, the Poles being bound by no treaty obligation as to the importation of arms. The matter was brought before the Council, as the execution of the Disarmament clause in the peace treaties was placed under its supervision when the Allied Military Commission ceased to exist. But action was taken so late and in such a timid way that perfect darkness still prevails about the case, and certainly the incident has added nothing to the prestige of the Council.

Opinions expressed on this question differ widely. It was said in some quarters: 'Why should you annoy the Hungarians about this? Those who made an international incident out of it are the real culprits, because by fostering ill-feeling they are disturbing the peace of the world.' From other quarters it was answered: 'Whether the disarmament clauses in the peace treaties were drafted as they should have been is open to discussion, but if it is found impossible by the existing international means to make sure that pledges taken under the treaties are kept, how can we be satisfied that more general pledges (if and when they are taken) will be kept? For if the facts concerning an alleged violation of disarmament clauses cannot be ascertained, what is to guarantee the execution of a general disarmament convention, when at last arrived at?'

This creates an unfortunate impression which no mere speeches, reports, or motions for disarmament can remove. The great question of a general reduction of armaments, connected with the question of security and of the peaceful settlement of disputes, has been the object of innumerable meetings of committees and sub-committees, preparatory, consultative, technical, and otherwise. This year important studies have taken place, and draft treaties have been prepared by competent jurists, to serve as models for future Locarnos. But nothing has been achieved as yet, and no one knows when the general Conference for the reduction of armaments can meet. As this is now held by many to be the greatest political task before the Council of the League, it is not surprising that its repeated postponement should lead to some disappointment among those who believe in League ideals.

iii. *A comparison corrected.*

The contrast is great when the political work of the Council in 1928 is compared with the activity of the technical organizations—a subject which I do not propose to deal with to-day. If I were to describe what has been done by the

Economic Committee and its different branches, the work of the special committee appointed to watch over the consequences of the Economic Conference, and the proceedings of the recent Conference on Export Prohibitions, you would realize that in that direction something is being done. The same is true of the loans with the help of which Greece was able to house and employ her refugees, and of the progress made in the Bulgarian problem, although the Bulgarian Government recently refused to accept the scheme for the reform of its national bank. The activities of the Health Organization and of the Transit and Communications Organization are many and deserve admiration.

Thus arises the impression that in everything it does or does not in the political field the Council shows insufficient vision and power, while the work of the technical organizations means achievement and success. If you think of it for a moment, however, you will find that the difference is perhaps not so great as is generally thought. Are the results obtained by the Economic and other technical organizations immediate and complete? By no means, except in a few special cases like those of loans for the settlement of refugees, which the Council made possible by its recommendations, but for which final arrangements had to be made between Governments and banks outside the League. The work of the technical organizations consists of an organized and regular effort towards the solution of lasting international questions. In the technical field we feel that those methods are right: we say that should not the result be immediately forthcoming much has been done already, and no one complains that the League has failed when it has only made preparations for desirable improvements. In the political field the public is more impatient. They want things to happen immediately. There is, of course, one thing that must be immediately prevented from happening, and that is war. As for the other tasks of the League, such as bringing together nations who are now divided by interest, feeling, and long memories of past injuries, they cannot be achieved without the help of time. If we applied to the political work of the League the same criterion which we use for its technical work we might find that although there is some difference in the progress made it is not as great as might be thought.

We should never forget that the League's first duty, as an international organization, is to create international habits, and the creation of good habits (bad ones being easy enough to acquire) is a long, tiresome, trying task. All we are entitled to ask for is that the work done should be in the right direction. Is that always the case with the League of Nations? Probably not. I have just pointed to some defects in the machinery and also in the tendencies of various Governments who, after taking little interest in the League at the beginning, now think they can run their ordinary policies through the League without paying too much attention to League rules or League principles. As it is essential to develop international habits we should take care that good and not bad habits are created, and this can be done only by educating public opinion in each country—for which the ultimate responsibility rests on each of us.

Those who are now conscious of the existence of international duties can do a great service to their own country as well as to the world by taking part in that indispensable work of education. It would be a bold assumption at present to believe in the permanent existence of any such thing as an international public opinion. No nation will be impressed by articles in the foreign press or by addresses from a few

E

well-meaning private societies when anything that is considered by that nation as a vital question is at stake, unless in that nation itself a growing body of responsible and active men and women are ready to support a League of Nations policy. International achievements and international habits will grow together, but they can grow only gradually. We should take this into account when we are inclined to pass sentence over what is being done in Geneva. International habits cannot develop unless helped by the action in each country of an active and growing body of opinion, and then only can the pressure of an international opinion be felt, and make it possible for the League Council to fulfil the hopes of its founders.

CHAPTER III

DISARMAMENT: THE ROLE OF THE ANGLO-SAXON NATIONS

Señor DE MADARIAGA:

A LECTURE on Disarmament has been a hardy annual of your Institute for several years, and the victim of it from one point of view and the torturer from another has been the person who is at present honoured with the task of addressing you. It puts me in a special difficulty. I believe that the fundamentals of the problem have been dealt with adequately in previous years, and I believe that because it was I who dealt with them. I do not see, therefore, how I can treat again a subject which I have thoroughly exhausted. Having since then become a professor, I might have taken refuge in a tradition already honoured both in the observance and in the breach, and merely repeat my last year's lecture, or the one I gave the year before, even to the extent of reproducing the jokes suddenly improvised before you, after mature reflection. However, your Institute has countered that solution to my problem by deciding that these lectures are to be published, and I cannot very well publish in this year's volume the lecture which you can find in last year's.

Having looked round for a way, so to speak, of renewing my subject, it occurred to me that perhaps the best thing to do was, since I had already dealt with the subject in general, to deal with it now in particular, and since the Institute is mostly composed of members of the two great Anglo-Saxon nations, I thought you might possibly like to hear a considered and, I hope, impartial and as little incomplete as possible review of the role played in the history of disarmament in the last ten years by the two great Anglo-Saxon nations.

Before I deal with my subject, however, I should like to say a word as to the spirit in which I intend to approach it. There is a Spanish story of a well-to-do middle-class Catalan who had a little house in the country. He was converted to socialism. 'For', he said, 'I hope, when the wealth of the country is distributed all round, with the part that will fall to me of the common wealth, plus the house I have in the country, I shall be quite well off.' That story is very useful when dealing with international relations. It applies very often, if I may judge by the number of times I have told it. It applies very aptly to the present case, for I have observed that there are many people—I do not say many peoples but many people—who consider the establishment of the League of Nations and in general the growth of the spirit of the world community as rather a way for increasing their feeling of sovereignty over others than for decreasing the feeling of sovereignty of their own nation. There are many people, indeed, for whom the League of Nations and its atmosphere are merely another way of satisfying their innate craving for imperialism. There is such a thing as the imperialism of idealism. Well, I flatter myself that I do not suffer from that defect, perhaps because there is no room for more defects in me. I do not intend, in developing my subject, to lecture the two Anglo-Saxon nations about all the wrong things they have done. I am sure they have done lots of them, and I am sure they will do lots of them in the future, and I hope they will, because I have observed that doing wrong is one of the ways of living.

i. *The Direct and the Indirect Approach to Disarmament.*

Now when I consider the question a little more closely I find that I cannot get away from the necessity of giving at least in outline a very brief summary of the conclusions of my experience in the problem of disarmament. I will give them very bluntly and shortly. If any one of you has any doubts as to the wisdom of my conclusions I advise him or her to look up the lectures I gave last year and the year before, or, if they think it briefer, to put some questions to me at the end of this meeting.

The first of my conclusions is that the problem of disarmament is not the problem of disarmament; it is the problem of the setting up and the organization of the world community. We cannot expect nations to disarm until there is an organized, continuous, and methodical system for dealing with difficulties even before they have arisen, and, if this method fails, for dealing with them after they have arisen. Armaments are the manifestation of the tendency to solve problems by violence. If you want to give up the method of solving problems by violence it is not enough to try to abolish the instruments of violence: you must try to find the cause why such instruments are wielded, and therefore you must discover some method other than that of violence. If you give up the method of force, there is but one method which remains, and that is the method of reason. But reason is not merely to be used *a posteriori.* That is, in my opinion, one of the greatest obstacles in the development of disarmament—some people still insist on reserving the use of reason for a kind of *a posteriori* method, which means that you will be very careless about your petrol and matches on the understanding that you can organize a very good system of dealing with fires when they have already burnt your house. That being so, it is obvious that the technical or direct method of dealing with disarmament is not the one which is going to lead us to the end desired. It is rather the political and indirect method which tends to the creation of a well-organized world-community that we must look to, and therefore, the problem being thus defined, if we want to consider the history of the role played by the two great Anglo-Saxon nations in this problem during the last ten years, we shall have to look into the matter from several successive points of view.

ii. *The Armaments of the Anglo-Saxon Nations.*

We might take them in any order you like, but I propose to begin by the actual facts, the actual state of their armaments, then to deal with the contribution of the two great nations to the efforts towards a technical solution, then with the sense and tendency of the two nations in the effort towards the true solution, namely, the organization of the world-community. Finally, I shall deal with what, in my opinion, is the most important factor of all, namely, the spirit of their policy; for it is the spirit that regulates the letter, and even the setting up of systems, legal or juridical, for the establishment of a world-community is not half as important as the life that animates not only these efforts but every other activity of the nations concerned.

As to the present system, let me say at once that the two Anglo-Saxon nations are at the head of the armament list. Their military budgets are by far the highest in the world in absolute figures; I believe they stand at about three thousand million Swiss francs for each of them. Per head of population the figures do not seem as bad as that, and after all it is fair to realize the immense responsibilities of the British Empire and the tremendous population of the American nation. If my figures are correct—and in questions of figures it is always very difficult to be correct, for there are numbers of considerations to take into account—Great Britain spends per head of population $12·2 in what is called euphemistically 'national defence', and the United States not quite $5. Great Britain is at the head in statistics of this kind and the United States comes after a certain number of nations, one of which is Spain. Between Great Britain and the United States from the point of view of military expenditure per head of population there comes France, Chile, Italy, Sweden, Spain, and the Netherlands.

My second point is, What is the tendency of these armaments? Is it to grow or to decrease? The answer is rather complex. It tends to decrease in an absolute sense and to increase in a relative sense. With regard to these two nations if one tries to arrive at a synthetic conclusion comprising both the tendencies of their military departments and those of their foreign offices, their policy would appear to be dominated by a set of conflicting forces, one being the desire to spend as little as possible on armaments and the other the desire to remain relatively as strong as possible in armaments. Hence a reduction in absolute armaments, whenever possible, without a proportionate reduction in relative armaments. That is, I think, a fair explanation of the trend of policy in both Great Britain and the United States, and it will explain to you at the same time the rather bewildering fact that now and then you see these countries are reducing their armaments and now and then you find them extremely anxious to increase them. In to-day's *Journal de Genève* I find a speech by the First Lord of the Admiralty explaining

how England has reduced her navy, and also a speech by
President Coolidge pointing out that it is absurd to expect
that the Kellogg Pact is going to have any consequences at
all in the reduction of American armaments.

Finally, what is the position of these two great countries
in the trade in armaments? Well, they are far and away at
the head of it. The two greatest exporters of armaments in
the world are Great Britain and the United States. Great
Britain exported in 1926 $14,000,000 worth, or 25 per cent.
of the total exports of the world, whereas the United States
exported $10,500,000 worth, or about 18 per cent.

So far I have dealt with figures. There is a cynical saying
that figures never lie: those who lie are those who use them.
I must say that I never feel comfortable in the field of
figures. To begin with I am apt now and then to take a
hundred for a thousand, and moreover I cannot help feeling
that figures are the best index to facts, and I have a peculiar
tendency not to believe in the existence of facts. Views
appear to me much more important than facts, and tendencies much more important than views.

iii. *The Contribution of the Anglo-Saxon Nations to the Direct
Method.*

I should like, therefore, to give you an outline of my views
on the tendencies of the two Anglo-Saxon countries in the
second plane in which the problem can be examined, namely
that of the technical efforts that have been made both in
Geneva and elsewhere to solve the problem by what I call
the direct method. You all know that from a relatively
early date the United States of America agreed to collaborate
with the League in trying to set up a Convention for the
reduction and limitation of armaments. When I say a rela-

tively early date I am speaking also relatively, for it was in fact at a rather late period that America decided to join. Be that as it may, there is no question that the arrival of the American Delegation and its participation in the work of the Commission and the Sub-Commissions which prepared the Convention for the Reduction and Limitation of Armaments was a great addition of strength to those bodies, for during the first years in which the League organization worked without America the work of the League was heavily handicapped by the fact that one of the most important nations in the field of armaments and the most important in the field of politics was absent from its counsels.

We may examine this matter under several headings. First of all, let us consider what has been done towards setting up a Convention for the reduction and limitation of armaments, that is to say, towards solving the problem in its strictest sense. The Preparatory Commission for the Disarmament Conference, created to that effect, has been working for several years now and, technically, is still working. This Commission has worked mostly on the basis provided by a French and an English draft. Theoretically the reduction of armaments must cover three points—men, material, and money. As far as men are concerned, it was obvious to me— and I believe it would be obvious to any impartial observer reading the minutes of the Commission—that both the Anglo-Saxon nations took up a role which it was, in my opinion, inevitable they should take. If you will allow me to go back to my opening remarks I said then, I think, that no substantial measure of disarmament could be expected without the adequate organization of the world-community. I should like now to draw a conclusion from that which is very aptly illustrated by what happens and keeps happening in the Disarmament Commission of the League and, indeed, in every other conference that has taken or shall take place. In the absence of any method for solving the problems that arise every day among nations, armaments are an indispensable element in national policy, and therefore no nation can afford to see them reduced in the only way in which it matters to have them reduced, namely, in a relative way. Every nation can agree to have its armaments reduced in an absolute way. If the nation's armaments are fifty, she does not mind having them reduced to forty-five on condition that the armaments of her potential adversary, which were forty-five, are reduced to twenty-two, because in the aggregate these two operations culminate in an accession of strength to the nation concerned. That is the inescapable law of the mind in which all disarmament conferences work in the absence of a world-community. Which leads me to this conclusion, paradoxical though it may seem, that *in the absence of an organized world-community all disarmament conferences are armament conferences.* If I wanted a definite illustration to back this law, which in my opinion is self-evident and needs no backing, I would ask you to invest the modest sum of ten Swiss centimes and purchase the *Journal de Genève* of the 15 August, and read the declarations made in an authoritative way by the Italian Prime Minister to the Rome correspondent of the *Popolo d'Italia.* In these declarations the Prime Minister is interpreted as saying what I indeed heard his official representative say many a time in League Committees, namely that Italy is ready to have her own armaments reduced to any level that may be wished, on condition that Italy's armaments remain equal to the armaments of the most armed nation in Europe.

Well, ladies and gentlemen, the difference there between

the Italian delegate and the others was not one of substance: it was one of method. He selected the frank and sincere way of putting the problem before the world. The others preferred a more discreet way.

I do not know that it will serve any useful purpose to occupy your time in speaking of details, in elaborating the conclusions of this law. So far as Anglo-Saxon collaboration in the Disarmament Commission is concerned all I need say is that even the most powerful nation in the world is bound to obey a law of reality, and that therefore whenever there was a question of power, whenever a principle was under discussion which might affect adversely the relative power of any one of these nations, we had immediately a very definite opposition taken in the Commission against that particular matter. Afterwards, in due time, a considerable number of arguments were discovered, a fact which it is never beyond the possibilities of the human intellect to do.

Take an example in the English attitude towards trained reserves. The English made a strenuous effort to force the French to accept the position that trained reserves in the Army should be severely reduced, but when it came to discussing the French counter-claim that trained reserves in the Navy should be reduced the question was found to be considerably different. It is extraordinary how arguments will lend themselves to be manipulated by men! Take again the attitude on questions of money. I am firmly convinced that no convention on disarmament will be worth the paper on which it is written if it does not contain at the same time a reduction in men, a reduction in material, and a reduction in money; that is to say, in budgets. We were never able to make the American or English members of the Commission look at the idea of limiting budgets. They would not look at it. There I must say their arguments were very poor. The idea was that the rich nation with the high cost of living would have to spend far more than the poorer nation, and therefore it was unfair to limit the budgets. It was no use explaining *ad nauseam* that budgets would be limited taking into consideration these differences in the purchasing value of money. The same argument was trotted out in the absence of any better one.

I will take now the point of what was done in regard to limiting the freedom of commerce in arms. We worked in Geneva towards a Convention of this kind, and we had the collaboration of both the British and the American Governments. I can give you only my conclusion as, I hope, an impartial and independent observer; the details would take too long to elaborate. I would ask those of you who want to challenge my conclusion to study the documents and discuss the matter with me, either privately or publicly.

The English nation was predominantly interested in controlling the traffic in arms in the Indian Ocean and other parts of the world in which it happens to be particularly interested, so that arms should not go to the particular peoples whom it is in the interests of the British Empire, and I may say of the whole world, to keep on good behaviour. There is nothing wrong in this attitude, which is for the good of the peace of the world and is one which the British Empire, with its great responsibilities, is fully entitled to take up in Geneva. I cannot say, however, that the British delegation manifested the same interest in the other aspect of the question, namely the control of the traffic in arms so that arms shall not be sent all over the world to peoples who should not have them in order to foster possible wars.

As for the American Government, their collaboration was

very much on the same lines as that of the British; they were quite ready to set up a Convention, they were very friendly in difficulties, and quite agreeable to all proposals which would not create what in my opinion was the most important point of all—a very efficient international control of what was happening.

Owing to the conservative views taken by these and other nations (for I must not give the impression that these two nations represented the 'extreme right' of the world; far from it; there were others who exceeded them in their anxiety not to do too much) the most valuable element of the Convention, namely the international institutions of control, were reduced to a very mild form which is nevertheless in my opinion, a very good step in advance; that is to say, there is to be publicity in regard to all that is done in the matter and the submitting of all exports of arms to a licence.

When it came to the actual 'delivering of the goods', however, things became less interesting. This Convention was signed in 1925. It has been ratified by France and Venezuela, and by no one else. The United States has not ratified it; Great Britain has not ratified it; and, as you see, they are in abundant and excellent company.

One of the reasons why the Convention has not been ratified is a reason for which Great Britain or America are but indirectly responsible. The Convention obliges the exporting nations to report the arms they are exporting and to say to whom they are being exported. The right to export is moreover limited to Governments only. Such a Convention is, therefore, bound to create absolute publicity in regard to armaments bought by nations that cannot manufacture their own arms, for as soon as a nation buys a gun or an aeroplane or a ship outside its frontiers it is bound by the Convention to appear in the statistics of the League of Nations as the purchaser, on being reported by the vendor. The argument of the nations which do not manufacture armaments was that that was very nice and they were willing to accept it, but why should they be treated more severely than nations which could buy their armaments on their own territory and remain very discreet about it? It was therefore decided to insert in one of the diplomatic instruments of the Conference a declaration to the effect that the Convention would be considered as a step towards a more general regulation of armaments, which would include another convention controlling all manufacture of arms, in order that the nations which bought armaments in their own territory should also have to report them statistically.

This happened in 1925. We are now in 1928, and a Commission has been hard at work during the intervening years trying to decide whether anything can be done in the matter. Here again I can express only a frank and sincere and open opinion. In my opinion, neither the British nor the American Government has been very helpful in the matter. Again I add I do not believe they were the only ones, nor, maybe, the least helpful. But neither can be said to have shown much enthusiasm for the idea.

I now come to the last point of this chapter, namely the efforts towards Naval Conventions. Let me say first that the relation between the various arms seems to me a little complicated. The school that claims that all armaments must be treated together has a very sound technical basis, namely that the forces of a nation are so intertwined that you never can tell whether the Navy is a wing of the Army or vice versa. When account is taken of the importance of

Navies for guarding communications which may be vital for Armies it is very difficult to treat them separately. On the other hand, it is no less true that such an argument is entirely a war argument and not a peace argument. You will see how reality always brings us back to the law I mentioned a minute ago: all arguments used in disarmament are arguments of armament.

Remember what happened in the Washington Conference. Mr. Hughes sprang his bomb of peace on the delegations, who were rather stunned by it. The amount of ill-feeling which resulted from this Conference is astounding. It is necessary, for instance, to know French public opinion well to realize how great was the harm done to the opinion in which France held both America and England by the way in which she was manœuvred into accepting a position which she considers inferior to that which she thought she ought to have. I am not taking sides with France or with the others, mostly because I fail to see how an objective standard could be found to judge what should be the respective naval armaments of the nations concerned; I am merely pointing out as an illustration that as long as you do not go about the problem of disarmament by the long way, by trying to reform the political constitution of the world before you try to make people drop their armaments, all you get is ill-feeling, discussions about 'what I ought to have and do not get', fear, prestige, power, and feelings of that kind which cannot be eliminated, which are human and which have a right to exist so long as nothing is done to banish the reason for their existence.

Exactly the same applies to the Geneva Conference. I was here during that Conference, though I am entirely innocent of it. The Geneva Naval Conference, in which Japan, Great

Britain, and the United States discussed the reduction of naval armaments, having an Italian and a French observer to enjoy the sights, did not take place under the aegis of the League of Nations, though it took place in a town with which the League of Nations is connected. The Head of the Disarmament Section of the Secretariat was admitted to the three public sittings which the Conference held (for not being a League Conference it did most of its work in secret), and he was admitted to these public sittings as an ordinary member of the public and received the public documents at the same time as they were distributed to the general public. I say that because I want you to be quite clear that the League had nothing to do with that Conference. Not that I mean that it is because the League was not there that it failed. No, the League has been failing at disarmament these eight years. It was not because the League was not there—no one is more unpleasant than a League fanatic—it was because the method was wrong. Where was the basis of agreement? There was none. The three nations came to Geneva with the subconscious, if not conscious, aim of reducing in general the naval armaments of the world, while increasing their own particular armaments relatively to those of the other two, and this was inevitable. This is a law of nature. I well remember that the discussion of the unthinkable—in fact, the thinking of the unthinkable—was never more intense than during those days when attempts were being made to do the impossible. All the arguments used in that Conference were based on the hypothesis of an Anglo-American war, and whoever says the contrary is either fooling himself or fooling others. Indeed, how could it be otherwise? Let me repeat it, because it is the essential thing: In the absence of a system for dealing with world conflicts otherwise than by force, all discussions and arguments must aim at the increase of power of every one concerned.

iv. *The Contribution of the Anglo-Saxon Nations to the Indirect Method.*

Let us now quit this dismal plane, and come to higher regions. The true road to disarmament is through the setting up of a world community. Now, it seems to me obvious, and of the most elementary justice, to say that on this plane the world owes an immense debt to the Anglo-Saxon nations. There is nothing in the history of mankind to equal the service that was done to the world by President Wilson in insisting that the League Covenant should go through during the Peace Conference. I do not want to commit myself to any evaluations; I want to speak in absolute calm and coolness of thought. I believe that America could still afford to carry on fifty years of blatant imperialism and still remain our moral creditors on the strength of President Wilson's achievement. In fact, the thing was so stupendous that we have not yet realized how big it was, and we have been living since 1920 in such an atmosphere of wonder that we do not realize how wonderful it is. I believe that when the history of the gradual disarmament of the world—because I am convinced it is going to disarm—is written, this one act of President Wilson's will stand as the greatest step on the road to disarmament in the whole evolution of disarmament, although that evolution may still take another hundred years, for there is nothing that has been done before or since to equal the boldness of the conception and the wisdom of the insistence on bringing it forth in the midst of the impurity of the Treaty. Some people described President Wilson as an idealist without a sense of realities. How could anything more realistic be found in an idealist, as he was, than that way of bribing every nation—including his own—into accepting the Covenant by giving them all sorts of things which had better not be discussed now? Therefore the Covenant, and all it means, and particularly the will behind the Covenant (which was Wilson's) is, in my opinion, far and away the greatest asset which the American nation can show in this account, otherwise not very favourable to her cause. And as for England, no one who knows the history of the first years of the League can fail to realize that the nation which has given the League the services of Viscount Cecil has an almost equal claim to immortality. I have had the honour of working in close association with Viscount Cecil for many years, and I am convinced that he is one of those men who honour not only their country but the human race in general. That he has his limitations is only another way of saying that he is a man. I am rather glad he has his limitations, for otherwise he would not be with us. But in spite of many accusations which have been raised against his action in Geneva, and in spite of many an accusation levelled against him even in his own country—particularly in his own country—again on the same lines as the accusations levelled against President Wilson, that he is an idealist without sense of realities, I hold Viscount Cecil to be one of the true and best types of Conservative that I have ever known—that is to say, a man who knows what is worth conserving, and what are the best methods for conserving it. On that definition, most Conservatives had better quit the ticket.

These two men, Wilson and Cecil, were far and away the most important supporters of the Covenant, and the Covenant, when well studied—a most important qualification, and very seldom followed—is, I believe, the most statesmanlike and the most complete effort for the solution of the problem of disarmament that has been devised or, indeed, probably can be devised. When well studied, the Covenant reveals itself as the solution of the problem of disarmament, for it is the charter whereby the world community is set up, with three aims in view: first, prohibiting a conflict without consideration of causes; secondly, establishing a system for the consideration of causes of conflict, and if possible, their solution; and thirdly, establishing a system for foreseeing conflicts by taking over as many of the national activities of the world on an international basis as is possible. I have been working at Disarmament since 1921, and I confess that I do not see any other road to disarmament than the *simultaneous* application of these three methods. I insist on the *simultaneous*. I am therefore convinced that the most important step towards disarmament, incomparably superior to anything ever previously dreamt of, was taken by the men who drafted the Covenant, and by the great man who insisted on having it put down in black and white and ratified.

After that, everything else is minor. But there is one thing which stands out, for it is, since the Covenant was signed and ratified by practically everybody, evidently the gravest step backward; and you naturally guess that I refer to the refusal of the American Senate to ratify the Covenant. That stands to the debit side of the American nation very heavily indeed, and I do not see how any precautions of international courtesy, or any tendency to safeguard the civilities, or even any tendency to make oneself agreeable to one's audience could minimize in any way the terrible responsibility which the American nation has incurred by nullifying, to a considerable extent, the great and statesmanlike step taken by one of the greatest of its Presidents. As for England, we had the valuable support of Lord Cecil's thought in Geneva for several years, and I am sure that to that thought the League owes and the world owes most of the progress that has been achieved in the education of the world in this problem. When all is said and done, it is mostly a problem of education of the mind, of public opinion. The evolution of League work, through the Treaty of Guarantee and the Protocol to Locarno—a mere episode, but an episode in the right direction—must be traced back to Resolution 14 of the Assembly of 1922, which was due to the statesmanlike imagination and wisdom of Lord Cecil. This evolution aims at perfecting in its details the system which the Covenant sets up, and which I summarized a minute ago. Personally I do not think that the whole of the Protocol is indispensable for the solution of the problem. I hold what perhaps Lord Cecil would consider unorthodox views on the subject. If I interpret him aright, he would attach great importance to the fact that any surrender of national rights to an international system of judiciary arbitration and conciliation should be subordinated to the success of a Disarmament Conference. I consider disarmament as a natural function of nations, which will be performed by those nations on the day that armaments become irksome and useless to them, and if nations accepted the Protocol without its disarmament clauses, and gave it a trial for several years, I hold the view that very likely a disarmament conference would not be necessary, for armaments would begin to drop right and left as people began to think that they did not want to spend money on useless and heavy implements.

Here I should like to say a word about the attitude of England and America in relation to the Protocol. England turned down the Protocol in a letter addressed to the Council of the League of Nations, a letter in which the feebleness of the substance was only rivalled by the brilliancy of the form; and yet, when that letter is studied, one detects in it two preoccupations, both of which deserve to be considered. One is the extremely complex and vague nature of the world interests which the British Empire can plausibly call 'vital', and the other one is a strong preoccupation with the possible consequences of the Protocol in cases in which the United States of America finds itself on the wrong side of the barricade. So that when the attitude of the British Empire towards the Protocol is considered, it is only fair to say that at least 50 per cent. of its negative attitude is due to a fear that nothing can be done on that road until the United States has fully joined the world community. I think, therefore, I am justified in associating the two nations in the failure of the Protocol. As I said a moment ago, I am not committed to the full Protocol, and in my opinion what should have been done at the time by the two Anglo-Saxon peoples, if they had remained faithful to the Wilson tradition, would have been to suggest that the disarmament and the sanctions clauses should be dropped—but to insist very strongly that the Protocol, in so far as it sets up a system for the peaceful solution of conflicts and for the designation of the aggressor nation, should remain in full force. If the two Anglo-Saxon nations had given that answer at the time, I think we should be on the very rapid way towards disarmament. Instead of that, they turned it down. Why? Because for a number of reasons, some of which are known, neither of these two nations is enthusiastic about a complete system for the peaceful solution of conflicts. It is no use watering down that statement. That is a fact. Look at the facts. There are to-day at least twenty-five treaties in the world between nations submitting absolutely all their disputes to peaceful settlement. All of them without exception. Now several of these nations, including Switzerland, have offered England such treaties. England has turned them down. England has only made one such treaty, with Uruguay, and I believe that the Foreign Office was bold enough at the time even not to except from the Treaty frontier difficulties with Uruguay. What is the record of America? President Roosevelt made an effort to set up treaties of complete arbitration. The Senate brought in an amendment, of which President Roosevelt himself, who, after all, was not particularly squeamish in international matters, said textually: 'I think this amendment makes the treaties shams, and my present impression is that we had better abandon the whole business rather than give the impression of trickiness and insincerity which would be produced by solemnly promulgating a sham.'

That brings me to policy. I believe that if the record in arbitrational matters of these two great nations is not as satisfactory as we might expect from the strong body of idealism which both of them contain—for, after all, Anglo-Saxon idealism is one of the strongest forces in the movement of the League of Nations—it is due to the fact that their policy is not fully in harmony with the present trend of international life. To begin with, both these great nations base their policy to a considerable extent on the strict keeping of the narrow waterways of the world. The British policy of Gibraltar, the Suez Canal, the narrows of Asia, has been inherited by the United States, and explains all that goes under those two significant names, Panama and Nicaragua. The Monroe Doctrine has evolved from a system whereby a whole continent was defended and protected against European ambition, into one whereby the whole continent is undefended against American ambition. I do not know how many of you are aware that the only recent case in which any award given by an international court has been flouted stands to the debit of the United States. When the United States Government made a treaty with a Government which was set up in Nicaragua under the protection of American marines, whereby the sole rights for the building of a Nicaraguan Canal through the San Juan river were granted to the United States, and the Bay of Fonseca was given over for ninety-nine years as a naval base to the United States, three other States—Costa Rica, Salvador, and Honduras—protested on the ground that this treaty was against their rights. Costa Rica had a Treaty with Nicaragua dating back more than fifty years, in which Nicaragua agreed that the river navigation Treaties would be reserved for Costa Rica, and that nothing could be done without consulting her in the matter. As for the other two States, being riparian to the bay and inheritors of its rights, as both members of the old Central American Federation, they insisted that nothing should be done in the Bay without consulting them. Washington tried to buy them out with money. They refused. Washington—for this is the curious thing about Washington, that it is at the same time running this kind of policy and highly idealistic in other ways—Washington had induced these five States to set up a Court for solving their difficulties, and this Court existed. These States therefore said, 'Very well, let us go to the Court,' and they took the matter before the Court. The Court, in 1916, decided the case about Costa Rica, and in 1917 the case about Guatemala, and in both cases the Court said that a treaty was evidently against the rights of those States, and that Nicaragua was in the wrong; but being a small Court, of a small Central American

Federation, it did not feel adequate to deal with its great neighbour of the north, and said that it had no competence to decide—having said that—whether the Treaty with the United States was valid or not. All it could say was that the Treaty violated the rights of a State over which that Court had jurisdiction. The Treaty was nevertheless upheld by Washington. Ladies and gentlemen, I said at the beginning that I was going to speak with as much impartiality and coldness as possible, and I am doing it. I am only referring you to facts which are known, and which can be got at by a very moderate amount of exertion, as is proved by the fact that I have got them.

Now, policy, it seems to me, is in the last resort the essential in these matters. The letter of the law is dead compared to the life, to the trend of policy. In my opinion, on the day on which the British Government sends an ultimatum couched in terms of absolute sovereignty to the Egyptian Government, it does not matter whether legally Egypt is not a member of the League, it does not matter whether Egypt is theoretically not altogether an absolutely independent State, but only a State more or less semi-independent while not being dependent, the fact remains that the world has heard the growl of the lion, and when the world hears the growl of the lion, the lion in every one of us wakes up, and that is the main point. I am not so much concerned with the injury done to Egypt as with the injury done to the world community. One action against the Covenant means ten years of retrocession on the road to disarmament, and when I say one action against the Covenant I do not mean against the letter of the Covenant, I mean against the spirit of the Covenant. We have all heard that a Pact is going to be signed in Paris in a few days outlawing war.

Very well. I personally thought that war had been outlawed by the Covenant. It seems that the Covenant still leaves open what Sir Austen Chamberlain has been pleased to call the windows for letting in air to breathe, and what I should like to call the windows for letting poison gas in. I am quite pleased that Mr. Kellogg should come along with some putty and try to block up those windows. Sir Austen Chamberlain, being committed to the policy of the open window, and yet being anxious to keep on good terms with his American cousins, has found an elegant solution. He accepts this putty being put on his windows, and then he proceeds to perforate it with reservations. Well, it may be, in fact I believe that it is, if not all to the good, on balance to the good. People will keep talking, efficiently or inefficiently, about stopping war for a long time before they actually do it, and therefore I am ready to applaud with both hands while the ceremony takes place in Paris. But I remember the holes in the putty, and so far as I am concerned I cannot help feeling that Mr. Kellogg must have been rather glad of those holes, thinking of the holes that he at least had mentally perforated in his own putty.

I have spoken too long, and I want to sum up. On the debit side, I believe the two great Anglo-Saxon nations have the heaviest responsibility for slowness in the progress of the work of disarmament; the heaviest for two reasons: first, because I believe that on the whole it is intrinsically the heaviest, and secondly, because being the two leaders of the world, their responsibility is relatively higher. On the positive side, there is no question that the two nations that have given the Covenant, President Wilson, and Lord Cecil to the world, not only show thereby that they have already contributed definitely what is probably the greatest asset in the problem of disarmament; they show something more. They show that there is in them a spirit, that spirit which created those men, and that that spirit must conquer the other, and bring about the desired result. I personally, knowing one of them well and the other one fairly well, for, after all, most of America comes to Geneva—feel very optimistic. The only element of doubt I see, in the possibility (which I believe is strong) that the two Anglo-Saxon nations may finally take the lead forward and bring about the desired end, is that I believe that Anglo-Saxon idealism is apt sometimes to accept too readily the lame explanations of Anglo-Saxon—the other thing. That is evidently a tangible danger; but I come back to my first note. The world has not even yet realized the greatness, the moral and political and statesmanlike greatness, of the men who created the Covenant, a Covenant which was mostly an Anglo-Saxon inspiration at the time—I am not speaking of historical origins. The greatness of these men is a token, a guarantee, that there is, in those two great nations, enough idealism to create the world community. Well, let them do it.

CHAPTER IV

THE FIRST RESULTS OF THE WORLD ECONOMIC CONFERENCE

Sir Arthur Salter:

MY subject, as the Chairman has reminded you, is *The First Results of the World Economic Conference*. I have had the pleasure of lecturing to this Institute for the last few years, and I am anxious not to repeat unnecessarily anything I have said on former occasions. But I cannot present intelligibly the first results of this Economic Conference without attempting first to set the Conference itself in its proper background and perspective. I propose, therefore, this afternoon to attempt first to place the Economic Conference in its proper place in relation to the general economic and financial work of the League. In the second place, I shall remind you, I hope briefly, of what the Conference was and what in main substance it recommended. Then in the third place I shall come to my principal subject: the subsequent developments,—what has happened since the Conference. Next I propose to say something about prospects for the future and the more important conditions of success. And lastly I shall attempt to suggest the relation of the whole of the work of this kind to the general work of the League and to the general problem of the peace of the world.

i. *The Perspective of the Economic Conference.*

First, then, What is the relation of this Economic Conference to the general economic and financial work of the League? You will remember that after the first confusion of the years immediately succeeding the war, when there

had been time for the transitional and trivial obstacles to
the recovery of Europe and of the world to disappear, two
great impediments to future recovery came into prominence.
The first was the financial chaos and the fluctuations and
wasting of currencies, and the second, both in time and, for
the time, in importance, was the emergence of increased
trade barriers and in particular the increased height of tariffs
since the war. Each of these impediments to recovery resulted from governmental action and needed for its removal
both national and international action. They were both,
therefore, suitable cases for League intervention. I need
not remind you of the important part the League has
taken in the removal of the first of these obstacles. The
League did pioneer work, both by precept at the Brussels
Financial Conference and by example in the reconstruction
of Austria and of Hungary, to lead the world back to sound
finances and stable currencies. While that work was still
requiring to be done it was so much the most important
that it would have been useless and futile for the League to
attempt its second task of dealing with specifically economic
troubles, such as trade barriers.

Up to about 1924–5 we might say that fluctuating and
wasting currencies were the principal obstacle to the economic recovery of the world. By 1925 that had ceased to be
the case, and trade barriers were becoming the most serious
obstacle. At the present date, in August 1928, we may say
that the first task of stabilizing currencies and securing that
stable foundation, upon which alone any stable rebuilding
of the structure of the world's economic life is possible,
has been achieved with the stabilization of the French franc.
Although, however, the goal was not completely attained,
it was clearly in sight in the year 1925, and in 1925, therefore,

the League of Nations, carefully choosing its time, decided upon a general review of the whole economic position of the world in order to see whether the adoption of new principles of economic policy could substantially accelerate the progress of the world's recovery. After more than a year's preparation, therefore, the great World Economic Conference was held in May 1927. I would remind you that that Conference, though not consisting of representatives directly accredited to the different Governments, consisted of some two hundred persons, chosen from every possible sphere of qualification and experience by the fifty Governments who participated in the Conference. Economists, industrialists, workers and consumers, agriculturists, men of every relevant type of experience were all included among its members. The distinctive character of that Conference, therefore, as Monsieur Theunis, I think, happily phrased it in his speech to the Conference at the time was that it was 'responsible though not official, expert while not academic'. The unanimous agreement of two hundred people so chosen and qualified upon what the world most needed to enable it to return more quickly to prosperity, gave an incontestable authority to the recommendations. The advice was, I think, at once more authoritative and more definite than any which has ever proceeded from a Conference appointed to consider economic problems. It was, in a word, something as near certainty as we can ever hope to attain in this fallible world.

ii. *The Recommendations of the Economic Conference.*

What, in main substance, did that Conference recommend? I will mention, only to pass briefly by, the less important and secondary recommendations. The Conference traversed the sphere of industry. It considered as the most important subject in that sphere the question of what are usually called international cartels, 'international industrial agreements' as the official text calls them. Now there were many at the moment when the Conference was summoned who thought that the encouragement of such cartels by the League would perhaps be the chief and most important result of the World Economic Conference. It was, indeed, easy to imagine cases in which a cartel run in a certain way and inspired by certain motives might prove a solution to some of the most pressing and the most obvious problems of unemployment and dislocation with which the world was faced. As we got nearer to the Conference, however, another and rather a different trend of opinion developed. It was felt that while, indeed, some cartels might be useful and might be so designed, controlled, and directed as to be of general public utility and profit, not only to the employers and men in the industry concerned but also to the consuming public, it was at the same time extremely difficult to secure that result. It was felt that it would be a very difficult and dangerous thing for the League of Nations, representing, as it must, all countries and all classes, consumers as well as producers, consuming countries as well as producing countries, to bring into existence forms of collective organization whose ultimate development it could perhaps not control or direct. It was felt that possibly if the League did that, without powers of control which it was unlikely to obtain, the cloak of the League might be thrown over organizations for which it would be most improper for the League to take responsibility. When therefore the Conference met, the question of international cartels took a quite secondary place, and the Conference recommended not so much encouragement as an attitude of caution and vigilance. The League was advised to examine, report, and publish information as to development and effects of such cartels. For reasons into which I need not now go, no substantial work has yet been done by the League or under League auspices in relation to the movement of international cartels. We are now beginning, on the advice of the Consultative Committee which met this year, to make a study of certain aspects of these problems, but no results have yet been reached.

The position is much the same with regard to the second sphere, of agriculture. The Conference brought out in a very useful fashion the relation and the crucial importance of agriculture to the general economic life of the world. It made a number of recommendations as to lines on which action might usefully proceed. But in general the recommendations were rather for the continuance of action already undertaken, undertaken in some cases by or through the Institute of Agriculture at Rome, rather than advice that the League itself should initiate new action. There again no substantial work has been done by the League in the year and a half to which I am now referring. We are now engaged in conversations with the Institute of Agriculture as to the best way in which our respective functions of work should be divided. Here again, therefore, I have no results to report during this last year.

Passing rapidly these two spheres I wish to place the whole weight of emphasis this afternoon upon the third sphere, that of commercial policy. What the World Conference really said, is in essence very simple. Surveying the whole sphere of the world's economic life, surveying the whole range of post-war commercial and economic policy, it said unanimously, with incontestable authority and with unusual and surprising decision and definiteness, just this.

Trade barriers, and in particular increased tariffs, are the chief of the removable obstacles to the more rapid recovery of the world's prosperity. They are too unstable; they are too complicated; and they are too high. They ought to be more stable; they ought to be simplified; and they ought to be reduced.

Now to indicate by just a few figures the character of those obstacles which the Conference had in mind when it made these recommendations. First as to simplicity. I was looking at a few figures the other day as to the number of items of different categories in some of the principal countries' tariff régimes, and the way in which these numbers had increased. I see that in Germany, for example, instead of 400 items in 1888 there were 2,300 in 1925. In Italy instead of 535 in 1878 there were 2,777 in 1921. In Belgium instead of 235 in 1884 there were 2,000 odd in 1924. In France instead of some 1,500 in 1892 there were 4,000 odd in 1927. I have taken these four countries not because they are worse than others but just at random as four important countries whose case very well illustrates a very general tendency. If you imagine these enormous numbers of separate items in each of the countries' tariffs, and remember that they are phrased and defined with a nomenclature that means different things in different cases, that does not fit, and that overlaps, you will realize something of the complication that comes from the mere diversities and complications of tariff nomenclature. Then as to stability. Before the war it was customary to make a commercial treaty and to have suitable arrangements for at least something like ten years, but of 180 treaties examined after the war in connexion with the Economic Conference it was found that 153 were subject to change within a year. Now it is perfectly obvious that you cannot build any form of constructive and continuous trade relationship, you cannot build any industry, for a world market subject to interference, and perhaps fatal interference, by tariff changes made within such short periods as a year. Lastly, as to height: tariffs vary, of course, from 1 or 2 per cent. to 100 per cent. or more in value. But there has been a tendency on the whole for the real weight of the tariff to increase on the average by something like 30 per cent. since before the war.

Now to estimate the importance of the tariff obstacle to the trade of the world, you must, of course, take these difficulties not separately but cumulatively. I wish I could draw for you an adequate picture of what cumulatively and in total the trade barriers of every kind mean as a weight upon the productive capacity of the world. Just think for a moment of those thousands of items in each country's tariff, meaning something different from the thousands of items in other countries' tariffs. Think of the clerks in the Customs administrations working on these complicated documents. Think of the clerks in the offices of the industrialists and of the exporting merchants trying to understand them for each of the countries to which they wish to export their goods. Imagine behind them the army of officials required to collect, and directly or indirectly take their toll, at every railway junction in all the thirty or so frontiers round Europe, to say nothing of other continents; the officials at every railway junction and every frontier cross-road examining, unloading, studying, and applying these complicated tariffs. Try to realize the intricacy of the task of the exporting industry, faced with all these complexities, further aggravated sometimes by every kind of personal factor, from oriental corruption to occidental pedantry. Add all these together, and

G

imagine that they are pressing with a cumulative and collective weight upon the productive life of the world. When I think of these and try to visualize what they mean to myself, I am amazed that there should be any international trade at all.

I draw two conclusions: first of all, that if international trade remains enormous, and for the world as a whole is increasing in spite of this, it shows in a striking and undeniable fashion the enormous economic advantage there is in the differentiation of function in production as between different countries; and it shows also from another angle how overwhelmingly and obviously true is the view of the Economic Conference that if this weight could be removed, or even substantially reduced, the prosperity of the world would take a great leap forward.

iii. *The Results of the Economic Conference.*

So much for the policy. How far is it being applied? Now, what has happened since the Economic Conference? In answering that question, I have the advantage of the Report of the Consultative Committee which met in May of this year, a year after the meeting of the original Conference. This Committee was a body composed very much of people of the same qualifications as the Conference itself, although with a smaller range of numbers and a somewhat smaller range of nationality; but in effect it was a kind of miniature World Conference, and if it meets (as is at present the intention) each year, in the May of each year, it will become a kind of World Annual Economic Conference. This body reviewed the whole progress of what had happened in the year which had succeeded the Conference of May of 1927.

The Committee first reviewed the world's economic development in the preceding year. One interesting fact came to light. The Economic Conference had pointed out that already by 1926 the average level of prosperity was higher than before the war. This result was, however, due to a great advance of the other continents than Europe. Europe had fallen behind; and in Europe the Eastern part had fallen behind the West. Now the review of last May showed that in 1927 the backward parts of the world were beginning to catch up. Europe was not only substantially more prosperous in 1927 than she had been in 1926 and previous years, but she had begun to catch up a little on America. She had made an advance in 1927; America had about stayed where she was. And what is true of Europe in relation to the rest of the world was also true of the less prosperous parts of Europe in relation to the more prosperous parts; that is to say, the advance in 1927 of Eastern Europe had been greater relatively in comparison with the advance of Western Europe; so you had some tendency towards an evening up, a tendency which, I need hardly say, is very far indeed from having brought the position to anything like equality.

So much for general economic progress. But our special subject is what has been the attitude of the world towards the advice and recommendations of the Economic Conference. Well, as to acceptance by Governments, we have every reason, certainly, to be satisfied. Nearly all the Governments who took part in the Conference have accepted, in some form or another, the main substance of the Conference recommendations, accepted them in the sense at least of agreeing in principle. If one goes outside the Governments, we have the very remarkable endorsement of such bodies as the International Chamber of Commerce, which has enthusiastically supported the main thesis and the main advice of the Conference. We have also such pronouncements of opinion as that of the Economic Council of the German Reich, who have thrown themselves whole-heartedly behind the policy of the Conference; and, that of the Australian Tariff Board, set up to examine the effect of the working of the very high Australian tariff. The already responsible advice of the Economic Conference has therefore been made even more authoritative by official acceptance and by the endorsement of large and important outside bodies. So far, so good. But now as to action. As to what has actually happened, as to what has been the effect on the policies of the various Governments, I have to choose my words carefully. The best way to show the effect on policy is perhaps to cite from the official documents which attempt to give a measured statement of the situation. There are two documents which deal with this matter. In the first place, the Secretariat of the League prepared, for the Consultative Committee in May, a brief appreciation of the general situation, which may be summarized as follows. (a) In May 1927 the tariffs in the basic tariff systems of the different countries were perhaps slightly higher than a year before, in 1927. (b) In May 1927, however, a number of new tariffs were in preparation or before the respective parliaments which were much higher than the tariffs hitherto in force, and the tariffs actually adopted during the year 1927 were, on the whole, considerably lower than the tariffs that were then so proposed. (c) Moreover, a considerable number of commercial agreements providing for reductions in a number of items, either directly or indirectly through the operation of the most-favoured-nation clause, had been contracted during the year; and a number of important demands for increased tariffs made during the year had been rejected. (*d*) Further, with the adhesion of France, the most-favoured-nation clause had again become a central feature in the commercial policy of the world.

This report was, on the whole, endorsed by the much more authoritative statement of the Consultative Committee to which I have referred, and I should just like to quote to you a few words from the Report of that Committee. 'On balance', says the Report, 'there appears to have been some improvement during the year. Many prohibitions were re-laxed or removed, though the actual reductions of tariffs made during the year have to be offset by a number of increases in different countries, and though the increases embodied in tariff laws have perhaps outnumbered the reductions, the conclusion of numerous commercial treaties and the general adoption in them of the most-favoured-nation clause moderated the level of duties to which trade has actually been subjected. Coming after a series of years in which tariffs have been tending upward, many restrictive practices have been in force, and currencies have been in a state of chaos, the comparative stability of tariffs and of exchanges is largely responsible for the trade improvement that has actually occurred.' And if you may think that that, after all, is not a very encouraging result, I would quote one further sentence from this Report. The Committee pointed out that 'it was several years after the Brussels Financial Conference of 1920 before the Finance Committee of the League was able to put on record concrete achievements in the sphere of financial reconstruction in Europe. In the case of the recommendations of the World Economic Conference, action has been considerably more rapid, for it may be said that the effect of the Conference has already substantially checked the upward movement of tariffs, which was in full swing in May 1927.'

Now, if I am to sum up in a single phrase what that comes to in net result, I think I cannot do better than use, with some modification, a metaphor which the President of the Conference, M. Theunis, has constantly used during this last year. During the year 1927, he was accustomed to say, 'we found an upward tariff movement in process like a motor-car running away. We jumped on the car, we jammed on the brakes; we have certainly slowed the pace, but we have not yet stopped the car, still less have we reversed it.' But if you apply the same metaphor to the actual results found and reported on the authoritative examination of this Consultative Committee, you will be entitled to say that the 'motor-car has been stopped, and the reverse movement has just begun, but it is still not quite certain that the car will not slip down again'. The issue is hopeful, but not yet certain. That, I think, so far as I can interpret and present the collective view of this authoritative Committee, is the net result of this last year.

The actual method by which that result has been achieved has been a twofold one. In part, we have by collective action removed, or secured Conventions which, if ratified, will finally remove, many of the trade impediments, such as prohibitions and restrictions other than tariffs. But in the second place, the year 1927 was pre-eminently a year of commercial treaties. The foremost in importance of those, of course, was the Franco-German Treaty of August 1927. This Treaty, it is true, gave to France the opportunity of making an upward revision in her tariffs which had long been in contemplation. But this increase was much less than that planned before the Conference. Moreover, it has been subsequently modified by tariff reductions made by France in her commercial treaties with Belgium, Switzerland, Italy, and Austria, and the benefit of these reductions has been extended to nearly every State by virtue of the 'most-favoured-nation clause'. In addition to those treaties, treaties have been also concluded between Germany and the Serb-Croat-Slovene State, between Germany and Greece, between Austria and Hungary, and between Hungary and Czecho-slovakia. These treaties also have been based on the unconditional most-favoured-nation clause.

You therefore have, as a very distinctive note in the whole of this year, the conclusion of bilateral conventions between pairs of countries, of which the effect has been spread, by the operation of most-favoured-nation clauses, to countries not parties to the particular convention.

I have no time now to describe to you in detail the very large amount of other action outside the sphere of tariffs themselves, action which is briefly summarized by the Consultative Committee as follows: 'the elaboration in conjunction with the International Chamber of Commerce of a draft international convention on the treatment of foreigners, which is now before the Governments; the drawing up of a general outline of a uniform Customs nomenclature'—the importance of which I have just described; ' the initiation of inquiries into treaty methods, into the most-favoured-nation clause, and into the possibility of collective action in tariff matters. Conventions for the execution of foreign arbitral awards and the work on the assimilation of legislation on bills of exchange.'

There is just one form of action to which I must refer in rather more detail. Finding that the time was not ripe for anything like a general tariff reduction conference, the League has attempted to take particular trades and see whether some progress could not be made within a limited sphere. They have had considerable success in one rather important category of raw materials, skins and hides: so much so, that they are now considering the extension of this same method domain by domain to other trades. Let me repeat that the net result of all this action up to the present is that the rapid upward movement of trade barriers in 1927 has been arrested, and perhaps just reversed; but the struggle is even, the forces equal, the issue uncertain. The situation is such as to give every encouragement for effort, but no encouragement for complacency.

In the course of these events, a number of rather interesting pieces of experience came to light. I will quote two. The first is the case of Sweden. Sweden of all European countries has made about the biggest reduction in the weight of her tariffs as compared with before the war, and she has secured the biggest increase in her international trade, an increase of almost 100 per cent. I will give you one more interesting piece of experience—(I am just giving you odd fragments of experience, which I might, of course, develop and multiply a good deal). We found that one very common argument used against proposals to reduce tariffs was that if you reduced the tariffs you would lose so much revenue which the country could ill spare. Now in the course of last year Hungary made considerable reductions by means of commercial agreements with her neighbours, and to the surprise, I think, of most of the people in Hungary itself, even those who had advocated the reduction, the result, and the immediate result, was not a decrease but an increase in the revenue. The increased consumption, resulting from the reduced price that had followed from the reduced tariff, more than compensated the revenue for the reduction in the rate of duty on each article. Those are two small, but I think very instructive, examples of recent experience.

Well, so much as to the actual results of the last year.

iv. *The Prospects for the Future.*

I now want to have a word as to the prospects of the future. I have said that in my view, and I think in the general view, the struggle is equal, the forces well matched, the issue uncertain. There is matter for hope, but not for complacency. That means, in effect, that there must be another and a renewed effort if this policy of the Economic Conference is to be assured of success. I should like to make a few suggestions as to the way in which high tariff countries and low tariff countries respectively might help. If I were speaking to a series of high tariff countries, I should say something like this: 'You must not expect, having a very high tariff yourself, that you can get a general reduction in tariffs by reductions in equal proportions. You must no more expect that than you would expect the same proportion of his income in income tax from a poor man as you would expect from a rich man. Reduction from all, perhaps, but not equal or even proportionate reduction.' I would say this, in the second place: 'Of course, the other members of the Economic Conference realize the extent to which your economic life is based, or partly based, on tariffs. Nobody expects that you can suddenly return to free trade, nor does the Economic Conference necessarily mean that you should make equal reductions, or reductions for all your industries. But would not it be well for you to look at the different industries you are protecting, and try to discover and work upon some reasonable and logical principle, distinguishing between those industries which it is really worth while for the country to protect and those for whose protection you are paying excessive prices? Will you not examine in turn whether each industry which you are keeping in existence by a high tariff really has any affinity either to the resources of your country or to the inherited or acquired skill of the inhabitants of it? If not, will you consider whether it really is worth while for you to pay the price, and the very big price, that is required to keep that industry? Because think what it means. You, Ruritania (shall we say), are keeping in existence a textile industry which you never had before the war, and for which you have no natural resources. What are you doing? What is the price you are paying? In the first place, you must secure capital for the new plant of this new industry. In so doing, you are taking away capital from your basic industries, perhaps agriculture, and you are causing those industries to pay a higher price for their capital. That is the first result. The second result is that you are necessarily increasing the price of textiles, and directly and indirectly the whole cost of living for the whole of your country, and therefore the competitive power of your other industries. In the third place, you want to make commercial agreements with your neighbours, but how can you hope to get them to reduce the tariffs protecting industries which are as alien to them as this industry is to you, unless you are prepared to make a similar concession? And lastly, a reduction in imports *must* mean a reduction in exports, and if you prevent your nationals from importing you are certainly reducing to an equivalent extent their opportunities of exporting, and in addition, you are suffering the losses to which I have already referred.' Well, that is the kind of thing I should like to say to the high tariff countries.

But I should like to say something also to the low tariff country. I would say: 'If you really want this policy to succeed (and nobody is likely to score more from the general adoption of this policy of a general movement towards lower tariffs and lower barriers than the existing low tariff countries of the world) you must do something to help it. Now, it is no use for you to say, "We already have lower tariffs; all we have to do is to point out to the rest of the world how much more virtuous we are than they are." The rest of the world will reply, "If you have had a low tariff in the past, it is presumably because the best advisers you could find (and they may have been right) thought that it was in your national interest to have that low tariff, even though the rest of the world had a high tariff; we cannot take it that you had that low tariff simply because you desired not to impede our trade. We must therefore assume that a low tariff was in accordance with your interests, in the past, as you must assume that our higher tariff was in accordance with our interests. But now comes the proposal for a general world movement which will benefit all of us, you as much as us. If you want that to succeed, you must contribute. That does not necessarily mean that you should make as big a reduction, or as big a proportionate reduction, as we do; but you must *contribute*, and contribute does not mean saying how much more virtuous you are than we; it means something quite simple and quite definite. A contribution by a country to the success of the World Conference's policy means just this. It means bringing its policy closer to the policy recommended in the Economic Conference than it would otherwise have been." '
That is what I should say to low tariff countries.

I have one further thing to say as to what, in my view, is an essential condition of an assured success for the future movement towards lower trade barriers, and it is this. If we were starting now with a clean slate, without trade barriers, without tariffs, without vested interests, the authoritative verdict of a body such as the Economic Conference, and the recognition of the direction in which the general public interest of the world lies, might perhaps suffice; but we are not. We are dealing, and necessarily dealing, with a situation in which every barrier is buttressed by a vested interest. We must expect, and of course we shall find, the opposition of those whose interests are threatened by a movement in the other direction. Now, against that, the advice, however authoritative, of the Conference, the goodwill, however sincere, of Governments, the public interest, however real, but diffused, less organized, and therefore weaker, is not likely to prevail. We must have one more thing to support those forces, real as they, but in themselves not sufficient: we must have the organized and collective effort of those interests which stand to gain by the policy recommended by the Economic Conference just as directly as other interests may think they have gained by the opposite policy. There are very large interests in the world, the interests of exporting industries—(I mean by exporting industries, industries which depend, and know that they must depend, more upon export than they can hope to depend upon a protected home market)—export merchants, the shipping trade, finance and banking, and in addition all the industries to whom a protected article is a raw material; and, lastly of course, the general public themselves, organized, if in no other place, in the electorates of their several countries. If this movement is to be successful, all these classes of interests who stand indubitably to gain, and gain greatly, from the adoption of this policy, must do their part. The issue is still uncertain, the cause promising but not assured. If any one hesitates as to the importance of doing whatever lies in his own power to forward this policy, let him reflect upon the reward promised not only in the prosperity of the world but in the peace of the world. As to prosperity, there can surely be no gain-saying—no one has attempted to gainsay—the advice and the opinion of the World Economic Conference itself, an opinion which, when translated into human terms, means that the adoption of this policy will result, for millions of mankind, in prosperity instead of poverty, sustenance instead of starvation, employment instead of the degradation of unemployment. But apart from that, let him remember, finally, that it means a contribution, and a substantial contribution, towards the future peace of the world.

v. *The Economic Problem and the Problem of Peace.*

The World Economic Conference of 1927 was appointed for two objects—to find a policy which would help the prosperity of the world, and to find a policy which would help to strengthen the foundations of the peace of the world. The Conference believed that the principles which they advocated would conduce equally to both. When we are thinking of the relation between economic policies and the peace of the world, I hope we shall not say lightly and lazily, 'Oh, there is the League of Nations, with its machinery for settling disputes, to save us from the disaster of another war.' The League of Nations can do much under certain conditions, but it certainly cannot preserve the peace under every possible condition. I would like to quote to you the weighty and important remarks of M. Theunis, the President of the Conference, in this connexion. He said: 'Economic conflicts and divergence of economic interest are perhaps the most serious and the most permanent of all the dangers which are likely to threaten the peace of the world. No machinery for the settlement of international disputes can be relied upon to maintain peace if the economic policies of the world so develop as to create not only deep divergencies of economic interest between different masses of the world's population but a sense of intolerable injury and injustice. No task is more urgent or more vital than that of securing agreement on certain principles of policy which are necessary in the interests of future peace. And there is perhaps no question which, in comparison with its intrinsic importance, has had so little careful and collective deliberation.'

In a word, if we want peace we must not merely rely upon a machinery for the settlement of disputes when they arise; we must so lay the foundations of peace that the disputes which do arise will be relatively unenvenomed by previous dissension, and will not be deeply rooted in a long-standing sense of divergent interest and injustice. The League certainly cannot, like a quack medicine, undertake to cure an illness however long it has been allowed to develop. I read a week or two ago an advertisement of a quack medicine which made this somewhat alluring offer to its potential purchasers. 'This medicine', said the advertisement, 'permits every excess and saves you from the consequences.' Well, that is a very alluring offer; the trouble is that it is a lie. If you habitually conduct your life in defiance of all the rules of health, you are not going to find a quack medicine, or a medicine of any kind, that is going to save you from all the consequences; and if we, comfortably believing that there is a machinery for stopping war, are content to allow the economic forces of the world to move along lines which lead and guide to war, even the machinery of the

League will not, at the last moment, save us from the consequences.

When we consider therefore the future issues involved in the success or failure of this World Economic Conference, and whether or not it is worth our while to do, each in our own sphere, what we can to make this policy successful, let us remember that if we do decide to put our effort into the task, we are not only helping the prosperity of the world, but we are establishing the foundations of the peace of the world. And if, again, we wonder whether our aid is required, remember that on the review of the situation which has been made by the most authoritative body we could find to make it, the position at this moment is clear, perhaps only too clear, to this extent. The experience of this last year or eighteen months has shown, and shown indubitably, that success is possible—but it has not shown that success will come. We have, therefore, at once an encouragement and a stimulus to effort.

CHAPTER V

TENDENCIES IN INTERNATIONAL LABOUR LEGISLATION

i. *The Progress of Ratifications.*

Mr. E. J. PHELAN:

INTERNATIONAL Labour Legislation is a body of Treaties, or as they are technically called international labour conventions. Where nationally we have legislation, internationally we have treaties. The area over which treaties are applied depends on the number of States which formally bind themselves to observe their provisions. States bind themselves to observe a treaty by the act of ratification. The International Labour Conference adopts drafts conventions: it performs the function which is performed by a meeting of plenipotentiaries when they draw up the terms of a treaty. But it is the ratifications of the States which bring the treaty into operation. The number of ratifications of Labour Conventions is accordingly a measure of the extent of international labour legislation.

We may take the number of ratifications of labour conventions, therefore, as a quantitative indication of the transformation of international proposals regarding labour conditions into national obligations to observe those conditions. The following table shows the progress of ratifications:

	August 1926.	August 1927.	August 1928.
Ratifications registered . .	208	230	325
Ratifications authorized .	28	36	28
Ratifications recommended .	153	172	150
Total ratifications registered or in sight[1] . . .	389	438	503

[1] There are usually three stages in a national decision to ratify a labour

Thus between August 1926 and August 1927 twenty-four new ratifications were registered.

Between August 1927 and August 1928 there were ninety-five, or practically four times as many.

Thus the first tendency we may notice is that there has been a remarkable increase in the total number of ratifications and in the *rate* at which ratifications are coming in.

Moreover, national activity as regards the labour conventions has increased in an even more remarkable degree. The new ratifications are not as it were ripe fruit which was ready to fall from the tree and which accidentally happened to be shaken off in the period under review.

If we analyse the figures given above [1] we shall see that whereas 99 governmental or parliamentary decisions in favour of ratification were taken between August 1926 and August 1927 no less than 251 [2] similar decisions were taken in the period August 1927 to August 1928.

---

convention: (*a*) the Government brings the convention before Parliament with a recommendation that it be ratified; (*b*) Parliament authorizes ratification by approving the convention; (*c*) an instrument of ratification is transmitted to the Secretary-General of the League who registers it. A Government is of course free to recommend to its Parliament that a convention shall not be approved, but if its recommendation is in favour of ratification, ratification is usually achieved after the delay required for the subsequent operations.

[1] For details of this method of analysis see my article in *Problems of Peace* (Second Series).

[2] This is a minimum figure. It assumes that the 95 new ratifications were obtained by the 'promotion' of the 32 conventions which were authorized for ratification and of 73 of the conventions for which ratification was recommended. Some of the new ratifications, however, may have been ratifications which had made no progress at all a year ago, and if this is so the total number of decisions taken would be greater.

Can any reasons be assigned to explain this very satisfactory phenomenon?

It is difficult to give any complete explanation, but it is easy to show that certain reasons which might suggest themselves are wrong.

The increase is not due to the adoption of a large number of new conventions. Only *three* new conventions have been adopted since August 1926 and they have secured only five ratifications between them. The States have as yet hardly had time to decide whether they will or will not ratify them.

The increase is also not due to any change in the character of the conventions more recently adopted, and by more recently is meant, say, since 1923 or 1924. The suggestion has sometimes been made that the earlier proposals of the International Labour Conference were particularly idealistic, or that they did not, at all events sufficiently, take account of the real complexity of the problems for which they purported to provide an international solution. The Organization has perhaps learnt by experience to moderate its first fervour and to be content with more moderate proposals susceptible of wider and more ready acceptance. But if the ninety-five ratifications of the last twelve months are examined they lend no support to this theory. They are found to be distributed fairly evenly over the older and the newer conventions.

The explanation of the increase is not to be found therefore in any change in the character of the conventions. It would appear to be due, in part at all events, to two general factors.

First of all the provisions in Part XIII of the Treaty providing for the national consideration of the Conference's decisions are now no longer novel. They have become a recognized and habitual procedure. State machinery is a cumbersome and usually a congested thing. To adapt it to the obligations resulting from a new international organization took time. A certain inertia had to be overcome. The obligations had either to be exactly defined as regards the constitutional methods of each State, or new procedure had to be invented for their fulfilment. The international machinery had been created by the Treaty, but the national machinery which had to be geared up with it, as it were, demanded adjustment.[1] And until that adjustment had been made ratifications either were not possible or were only forthcoming with difficulty.

That this kind of adjustment has taken place is indicated by the fact that in many cases the new ratifications have come in in groups from a single country. Thus a block of twenty-five ratifications was sent for registration from Luxemburg. Luxemburg, a State with advanced labour conditions and legislation, had hitherto not ratified any labour convention. The difficulty obviously was not one of legislation but one of procedure.

We may take it therefore that the difficulties of procedure have been, or are being solved, and that henceforth labour conventions will fall more and more to be considered as a matter of course. It would seem possible to hope that, in consequence, an increased rate of ratifications will be main-

---

[1] In some cases it had even to be created. For example, in the case of the Serb-Croat-Slovene State during the early years of the Labour Organization there was no Parliament to which labour conventions could be submitted. It was only when the Constituent Assembly had drawn up the constitution, and the constitution had come into operation that the consideration of labour conventions could begin.

tained, although possibly not at the exceptional level attained during the last twelve months.

There is a second factor which no doubt has had its effect. The fate of international labour conventions must be intimately connected with the general level of economic prosperity. On the one hand the steady progress in economic reconstruction, as instanced for example by the stabilization of European currencies, has meant a return to conditions in which social charges play a greater part in international industrial competition. And on the other hand an increase in economic prosperity and stability removes one of the main obstacles to the advancement of social reform. Thus social reform may be expected to be carried on more actively and the protection given by international labour conventions to become more evident, and therefore more readily sought.

ii. *The Eight Hours Convention.*

While the new ratifications have been spread over the different conventions, including the Eight Hours Convention, the position of that Convention is a special one, and it cannot be included without certain further observations in the general tendencies noted above.

The present position is that it has been ratified by thirteen States, namely: Austria, Belgium, Bulgaria, Chili, Czechoslovakia, France, Greece, India, Italy, Latvia, Roumania, Luxemburg,[1] and Portugal.[1]

These ratifications, however, fall into three classes:

(*a*) The convention contains special provisions as regards *India.*

[1] Ratified during the period August 1927 to August 1928.

(*b*) *Belgium*, *Bulgaria*, *Chili*, *Czechoslovakia*, *Greece*,[1] *Roumania*,[1] *Luxemburg*, and *Portugal* have ratified unconditionally.

(*c*) *Austria*, *France*, *Italy*, and *Latvia* have ratified conditionally, i.e. their ratifications involve no obligations for them unless and until certain other States named in their ratifications also ratify.

The Convention is therefore only actually binding between eight States, and of these only Belgium and Czechoslovakia are of first-rate industrial importance.[2]

The ratifications of France and Italy depend on those of Great Britain and Germany. The attitude of the late Government in Germany was favourable to the Convention and that of the new Government may be expected to be equally or even more so. It was anticipated that the former would decide in favour of a ratification conditional on that of France and of Great Britain. If this decision is now taken the coming into force of the Convention as regards the great industrial Powers of Europe will depend on Great Britain. Her ratification would then make operative the ratifications of France and Germany, and probably also of Italy.[3]

The British Government has announced, however, that

---

[1] Roumania and Greece were given a special period to adapt their legislation, but that period has now elapsed and so they stand in the same position as the other States in (*b*).

[2] The ratification of Luxemburg should not, however, be left out of account. In proportion to its size its industry is important, and has to compete with that of its powerful industrial neighbours.

[3] The Italian 'condition' includes Austria, Belgium, Czechoslovakia, France, Germany, Great Britain, and Switzerland. It is unlikely that Italy would stand out because of Switzerland, and thus isolate herself from the other great industrial powers, or alternatively Switzerland might ratify.

it will not ratify the present Hours Convention, and proposes that it should be revised. All the labour Conventions
contain an article providing for the possibility of their revision, and the British Government proposes that advantage
should be taken of this provision to obtain a convention
embodying the principles of the Washington Convention
(the Eight-hour day and the Forty-eight-hour week), but
defining more clearly certain details of their application.
What these details are the British Government has not yet
specified.

The problem of the Hours Convention is thus at present
intimately bound up with the problem of 'revision', which
is dealt with below.[1]

iii. *The Application of Conventions.*

However satisfactory may be the increased rate of ratification of Labour Conventions, it would of course be of no real
utility unless Conventions when ratified were in fact applied.
Is there reason to believe that a reasonable degree of genuine
application will be enforced?

Last year I drew attention to the importance of Article
408 of the Treaty and of the possibility it gives of a kind of
audit of the balance-sheet of enforcement in each ratifying
State. The Conference had decided to set up a Committee
of independent experts to examine the detailed information
concerning the application of conventions furnished by States
which had ratified and to report on them, much as the Mandates Commission reports on the application of the Mandates.

This system was instituted with a good deal of hesitation.
Doubts were expressed as to whether the initiation of such
a system was not going beyond the terms of the Treaty, and

[1] See page 118.

agreement was only obtained on the basis of trying such a method for an experimental period of two years.

That period ended in May 1928. The experience proved wholly satisfactory, so much so that the Conference has recommended its continuance. Machinery to watch over the application of Labour Conventions [1] may now be regarded as a permanent and unquestioned part of the Organization, and the Conference has even encouraged the experts to pursue their task in greater detail and with complete frankness.

Thus the tendency towards a greater rate of ratification is accompanied by a tendency to secure more complete and effective application. The tendency is both towards an increase in the quantity of international legislation and towards an improvement in the quality of its results.

iv. *The Subjects of International Labour Legislation.*

Twenty-six conventions have so far been adopted by the International Labour Conference. An idea of the field they cover may be gathered from the following brief indications of the subjects with which they deal:

The limitation of hours in industrial undertakings.
Unemployment.
Employment of women before and after childbirth.
Employment of women during the night.
Employment of children and young persons at night.
Minimum age of admission of children to industrial employment.
Minimum age of admission of children to employment at sea.
Unemployment of seamen resulting from the loss of the ship.
Facilities for finding employment for seamen.
Minimum age of admission of children to employment in agriculture.

[1] This is of course independent of the provisions in Article 409 and the following articles for formal complaints and possible sanctions.

Rights of association and combination of workers in agriculture.

Workmen's compensation in agriculture.

Prohibition and regulation of the use of white lead in painting.

Weekly rest in industrial undertakings.

Minimum age of admission of young persons to employment as trimmers and stokers.

Compulsory medical examination of children and young persons employed at sea.

Workmen's compensation for accidents.

Workmen's compensation for certain occupational diseases.

Equality of treatment for national and foreign workers as regards workmen's compensation for accidents.

Prohibition of night work in bakeries.

Simplification of the inspection of emigrants on board ship.

Seamen's articles of agreement.

Repatriation of seamen.

Sickness Insurance for workers in industry and commerce.

Sickness Insurance for agricultural workers.

Minimum wage fixing machinery.

Of course the mere titles of these conventions do not convey any idea of the way in which the problem concerned may have been dealt with. Some conventions cover the ground very completely. Others deal only with one element of the problem which seems susceptible of international treatment. The Hours Convention, for example, deals with the regulation of hours in industry in considerable detail: it provides for different kinds of industry having different characteristics, e.g. seasonal industries and continuous processes; it is a complete system. The Unemployment Convention deals only with the furnishing of information, the creation of free employment agencies, and the principle of direct agreement between Governments which possess systems of unemployment insurance. It is by no means, and does not pretend to be, or to afford, a solution of the un-employment problem.

Without going into the detail of the content of the different conventions, we can, however, take the above list as indicating the subjects which the Conference has so far treated, and we can assume that the international solution of the problems they present has been carried as far as knowledge and opinion at present permits. In other words, if these subjects came before the International Labour Conference again at the present stage, though some details in the conventions might be altered, it is unlikely that any advance would or could be made at present in the principles so far incorporated in the conventions.

Secondly, we can see that although the list is by no means equivalent to a complete labour code, the Conference has already dealt or begun to deal with a considerable number of the fundamental questions which can be the subject of legislation. And it has not confined its efforts to industry, but has dealt also with agricultural workers and with seamen.

It should be added that two conventions which were brought before the Conference did not obtain the necessary two-thirds majority, namely, a convention on the Hours of Labour at sea, and a convention dealing with the stoppage of work for one day per week in glass works employing tank furnaces. A proposal for a convention on Freedom of Association was abandoned at the first discussion stage as there seemed to be no prospect of working out a satisfactory agreement in the following year.

Mention should also be made of the fact that the Conference has adopted thirty Recommendations, mainly dealing with the same subjects as those treated in the conventions, or with allied subjects, though in greater detail. A few, notably those dealing with the prevention of anthrax, with the protection of child and women emigrants, with factory inspection, and with the prevention of accidents, need, however, to be specially noted in this brief description as they represent an attempt to tackle another set of problems.

One conclusion to be drawn from this examination of the subjects which the Conference has had on its agenda is the extraordinarily high percentage of its successes.

Out of twenty-nine subjects brought before it for the adoption of a Draft Convention, twenty-six have been successfully dealt with in that way. In no case has the Conference failed to arrive at an agreement on the terms of a Recommendation.

When the composition of the Conference is remembered, the conflicting interests of the employers' and workers' groups, and the necessity of obtaining, not a simple, but a two-thirds majority, this is certainly a remarkable record. And as the percentage of successes has been so high and so constant, there is no reason to suppose that, at all events in the immediate future, it will greatly alter.

Before we attempt to discuss whether any definite tendency can be discerned in the choice of the subjects with which the Conference may be called upon to deal, we should note that two subjects of special interest have been placed on its agenda for 1929.

The first of these is the Hours of Labour of Commercial Employees. As may be seen from the above list, the Conference has not ignored commercial employees, but it has hitherto dealt with them incidentally, as, for example, in its treatment of sickness insurance. Now it is to attempt to secure an international agreement on the question to which commercial employees attach the greatest importance, namely the question of the regulation of hours.

The second question is of even greater interest and importance. It does not so much represent an attempt to deal with another subject or with a fresh category of workers, as with another world of labour presenting a whole series of new problems. It is the question of 'native' labour.

The nature of the issues which that question raises, its fundamental importance in the present world civilization, and the peculiar responsibilities of more advanced communities towards those more primitive societies whose products are daily becoming more essential, need not be developed here.[1] All that need be noted is that in placing Forced Labour on its agenda the Conference will be entering on an entirely new field with almost unlimited possibilities of development.

Can any general tendency be perceived as regards the questions which the Conference will deal with in the future? There is nothing like a generally accepted programme to which we can point.[2]

Problems connected with all the main categories of workers, women and children, workers in industry, in agriculture, in commerce and at sea, and native workers, have now been the subject of consideration by the Conference. There remain of course intellectual workers, and though no question speci-

[1] They form the subject of a special chapter in the present volume. See Mr. Grimshaw's lecture on pp. 130–55.

[2] A programme, or rather an order of priority was suggested by M. Lambert Ribot, the Delegate of the French Employers, at the 1928 Conference. He suggested that the order followed should be: i. protection of women and children; ii. safety and health; iii. *methods* of payment (not wages); iv. housing; v. apprenticeship; vi. hours, i.e. that the Conference should take up questions in the inverse order of their influence on production.

cially concerning them has yet figured in the agenda of the Conference, a special Committee on which their most important international organizations are represented, and which also includes representatives of the Committee on international intellectual co-operation, has recently been set up by the Governing Body and if, as is probable, it recommends subjects for treatment by the Conference we may expect that in the near future one or more questions dealing with intellectual workers will figure on the agenda of the Conference.

The Conference will then have touched all the main fields. Which of them it will decide to till more extensively will depend on the urgency of the problems which call for attention and on the probability at any given time of securing agreement on a reasonable solution.

It will also depend on the experience of 'revision'. If the revision procedure should in practice prove easily workable, and if the hesitation and distrust which the workers at present feel concerning it should be dissipated, new international legislation might come into being by the successive revision of the Conventions already adopted as they fall due year by year for consideration after their ten years' period has run. This kind of process would be an advance in the direction of emphasizing the quasi-legislative character of the work of the Conference. At present one can only say that in this respect the experience of revision may have an effect on the Conference's future programme. It can, however, even at most only be a partial effect. It is unlikely that further problems connected with native labour, as soon as the necessary knowledge has been collected and experts consulted, or the great general problems mentioned in the preamble, and in particular those of insurance, of health, and of safety, can fail to come up independently of any desire to perfect the work already done.

v. *The Problem of Unemployment and collaboration with the League.*

In the above discussion of the future programme of the Labour Conference no mention of the problem of unemployment has been made, because it is a problem that stands in a class by itself.

The Washington Conference adopted, as we have seen, a draft Convention on the communication of information to the International Labour Office and the establishment of free employment agencies. It also adopted a Recommendation on unemployment insurance and on the policy of co-ordinating the execution of public works so that it should be reserved so far as practicable for periods of unemployment.

No one of course was under the delusion that this effort of the Washington Conference had adequately dealt with more than the fringe of the problem, and since then it has been the constant preoccupation of the Organization.

The trouble is that no one knows the remedy for unemployment, and very little more about its cause. Unemployment may indeed be described as the cancer of the body economic. One thing, however, we do know, and that is that its prevalence is independent of any political system, or even of the resources within any one political unit. It exists in the United States which is a Republic, and in Great Britain which is a Monarchy: in the former which is protectionist and in the latter which is free trade. It exists in Russia where the workers control the State, and in Italy where the State controls the workers. It exists in the British Empire with its scores of colonies and in the German Reich which has no colonies. It existed in Great Britain under a Labour Government, just as it existed under its predecessor and still exists under the Government that has taken its place.

It is perhaps the clearest case of the impotency of the many political units to deal with a problem which is a problem of the single economic unit that the world has now become. No one State can hope to find within its borders either the complete cause or the complete remedy. Unemployment is something which is wrong with the economic organization of the world.

Thus it is primarily an economic problem, but one which, technical questions of competence apart,[1] must be a vital concern of the Labour Organization. For it is the worker who supports its most cruel consequences, not only materially, but morally and spiritually. What the problem of security is to the League the problem of unemployment is to the Labour Organization. It is in fact the problem of human economic insecurity, and just as a solution of the problem of security is a necessary condition of disarmament and the abolition of war, a solution of the problem of unemployment is the only basis on which we can hope to build a lasting social peace.

This is the explanation of a very marked tendency of the International Labour Organization to preoccupy itself more and more with economic problems.

We saw last year that it can be claimed that the holding of the World Economic Conference of 1926 may be directly traced to a resolution of the 1922 International Labour Con-

[1] The Permanent Court of International Justice decided that the International Labour Organization was not competent to deal with economic questions, in the sense of questions of production, except incidentally.

ference adopted after a long and detailed examination of all
the information which could be compiled concerning unemployment. The presence of workers' representatives nomi-
nated by the Governing Body in the Economic Conference
and in the Economic Consultative Committee to which it
gave rise, and the role of the International Labour Office in
participating in the secretariat of this latter body, represents
an almost inevitable development.

The detail of the intimate collaboration thus established
between the International Labour Office and the new economic organs of the League need not concern us here.[1] We
need only note it as something which is likely to develop,
which is natural and which is necessary. Necessary not only
because the economic organization might possibly relegate
the problem of unemployment to a secondary place if labour
representatives were not continually calling attention to it,
but because in the absence of collaboration of the kind indicated economic action might be taken which would be socially
dangerous. For example, when the Brussels Conference met,
and laid down with unquestionable authority those principles
of financial reform which have since played so decisive a part
in the financial reconstruction of Europe, it incidentally
went outside the limits of its uncontested financial competence and included in its report a recommendation that
unemployment insurance should be abolished. Fortunately
the International Labour Office was able to intervene and to
secure that Governments should be warned of the contradiction between this suggestion and the proposals of the Wash-

---

[1] As an example it may be indicated that the International Labour
Office has been asked to supply the Economic Consultative Committee
with figures concerning wages and hours in the coal mining industries of
the different countries.

ington Conference. But the danger of bodies of experts straying outside the exact limits of their special knowledge and precipitating social consequences which they were unable to foresee was emphasized. And the collaboration now established between the International Labour Office and the League in economic matters provides a safeguard against any such perils in the future.

vi. The Remedy for Unemployment.

Can it be said that any progress has been made towards finding the cause and the remedy for unemployment?

The answer is hopeful: progress has been made, enough at all events to indicate the direction of the goal if not exactly how it should be attained.

First of all the International Labour Office by means of the figures and documents supplied by the different Governments under the Washington Convention has been able to centralize information concerning the extent of the problem not hitherto available. And secondly, it has been able to publish a study of the steps taken in the various States to deal with it. Governments who wish to take national action can therefore draw on the experience of all their fellows.

But national action can at best have only very partial results, and usually can only be a palliative and not a remedy.

As regards the problem as a whole, the extent to which a solution can be found and the direction in which it should be sought is becoming clearer. Careful studies have shown that there are different kinds of unemployment, in the sense that different causes may operate to produce it. There is the unemployment which was caused by the general dislocation of the world's economic machinery caused by the war. There is the temporary unemployment caused by financial reconstruction. Just as a sick man may have to lose blood in a surgical operation before he is cured, so States which were financially ill had to deliberately face the problem of some unemployment during the period of their financial *redressement*. And there is the unemployment which is endemic in the present economic organization and which fluctuates in severity. And there are also various kinds of local unemployment due to special local causes.

The trouble is that all these kinds of unemployment overlap and interact. It is almost impossible to isolate them and to determine that a given group of workers is unemployed due to one or other of them. So although the causes may be identified in theory the effect of one of them may be masked by the operation of others acting at the same time.

The progress of economic reconstruction has been dealt with elsewhere by Sir Arthur Salter.[1] The financial problem may now be regarded as solved and a beginning, not yet decisive, has been made with the problem of trade barriers. As economic reconstruction progresses, the economic causes of unemployment due to the dislocation of the war will progressively disappear, as will those due to the stabilization of currencies.

There remains the endemic problem. Here the difficulty is greater. Modern economic civilization is so complex that its working is as yet but dimly understood. We take its marvels for granted without reflecting on the relatively miraculous smoothness with which they are produced. The simplest needs of each individual are met by a system which brings to him at all hours of the day contributions from the uttermost ends of the earth. Each individual is in fact the

---

[1] See his lecture in this volume, pp. 75–95 and his lecture in *Problems of Peace* (second series), pp. 104–23.

focus of innumerable economic activities scattered over the face of the globe. On the ordinary breakfast table may be found coffee from Brazil, tea from China, bacon from Canada, butter from Denmark, eggs from Ireland, sugar from Cuba, fruit from California, fish from Newfoundland, and bread made from American, Canadian, or Roumanian wheat. The economic machine that produces these results runs practically unperceived and what is more extraordinary it runs blindly and without any general control. Paradoxical as it may seem, the coffee bean appears on the plant in Brazil as a result of a much more conscious and definite human act than does the same bean on the breakfast table. The individual acts of production are highly organized and deliberately directed. But the whole system escapes any kind of control. When the system was thrown into confusion, as it was after the war, the remedies were not immediately apparent. They had to be sought for by international meetings of experts and then States had to be educated to apply them. That process is still going on.[1]

But it is much more difficult to attempt to control the normal running of the system than to get it running again when it has partially broken down, just as medical science finds it easier to mend a broken limb than to prevent the common cold.

Some progress has, however, been made. It has long been known that periodically fluctuations in economic activity occur—booms and slumps. And periodical slumps mean periodical unemployment. The problem is to find some method of control which will flatten out the humps and hollows in the curve of economic activity.

Assuming such a control to be possible we should need to

[1] See Sir Arthur Salter's lecture, pp. 75–95.

know when to apply it, for obviously it must be applied in advance. It is no use navigating the ship after it has struck the rock. Methods of foretelling economic booms and slumps have now been devised as the result of very technical studies in economic and industrial statistics.[1]

A Joint Committee of the League and the Labour Office has been working at the elaboration of what may be called economic barometers, and these are now being tested.

When they have been perfected the next problem is to avoid the dangerous hump or hollow which they may indicate to be approaching. Further investigations have shown that this could probably be done by an international control of credit. At present the banks feed credit to the booming industries, thus accentuating the rise of the wave till it reaches a dangerous height of over-production, and finally breaks into the chaos of bankruptcy and unemployment. The banks then draw back and refuse the credit which might prevent the disaster from spreading, and the slump is accordingly accelerated.[2]

The ramifications of economic activity being world wide, it would be little or no use for the banks in one country to try to apply a policy of credit control with the object of preventing crises, if their fellows elsewhere did not do likewise. The remedy, therefore, would have to take the form of an international agreement for common action.

[1] It is interesting to note Sir Josiah Stamps's prediction that the greatest hope for the progress of economic knowledge is now through the study of statistics. See 'The Statistical Verification of Social and Economic Theory.'

[2] This is a very summary description of a complex phenomenon. For a fuller treatment see Bellerby, 'Control of Credit as a Remedy for Unemployment' and Fuss, 'Money and Unemployment', *International Labour Review*, November 1927.

This solution is still very largely in the stage of theory.[1] But assuming that the theoretical investigations are pushed further with success the question of its application will undoubtedly arise. The negotiation of an international agreement concerning the control of credit would seem primarily to be a matter for the Economic Organization of the League. The International Labour Organization might, however, claim to be competent [2] if the Economic Organization were inactive. The present close collaboration between the two organizations would rather, however, seem to indicate that it will be by a continuation of that collaboration that the problem will be eventually tackled rather than by one or the other organization acting alone.

It should not of course be concluded that an international agreement for the control of credit would put an end to all unemployment. The system of forecasting will have to be perfected and in all probability it can never be more than very approximate: the machinery of control will require experiment and can only operate generally: the humps and hollows in the curve will be diminished, not removed: local control will have to be allowed a large latitude and may operate wisely or unwisely: local crises will continue: special industries may have their own problems: and changes in methods of production will always cause temporary unemployment.

But we are now within sight of the possibility of being

---

[1] There is some evidence that it has been an element in the decisions of the Federal Reserve Board in the United States. See Bellerby, *Stabilization of Employment in the United States.*

[2] The Permanent Court has laid down that the competence of the Organization is not to be decided by the exclusion of all non-labour matters.

able to attack one of the fundamental causes of unemployment, and to attack it as a general world problem instead of tinkering at it with ineffective national palliatives.

And as the problem is of the first importance it may be expected that the tendency which we have noted, of the preoccupation of the Labour Organization with economic problems, will be intensified, and that in consequence its intimate relationship with the work of the Economic Organization will be still further developed.

vii. *Emigration.*

Before leaving the subject of unemployment, a word should perhaps be said on the subject of emigration, if only to explain why it is not discussed. Emigration is at best only a palliative for unemployment, and not a satisfactory one in view of the immensely difficult political problems which it precipitates. It is in fact a problem of population rather than a problem of unemployment, and as such it requires separate consideration.

Space will not permit of a discussion of the activities of the International Labour Organization, within whose competence certain aspects of emigration necessarily enter. Those aspects are the non-political aspects, the questions of the protection of the emigrant on his journey and the securing for him of equality of treatment with nationals in the country to which he may have been permitted to go. Still, so delicate and so diverse are the political problems connected with emigration that it is difficult to get agreement for the treatment of the non-political aspects of the question lest incidentally political issues should arise and be prejudiced.

The work of the International Labour Office has therefore of necessity been largely concentrated on non-contentious activities, the publication of international migration statistics, and of the treaties, laws, and regulations dealing with emigration or immigration in the different countries. This latter publication has been of immense utility to emigrants and to the various private associations which exist to watch over the welfare of emigrants and whose work has frequently been rendered difficult in the past by the lack of precise information.

It seems likely that for some time at all events, until emigration problems become less charged with political electricity, the work of the International Labour Office will continue along lines of information and in particular towards the supply of reliable data which may be made available to the intending emigrant before he decides on his adventurous voyage.

viii. *Revision of Conventions.*

The work of the International Labour Organization began with the Organizing Committee of the Washington Conference in April 1919. There has now been, therefore, practically ten years' experience of the working of its machinery. The end of the first decade would seem to be a suitable time for examining how it has functioned and what new developments of procedure seem to be called for.

As a matter of fact such an examination is, as regards the conventions, a statutory necessity. Each convention contains the following article:

> 'At least once in ten years the Governing Body of the International Labour Office shall present to the General Conference a report on the working of this Convention and shall consider the desirability of placing on the agenda of the Conference the question of its revision or modification.'

This is the famous revision clause, to which so much attention has been directed as a result of the desire of the British Government to see it applied as regards the Hours Convention.

It will be noted that it deals with two distinct operations, first the submission of a report on the working of the Convention, which is in all cases obligatory, and secondly the placing of revision or modification of the Convention on the agenda, which is discretionary. So far as the report is concerned there is no difficulty, but considerable controversy has arisen over the second operation.

The Governing Body has had to work out the Standing Orders which will govern its procedure when dealing with this Article. Although apparently simple, they have been the subject of long and involved discussion. That discussion provides an interesting and instructive example of the tendency of international negotiation to take the form of a struggle about procedure. The game is fought and often decided by the smallest pieces on the board. The heavy pieces are rarely or never brought into play as they are in national politics. The reason is that a movement of the heavy pieces, or the shock between them might easily overbalance the somewhat fragile board on which the game is played. That is why the proceedings of the League often appear to the superficial observer as futile struggles about insignificant details waged with an intensity out of all proportion to their importance. The truth is that real issues are being dealt with but a special technique, not easily comprehensible to the casual observer, has to be employed.

The Governing Body seemed to be settling a small and simple point of procedure which was to apply to all the Conventions adopted by the Conference. In reality all of its members had in mind the Hours Convention and the effect which their decisions might have on its fate.

The real point at issue may be put briefly as follows. The problem of the general ratification and application of that Convention centres, as we have seen, round Great Britain. Great Britain demands a revised Convention while declaring that she accepts the principles of the Eight-hour day and the Forty-eight-hour week. The Employers' group are also in favour of a revised Convention and support Great Britain, though it may be doubted whether supposing revision is begun, they will see eye to eye with Great Britain as to its substance. The workers are solidly opposed to revision. They have got the Washington Convention, adopted practically unanimously.[1] They are reluctant to give it up in return for, not a fresh Convention the contents of which are known, but for a discussion which might lead to a much less favourable Convention from their point of view, or to no Convention at all.

To decide that the Washington Convention should be revised is undoubtedly to run the risk of destroying its present value. If revision, once begun, fails, the Washington Convention will have been declared defective and nothing will have taken its place. The attitude of the workers is therefore easily understandable.

The situation seems to be, at all events momentarily, in the nature of an *impasse*. It could be solved by a satisfactory revision, i.e. a revision which, as the British Government declares it desires, will respect the fundamental principles of the Convention. But the workers are unlikely to budge from their present position unless there can be some guaran-

[1] Only one employer voted against it and one abstained. The others voted for.

tee that the principles of the Convention will not be touched.

The problem of revision is therefore first of all that of procedure. Can revision be limited *in advance* to certain secondary questions, or must it be unlimited and left to the hazards of debate in the Conference?

The Governing Body's Standing Orders mark a slight though not a decisive advance in favour of the thesis of limited revision. If the Governing Body decides on revision it 'shall define exactly the question or questions which it places on the agenda of the Conference'.

The alternative formula, which was defeated, would have placed on the agenda the 'revision or modification of the Convention', thus putting the whole of the Convention into the melting-pot of the Conference.

As matters now stand the Governing Body may decide on each occasion whether it will put one or more questions of detail concerning a Convention on the agenda, or whether it will put a number of questions which in their totality might be equivalent to putting on the whole of the Convention, or whether, if it clearly desires total revision, it will put the whole Convention up for reconsideration.

Thus so far as the Governing Body is concerned the possibility of limited revision is kept open.

The next problem which has now to be dealt with will presumably be the examination of the procedure of the Conference as regards revision, and here the same issue arises though in a more difficult form. Could the action of the Conference turn what was intended to be a limited revision into what would be equivalent to total revision?

Let us suppose that the Governing Body puts on the agenda of the Conference only certain questions of secondary importance concerning an existing Convention and let us examine what might happen.

Whatever is put on the agenda of the Conference, the Conference can only deal with it in accordance with the provisions of the Treaty. It must give effect to a proposal for limited revision, if it accepts it, by adopting a draft Convention open to ratification by Member States.

The old Convention will still be in existence. The Conference has no power of repeal. Just as it cannot dictate to Members what obligations they shall assume, it equally cannot order them to abandon contracts into which they have entered.

The position would therefore be that the old Convention would continue in existence, and that a new Convention containing variants of some of its provisions would come into being. How can the coexistence of these be harmonized? If the old Convention had contained an article providing that any of its clauses when revised by the Conference should be considered as repealed and replaced by the new provisions, assuming these to be ratified, there would be no difficulty. But the old Conventions contain no such provisions.[1]

Moreover, the new clauses of secondary importance would be binding for at least ten years, while the unrevised principles of the Convention having already outlived their period of ten years, would be open to denunciation at any moment, and this would obviously be an absurd system.

Clearly, therefore, some method must be found whereby the new revised clauses and the old unrevised clauses become a coherent system of legal obligations for States which have ratified them.

---

[1] A provision of this kind can of course be inserted in future Conventions if the experience of revision is satisfactory and if the system is continued.

There would be no legal difficulty in incorporating the unrevised clauses in the new Convention, but it seems clear that the Conference cannot so incorporate them if the Governing Body has not put them on the agenda, and we have assumed that the Governing Body has not done so. Can an act of the Conference link up the unrevised clauses with the revised clauses without throwing the former open to discussion and to possible revision? We are thus back again at the fundamental political problem on which the whole question of revision turns.

It does not seem impossible to devise a system. Among the articles put down for revision might figure the article of the old Convention providing for its denunciation. That article might be revised so as to provide that the period for the denunciation of the Convention should be set forward so as to coincide with the period for the denunciation of the revised clauses. The Conference would only be competent to discuss the *period* of denunciation, and not the substance of the Convention other than those provisions of it which had been specifically placed on the agenda.

A State which had ratified the old Convention and which now ratified the new would agree to a new period of denunciation for the old Convention and to the substitution of certain articles contained in the new Convention for certain articles contained in the old. A State which had not ratified the old Convention but which was willing to accept it in its revised form would ratify both the old and the new Conventions and would thus undertake to observe the old Convention as modified by the new.

No difficulty need be anticipated in the application of such a system if all the States which had ratified the old Convention also ratified the new. But it might be asked what would be the position if only some of them do so. Let us see what might happen.

Suppose there are three States, *A*, *B*, and *C*, all of whom have ratified the old Convention but only *B* and *C* the new. *B* would then be obliged to observe the terms of the old Convention as regards *A* and the terms of the revised Convention as regards *C*. It is easy to imagine a case in which *B* would have assumed two series of contradictory obligations: it might find itself in the position of having contracted with *A* to do a certain thing, and of having contracted with *B* not to do it.

It is unlikely, however, that this difficulty will be encountered in the case of Labour Conventions. Labour Conventions lay down certain *minimum* standards. States when they ratify undertake that certain conditions shall not be worse than a certain standard. They are free to make them as much better as they like.

Thus the fact that the network of the old and new Conventions may not exactly overlap as regards ratifications is not likely to give rise to difficulties. And if such were likely to arise in a particular case they would in all probability be avoided when the terms of the new Convention were being settled. Moreover, if revision fulfils its purpose, namely to secure a Convention more generally acceptable, it is to be expected that States which have ratified the old Convention will in general ratify the new.

The above system is not the only one that could be devised, but it will serve to show what the difficulties are, and that although they are complicated it is not impossible to overcome them.

Whatever the solution adopted, however, it would seem that for political reasons it must allow of a guarantee of limited revision being given beforehand when such is recognized to be desirable. The procedure to be sought should allow of total revision or partial revision as circumstances may dictate. Limited revision can of course always become total revision, and therefore it is as regards limited revision that a system must be worked out. If it is not, there will always be strong opposition to certain proposals of revision, often those which may be most desirable in themselves, and the Conference will fail to secure that freedom in its legislative work which is possessed by Parliaments and which will be an important element in the development of international legislation.

It will also be a matter for consideration whether future Conventions should not contain a provision for their amendment in minor details by some simpler system than that of revision. A 'procedure of amendment' was proposed at the Conference in 1922 but was not accepted on account of legal objections. A somewhat similar procedure to that then proposed was inserted in the Convention on the Simplification of Customs Formalities and the Council of the League has since formally recommended the adoption of the procedure for technical Conventions. The legal scruples of certain delegates at the Labour Conference may therefore be assumed to have been removed, and when after the first experience of the 'revision' procedure the future form of Labour Conventions is considered, the utility of inserting provisions for a procedure of amendment might usefully be examined. Such a procedure would be a complement to a procedure of revision rather than a substitute for it.

Apart from the technical difficulties of revision which have been briefly commented on above there is another aspect of it which requires mention. There is a danger that the revision desired by different States may be so fully worked out and become the subject of such firm decisions or definite agreements within the States that their representatives will arrive at the Conference instructed to present what amounts to this or that ultimatum. Their instructions will be rigid and their powers of negotiation paralysed. This was precisely the kind of thing which happened under the old double reading procedure of the Conference, and it had to be abandoned, in consequence. Unless a certain freedom of give and take is allowed, international agreement is impossible, and there is a danger that the experiment of revision may fail, not because of the technical difficulties, which can be surmounted, but because a too definite crystallization of opinion as to its content has taken place without international discussion.

It is also desirable that on the question of procedure allowance should be made for the fact that it is the procedure of a new international body which has to be worked out to face an entirely new problem, and that that procedure may not necessarily conform to the long-established and minutely perfected procedures of certain national Parliaments. The attempt to force a purely national view either as to the content of revision or as to the procedure by which it is to be operated must almost inevitably lead to failure.

ix. *Conclusion.*

In summing up the various tendencies which we have reviewed we may generalize them by saying that it is the constitutional element which is predominant.

The increase in ratifications is at all events in part due to national constitutional adaptations or the adoption of what are now normal rules of procedure for the consideration of

Labour Conventions. The question of unemployment has led to developments in the relations between the League and the Labour Organization which tend to become organic. The fate of the Hours Convention has become intimately linked with the question of revision. And the question of revision brings with it the whole question of the machinery of treaties which are to the League and the Labour Organization what legislation is to a national Government.

The new international order must have as its basis a network of treaties and the whole system of treaty-making must necessarily play an important part in the future of civilization. The authors of Part XIII of the Treaty of Versailles when they designed the International Labour Organization paid particular attention to this essential instrument of its work. They devised a complete procedure for the adoption, national consideration, ratification, and application of Labour Conventions.[1] They did not as we have seen provide for revision, but they did immensely simplify the old procedure of treaty making and what is more important relate their new system to the Organization. Labour Conventions cannot be taken in isolation.[2] They are a coherently knit body of international legislation, and they take the form of obligations which bind the Members of the International Labour Organization.

In the case of the Covenant it was far otherwise. The League was set up with the primary object of promoting 'international collaboration', and that has in fact been the

[1] For a discussion of the system see 'Current Progress of International Labour Legislation' in *Problems of Peace* (first series).

[2] It would, for example, be difficult to conceive of a State outside the Organization ratifying a Labour Convention, not because of any constitutional rule to the contrary, but because the whole operation of the Convention is bound up with the operation of Part XIII.

most fruitful form of its activity. But international collaboration can only be promoted by Treaties and Conventions. It is only by Treaties and Conventions that the rules of collaboration can be laid down and the common measure of collaboration in a given field defined. The Covenant, however, contains no legislative provisions: the Assembly is given no power to adopt a Convention or even to propose one. In practice this difficulty has not been grave. Numerous Conventions have been drawn up under League auspices and are in fact in operation. But they have been drawn up in any and every form. Some definite form which would clearly stamp them as League treaties, as part of a body of international legislation promulgated by the League and operating primarily between its Members would surely be desirable.[1]

Possibly the experience in which the International Labour Conference is now entering in the matter of revision may lead to a general examination of the function and form of treaties as instruments of international collaboration, and thus provide the League with a recognized legislative machinery adapted to its special needs and constitution.

But it is not only as regards the problem of revision and the form of treaties that it would seem that a kind of international constitutional epoch has opened, or is in process of opening.[2]

[1] A uniform method has now been suggested by the Council on the motion of Sir Austen Chamberlain who laid before it a proposal approved by the Imperial Conference of 1926. The form of treaty in question was suggested originally to meet the special problem of the relationship between Members of the British Commonwealth, but it does not correspond to the constitution of the League, and it does not seem that a special problem of the Commonwealth which can be solved in other ways should decide the form of League Treaties.

[2] Since this address was delivered the questions raised at the Assembly

In the League we have had the crisis of the Council, and there is talk of the enlargement of the Court. In the Labour Organization only two ratifications are now required to bring about the enlargement of the Governing Body which presumably will soon be an accomplished fact.

The fundamental constitutional question of Membership arises out of the case of Brazil which, having resigned from the League, claims that her resignation does not affect her position in the International Labour Organization.

In the Labour Organization there is the question of how its machinery is to be adapted to the negotiation of Conventions of only a regional or definitely limited interest, and the problem of the relation between a Maritime Conference and the General Conference.[1]

And last but not least in its possible repercussions Costa Rica has asked the Council to define the extent to which the guarantees of the Covenant are affected by the reference to the Monroe Doctrine in Article 21.

Such a flood of constitutional issues is, however, a sign of health, and not a sign of crisis. It has been proved that the international organizations can work. It has been demonstrated that they can work effectively. The task that is now upon us is to discover how they can be still better adapted to the tasks which it is essential that they should perform if they are really to fulfil the hopes which humanity has placed in them.

of the League have fulfilled this prediction. To the examples which could be quoted in August there must now be added the question of the position of the Secretariat, the Revision of the Statute of the Permanent Court of International Justice, and the question as to whether unanimity is required in the Council to demand an advisory opinion.

[1] Seamen and shipowners object to having their problems treated in a Conference in which non-maritime States and other than seamen's and shipowners' organisations are represented.

CHAPTER VI

THE MANDATES SYSTEM AND THE PROBLEM OF NATIVE LABOUR

Mr. GRIMSHAW:

I DO not wish this afternoon to discuss the Mandates System and all its implications at large, but rather to put the emphasis on the second part of the title of my subject, and to examine the problem of native labour in relation to the Mandates System. I hope to show you how the creation of the Mandates System has come perhaps at a fortunate psychological moment in the history of native labour, and how it may be effective in creating in certain colonial areas, by its regard for conditions of labour, a form of society as different from that obtaining in similar areas to-day as Robert Owen's 'New Order of Society' differed from that in which he lived. And if that happens, we may hope that the benefits of the mandatory experience may be extended to other areas similarly situated.

i. *The Destructive and Constructive Importance of Labour Policy.*

Clearly, if I am to establish this thesis, I must convince you of the primordial importance of labour problems in any organized society. Our Chairman emphasized that importance a moment ago, but I must go somewhat further. In my study of colonial affairs I have come to one very definite conclusion, which is this: that if the labour conditions of the general population are right, administration is easy and can be good; if they are wrong, administration is always difficult and never good. You would probably admit this dictum in the case of more advanced industrial countries, where the social difficulties arising from evil labour conditions are apparent and at times clamant. You must, in my opinion, admit it as even more correct of colonial areas, and for this reason.

One certain result of continued contact between ourselves and the primitive systems of society found in colonial areas is the destruction of the latter. It is not my present purpose to discuss whether there may not be, in these systems, elements which are worth preserving. I might mention in passing that we British tend to nourish our reputation as a people loving aristocracy by attempting to preserve and even strengthen the aristocratic elements we find existent in native society. But I wish at this moment merely to note the fact that native social organization is profoundly affected, in a manner amounting to destruction, by contact with us.

What factor in that contact has the most powerful destructive force? It is without a shadow of doubt our demand for the labour of these primitive peoples. Other factors exist: missionary teaching, our repression of barbarous practices, our suppression of war, our introduction of gin. But these are not so fundamental in their effects as is our insistence on labour—labour, that is, as we know it, and not as the native knows it.

But whilst labour is thus the most powerful destroyer of a society in which it has hitherto been unknown (at least in the form in which we present it), it is also the most powerful agent in the construction of the *new* system of society. Of that also I think there can be no doubt in any mind acquainted with colonial history.

The new system of society is, in fact, founded upon what is to these primitive peoples a new factor in their existence—

the development of labour in our western sense. And if that be so, it is evident that only upon satisfactory conditions of labour can be built a satisfactory system of society, and only with a satisfactory organization of society can we have good administration.

Destructively and constructively, then, labour plays in colonial areas the leading role, and I come back to my dictum, now I hope proved, that where labour conditions in such areas are right, administration is easy and can be good, and that otherwise administration is always difficult and never good.

You will forgive me, I hope, for having spent so long on the matter. I regard it as a fundamental law upon which the administration of the affairs of all primitive peoples should be based, when the object of such administration is to lead them forward, to assure their 'well-being and development'. I shall return to the implications which follow upon the acceptance of this dictum when I have discussed other aspects of the labour problem.

For its importance can be shown in another way. Few of us realize to what an extent our western civilization—in that term I include the United States of America, although some of my American friends have an idea that I don't—is economically based on the labour of backward and primitive peoples. You have only to run through the list of your groceries or the things on your breakfast table and think of the origin of these things to agree with me on that point, and I could take you further if I were to show you the recent trade and commercial figures, for example, of Central Africa. There you find the output of rubber, copper, copra, cocoa, cotton, and almost everything else there produced, going up by leaps and bounds year after year and forming to a greater and greater degree the basis of our own industry and commerce and, in fact, of our own civilization. That makes me think often of the enormous debt we owe these peoples, sweltering under tropical suns and under labour conditions which we ourselves could not support and never would support, and I wonder whether we are not in some danger, consciously or unconsciously, of tending to produce the equivalent on a large scale of the ancient Greek civilization where a pleasant, agreeable, intellectually active democracy rested upon a slave class and the labours of a slave class. There is in my mind a close analogy between ancient Greece and the situation as I see it developing now, the situation of comparative ease in Western Europe (and of still greater ease in the United States), and on the other side of the picture more and more millions of backward peoples dragged into the industrial mill under conditions which are in general insupportably bad.

Is it inevitable that we should tend towards that situation, or can we change the route a little? Can we call a halt? My purpose in speaking this afternoon is to indicate that a halt may be called; that we may by a change in colonial policy with regard to labour produce something better than that which we have so far produced. It is not perhaps too impossible a task to produce something better than our Western order of society. At any rate, the imagination does not reel at the suggestion that the latter might be improved upon.

In these colonial areas and the areas under mandate we have the opportunity, if we like to take it, of avoiding the mistakes of our Western civilization. The creation of the Mandate System nearly ten years ago was an indication that thought was stirring on the point, that minds acquainted with colonial affairs were not easy. Our Chairman has referred to the ideals of President Wilson. They were shared by many people at the time, and on at least one point there was general agreement: that there were some things in colonial practice which should be stopped. There were certain things which should not be done. As to the things which should be done, minds were much less clear.

ii. *The Labour Policy of the Mandates System.*

When we examine the documents upon which the Mandate System is based and upon which it works, we find that when they are negative they are precise, but when they are positive and constructive they are vague. Take, for example, Article 22 of the Covenant itself, and we find it is purely negative in so far as labour conditions are concerned. It makes a reference to the prohibition of the slave trade and says not a word more on any labour matter. When we come to the texts which were drafted later, the 'mandates' as we call them now, which lay down the principles in accordance with which the Mandatory Powers carry on the administration of the various areas under their tutelage, we find the same thing. They are negative rather than positive. They would suppress the slave trade; they would stop abuses and fraud and force in the recruiting of labour: but as to any constructive policy there is not a word. Even so, the only ones which contain any reference to labour conditions at all are the 'B' and 'C' mandates, applicable to the more backward areas. In the 'A' mandates there is no reference whatever to labour questions.

What have we got on the positive side? In Article 22 we have the expression that the well-being and development of these peoples is a 'sacred trust of civilization'. Very nice indeed. It is the banner, isn't it—in the French sense, the *drapeau*—and it is very good to have it there, but when it comes to be translated into facts and into practice on the labour side, then it is only indirectly helpful. We get a little more in Article 23 of the Covenant, but this time with no precise reference to mandates, but to all areas, colonial and other, since the Signatories to the Covenant undertake to 'secure and maintain fair and humane conditions of labour for men, women, and children, both in their own countries and in all countries to which their commercial and industrial relations extend'. There we are a little more precise. We get at least an indication that conditions of labour should be fair and humane, but no guidance as to what fair and humane conditions are or might be. We get still a little more in the 'Labour Part' (Part XIII) of the Treaty, again with reference not specifically to areas under mandate but to all areas. I think I ought to quote the Preamble to this Part, though many of you must be familiar with it. It states that 'conditions of labour exist involving such injustice, hardship, and privation to large numbers of people as to produce unrest so great that the peace and harmony of the world are imperilled . . .', and for that reason the Signatories proceed to create the International Labour Organization. It takes us a little step further, in recognizing the existence of evil labour conditions and in setting up machinery to assist in righting them. Finally, in Article 421 of the same part of the Treaty, the Powers which have ratified international labour conventions undertake to apply them in so far as they can be applied to their colonies, protectorates, and other non-self-governing possessions, thus indicating how the machinery may be applied in the case of areas similar to those under mandate.

And that is all. It is the juridical basis of the international treatment of labour conditions under the Mandate System. As an indication of the policy to be followed, it is somewhat meagre; purely negative, though fairly precise, in regard to slavery, forced labour, and force or fraud in the recruiting of labour; for the rest, general phrases. As machinery, it is defective.

iii. *The Action of the Commission in regard to Labour Questions.*

It is on that basis, and of course more particularly on Article 22 of the Covenant and on the Mandates themselves, that the Mandates Commission has had to work in its examination of labour conditions. I would like firstly to spend a few minutes running through a few cases taken almost at random from the proceedings of the Mandates Commission during the last eight years in illustration of its application of the precise though negative points. Take the question of slavery, for example. In looking through the minutes of the Mandates Commission you will find that in the early years slavery bulked very largely, and that in recent years it tends to appear less and less frequently in discussion. The reason is simply that in these areas slavery has either disappeared entirely or is in course of disappearance, and the Commission appears to be satisfied that whatever can be done either has been or is being done. There are odds and ends of doubtful cases—debt slavery, purchasing of women as wives, occasional selling of children, and so on—which keep coming up, but the big question is settled, and with the gradually more complete administration of these areas under mandate the whole difficulty will disappear, I think, very rapidly.

Then there is the question of forced labour, which is very much more difficult, partly because the texts of the articles on the question of forced labour differ in certain of the mandates and are open to more than one interpretation. However, the Mandates Commission has worked out a doctrine on the matter by this time. It has never formulated that doctrine, so that I should be presumptuous, perhaps, in stating what that doctrine is, but I may perhaps be permitted to give a few indications as to its nature.

In accordance with the terms of the mandates forced labour is permitted only for 'essential public works and services', but there is a variety of interpretation put upon the word 'essential'. It is, as a matter of fact, rather a nebulous word. It may be argued, for example, that the construction of a railway in a Central African country would be highly beneficial to the population of that country at some distant date, or even at some less remote time. Can it be argued that therefore that work is 'essential', and that, justified by its essentiality, you may take your negroes by the scruff of their necks, tear them from their villages, put them to work for a year or more without wages or with very small wages, under conditions to which they are not at all accustomed? Personally, I doubt it very much. And I could base my attitude on a very practical argument: it may soon become an essential public work or service in Great Britain to tear up the railways. What I mean is, of course, that I am not sure that railways are the ideal mode of transport for colonial areas, and there are colonial experts who share my doubt. We may therefore be building railways costing thousands of lives to no great benefit.

Again, *to whom* is a certain public work or service essential? If it can be proved that it is essential for the direct well-being of the present community, then I think I should have nothing to say; but if it is claimed to be essential for the well-being of the community a hundred years hence I should ask, as we ask ourselves in regard to our own affairs, is it worth while putting this burden on the present population in order (possibly, for we are never certain in these matters) to benefit the future population? We all—individuals and communities—face that problem of how much of our present energy and work we can devote to the future. It worries me at the end of every month when I try to see whether I can devote anything at all to the future by leaving it in the Bank!

If we should be extremely prudent in this connexion in our own affairs, then I think no one will dispute my claim that we are morally bound to be even more so when the affairs of peoples under our tutelage are concerned. Particularly when the only absolutely *certain* result of forced labour is hardship, suffering, and death, not for us but for those confided to us under a 'sacred trust'.

The question of allowing forced labour for essential public works and services is, then, not so simple as it seems. For that reason I should advise that permission to have recourse to that form of forced labour should rest not entirely with the authorities on the spot but with somebody a little more remote who can look at things in a truer proportion. Otherwise, the nearer interests tend to have undue influence. I do not think I am being unfair in stating that I know of no case where great public works of the kinds we are discussing now have been carried out by forced labour—I would not say exclusively, but even *primarily*—in the interests of the native populations which have sweated them through. I do not of course deny that these populations, or rather that their descendants, have sometimes benefited, but I have no hesitation whatever in declaring that if they and their interests had been the only object in view, the works would never have been undertaken. To use a phrase only too familiar to us of the West, where social values are lost in the muddy marshes of economic phraseology, they 'would not have paid'.

You note that I said that the native populations *sometimes* benefited. It must not be assumed that they always benefit. On the contrary. With a colonial policy based on compulsion —for labour, for military service, for the supply of produce— the creation of a railway or a road has effects perhaps a little unexpected, though in reality we ought to anticipate them. The road or the railway becomes the channel by which compulsion arrives, and the neighbouring population, very naturally, takes to its heels. Then deserted roads, passing through vacant, uncultivated country, through forests rich in uncollected produce—and, as now in certain African areas, still more compulsion to bring villages and tribes back to 'civilization'. There are too many colonies in Africa with networks of roads upon which nothing ever runs, with railways which serve a few plantations owned by whites, roads and railways built by forced labour at an enormous expense of life and a not very enormous expense of money, for wages is a small item. Built in fact entirely by the labour, and almost entirely at the expense of the native population.

To go back to what the Mandates System means and to what the Mandates Commission would expect in regard to forced labour for public works, you will not, I hope, be surprised to hear that it tends more and more, in my experience, to give to the word 'essential' in the mandates an interpretation which includes not only real necessity, but also urgency.

At the other end of the scale of forced labour—I am employing the term to mean all kinds of compulsory labour, and may be extending it further than some of you are accustomed—we have the case of forced cultivation. When one begins with the belief that all natives are very lazy people who do not like work, it is easy to proceed to the next step and say that, in their own interests they must be made to like it. It is singularly easy to take this step when it is a matter of compelling the native to produce enough food for his own subsistence. And that, we find, is sometimes necessary, particularly in areas subject to crop failure and consequent famine, where the foresight of the native is not so highly developed as is our own. Many colonial areas have therefore introduced a system by which every adult native is compelled to cultivate a certain area of ground or cultivate a certain quantity of crops, in most cases keeping the crop or its value when sold for himself. But if compulsion in such a case is justified, is it permissible to take a further step, and impose forced cultivation as a *measure of education,* as is done in some areas? A slippery slope, of which we have had considerable experience. The Slavery Commission of three or four years ago, and the Sixth Commission of the Assembly when discussing the Slavery Convention, decided that forced labour as a measure of education was much too dangerous, leading to precisely those forms of labour which the Slavery Convention was designed to abolish. The Mandates Commission appears to adopt the same line. Then, there is the still further step of imposing the cultivation of crops *for export,* sometimes again with the provision that the value of the crop remains with the native cultivator (a provision, by the way, often very difficult to execute). As I said before, a slippery slope. The question as to whether this is permissible under the terms of the Mandates has been discussed frequently by the Commission. Let me recall that the only forced labour permissible is for essential public works and services, and then *only in return for adequate remuneration.*

I think I can say that the opinion of the Commission is that it is not permissible.

I might add, for my own part, that I regard it as particularly open to suspicion. As in the case of forced labour for public works, it is rare indeed that the interests *primarily* considered in such cases are those of the natives: they are much more likely to be those of, say, the British cotton manufacturing industry. Moreover, even with the best intentions, mistakes are made and compulsion to produce a crop for export has in more than one instance led to the neglect of crops for food, whence the necessity for yet more compulsion.

There is one form of forced labour—forced porterage—which comes up every year. It is a hardy annual, and probably the most difficult of all forced labour questions. It is also the worst scourge under which many native people suffer. You know what it means. Government stores are to be moved. The Government Medical Officer may have to be moved to some place where disease is raging. Travellers or merchants may wish to have their goods or themselves carried. In many areas railways and roads do not exist, and the goods must be carried on the backs or the heads of men. For every ten men who are carrying you must have three or four more to carry for these ten and for themselves. In practice, it means sometimes weeks and weeks of march from home, and it is so detested by the native population that compulsion has to be used in order to make them carry it out.

That opens a great many very difficult problems. The easy solution, most commonly adopted, is to conclude that there is here a vicious circle with no way out. Progress, in administration or in well-being, is not possible without transport: transport is not possible, in the absence of roads, without porterage. Therefore porterage is a necessity, if we would make progress. One might admit then, the permissibility of compulsion in this case, but the criteria I have tried to lay down in the case of forced labour for public works should hold good here—the service for which porterage is demanded should be an essential public service, necessary and urgent. And again as in the other cases, it should be adequately paid.

The Mandates lay that down, and the Commission has been exceedingly watchful in the matter. The ease with which compulsion, once admitted as a principle, is extended is nowhere better illustrated than in the enormous development of forced porterage. Travellers' luggage, the goods of merchants, the crops of planters are still in many parts of Africa carried by porters compelled to their tasks by the officials of the Administration or by their own chiefs, the latter either themselves acting under compulsion or willing to get into the good graces of the Administration. This mention of chiefs reminds me that it has always seemed to me more than a little hypocritical on the part of those Administrations who say, in effect, 'we have no forced labour; we ask the chiefs to send us the necessary men'. As if this were other than compulsion, and as if native chiefs were likely to exercise compulsion more wisely and justly than the administrative staff. You remember Lord Lugard's story of the headman, himself a butcher, who in similar circumstances packed off every other butcher in the community for forced labour?

Under the Mandates System forced porterage for the benefit of private individuals is not permissible. And, I am happy to say, forced porterage for the public service is in some areas under mandate being strictly limited by a number of wise measures. The vicious circle is being broken across. If time permitted, I could tell you of Sir Donald Cameron's efforts in that direction in Tanganyika, and of their success.

One last point on forced labour. It may now be said that forced labour for private employers does not exist in any direct and legal form in any of the areas under mandate. It is another question which the Mandates Commission has followed very carefully.

Here, then, is some account of the Commission's work in connexion with the negative provisions of the Mandates, but it has gone a good deal further in its attention to labour questions. Again I take some cases, almost at random, where the Commission has intervened with the object of securing better labour conditions and has had a measure of success. Most of these cases, I am bound to say, are rather dramatic. The Commission tends to hear of and to comment upon those cases which are rather bad. There is the case of the South-West African diamond mines, for example, where three-quarters of the revenue of the State was produced by the labour of some five or six thousand natives who died at the rate of 10 or 11 per cent. per annum. I know this does not mean much to people who have not thought over these things, but if you recall that the forces of the British Empire during the four years which the war lasted lost less than 14 per cent. *for the whole period* by death, this 10 or 11 per cent. per annum amongst natives working in diamond mines means a good deal. The Commission intervened on that point. The result is that the death rate is now about 4 per cent., which is more or less normal in the circumstances. Again, take the case of the railway in the French Cameroons where forced labourers were working on the Chemin de Fer du Centre, and where the death-rate reached a height of

12 per cent. at times. The Commission again intervened, and now the mortality given in recent reports is between 3 per cent. and 4 per cent.

In the middle of the Pacific you have the famous island of Nauru, a little island consisting almost entirely of phosphates, which has a small native population and a fairly large population of Chinese immigrant workers. Again and again the Commission has intervened with regard to the conditions of those Chinese. On the last occasion it asked that Chinese workers who are incapacitated by reason of their labour and are sent back to China shall have something in their pockets when they go. It was already assured some time ago that those who are injured by accident were compensated; it turned its attention this year to those who are incapacitated from further work by sickness. The reason was that it had noted that amongst the Chinese workers repatriated during the last two or three years a large number were stated to be incapacitated from further work, and naturally it asked itself, What are these poor fellows going to do when they get back to China?

Come a little nearer home, in Ruanda Urundi, that densely populated part of Central Africa bordering on the Belgian Congo and not far from the rich copper area round Katanga. The Belgian Congo, for reasons into which we will not enter, is short of people. They were there; they are not there. Consequently, the administration must seek for labour elsewhere, and it looks to Ruanda Urundi. Now Ruanda Urundi is under mandate, and methods employed there in the recruitment of labour come under the annual supervision of the Mandates Commission, which has been quick to ask questions about it. There is going on there now what is, I think, the most carefully carried out experiment in the recruitment and movement of labour of which I have ever read. Men are recruited voluntarily in Ruanda Urundi and, before being put to work in the mines, they are put through a long process of habituation: habituation to the climate, habituation to the new method of living, and gradual habituation to work. You must remember that these people, like other primitive peoples, are not accustomed to the eight-hour day, or to any other hour day. Their friends would say they live almost an ideal life, fishing and hunting and so on when they are hungry. Their enemies would say they spend a good deal of their time watching their wives work. In either case they are not accustomed to a factory hooter or a bell, and often enough when they are put in a factory they die.

These are odd cases. I could go on all the afternoon citing cases where the Mandates Commission intervenes, points out dangers, suggests other courses, and where the fact of its intervention is a little check on the complete freedom of action of the Mandatory Power in regard to labour conditions, or a little aid to that Power in its struggle to safeguard the worker against the evil of industrialization.

But there are more fundamental questions still. There is the question of the land, which plays an enormous part in regard to labour conditions in these areas. If the native has his land to fall back upon, then he cannot be driven to accept employment on miserable conditions. He goes back to his land. That is well-known in colonial practice, and it is not unknown in colonial practice that in these circumstances the native is deprived of his land and thus forced to accept conditions of labour which otherwise he would not. The Mandates Commission has been exceedingly watchful on that point, and although it exists in no document, it certainly exists both in theory and in practice in the Mandates System

L

that there shall be no alienation of land belonging to the natives; that such land shall not be considered to belong to the Mandatory Power but to belong to the community; that where there is communal ownership, although such ownership may at times render progress in agriculture very difficult, yet there shall be no upsetting it unless the Commission is assured that the native gets a *quid pro quo*. There are one or two members of the Mandates Commission who are almost fierce on that point, who stay up at night, I believe, thinking out how better they can safeguard the land of the native. They no doubt base their attitude firstly upon the fundamental doctrine that the interests of the natives themselves must be the primary concern of the mandatory administrations, and secondly upon their realization, based on long experience, of the overwhelming importance of the land in the construction of a better social organization.

Land and its ownership and use are then the bases upon which a labour policy should be built, but in the process of building the most important factor, in my view, is education. Into this we cannot to-day go very far, though education in arts and crafts is worth a moment's notice. The gracious and learned woman on the Mandates Commission who interested herself in educational matters, Madame Bugge-Wicksell, whose loss is so deeply to be deplored, insisted in season and out of season on training in labour, in arts and crafts. She was interpreting, I believe, the general sense of the Commission in so doing.

But in mentioning education here I meant something much wider, which Madame Bugge-Wicksell thoroughly comprehended. Any policy of education conceived in the light of a 'sacred trust' will look further than to the mere production of artisans or craftsmen. And perhaps the recently advocated education policies for Africa, welcome as they are, may mean in practice little more than a change of system, producing artisans and craftsmen instead of clerks and minor Government officials. Still, have we learned even in our own lands that the object of education is not that one may earn a living, but that one may live a life? Here, I think, we must be patient. Possibly there is still much education to be done amongst administrations, and even amongst the members of the Commission itself!

There is still one other side to the labour problem, a very, very important one, which may arise in at least one area under mandate, and which has arisen in certain British colonies. Are you to take labour and divide it into two and say to the natives, 'This, the worst paid, shall be your share, and the rest of it shall be our share?' Obviously that is unthinkable in an area under mandate with a mandatory power responsible to the League of Nations, where neither race nor colour is penalized or held inferior. That is another question which the Mandates Commission has watched, the question of the 'colour bar'. I cite this case to you to give you some evidence that the Commission, in adhering to the letter of the Mandates and the documents upon which it is working, attempts also to apply the spirit expressed in the phrase 'sacred trust of civilization'.

iv. *The Development of a new Policy: its Implications.*

The experience of the Commission in going through these isolated cases, of the kind I have outlined to you, which have no clear interconnexion, has led them to outline one declaration of policy to which I want to call your attention. Unhappily it exists in a document which the wisdom of the

Council of the League, on the motion, I regret to say, of my fellow countryman, Sir Austen Chamberlain, has turned down—the famous new questionnaire, which was a re-draft of a questionnaire made in the early days and which no longer exists except in the archives. A new question inserted in that document was the following:

'Does the local supply of labour, in quantity, physical powers of resistance, and aptitude for industrial and agricultural work conducted on modern lines appear to indicate that it is adequate, as far as can be foreseen, for the economic development of the territory?

'Or does the Government consider it possible that sooner or later a proper care for the preservation and development of the native races may make it necessary to restrict for a time the establishment of new enterprises or the extension of existing enterprises and to spread over a longer term of years the execution of such large public works as are not of immediate and urgent necessity?'

You see where the emphasis here is laid? Entirely upon the interests of the natives, and on 'a proper care for their preservation and development'. The establishment and extension of enterprises are definitely put in a second place, and quite properly. Development and progress, yes, but in the interests primarily of the inhabitants of the country concerned, not in that of the mother country, even less in that of private enterprises. It implies an orientation of policy different from that guiding most of the colonial administrations of the world. It is in the true spirit of the 'sacred trust'; its beginnings are apparent, I am glad to say, not only in areas under mandate, and its full application will, I firmly believe, ensure a future organization of society in these areas to which the word 'colonial' with all its associations of scandals, oppression, exploitation, and race prejudice will no longer apply.

What is the situation? These populations (I am speaking of colonial areas in general) apparently cannot be left out of our accounts. Mankind has need, or has persuaded itself that it has need, of the resources of the areas they inhabit, and of their labour in the development of those resources. The older colonial idea said that in these areas conditions were very backward, development quite inadequate, resources were left unexploited and wasted, the natives were inefficient, the existing populations could not develop the area. Others then must do it for the existing population or instead of the existing population and even in spite of the existing population, and methods of exploitation were thus justified which would never be permitted in regard to people capable of standing for themselves.

No population, I concede at once, should reserve its resources for itself or refuse to allow their development for the greater benefit of mankind in general. But the development must not be carried out at the expense of that country or of that population merely because that country or population is incapable of defending itself. Morally that situation would be exactly what it was a hundred and fifty years ago in England when we exploited children for our industrial expansion, and became rich at their expense.

Let us then think no more of the exploitation of resources but of the development of peoples as our primary object. The exploitation of resources, including labour, then falls into its proper place as the instrument by which the development of peoples may be aided, but as an instrument like a surgeon's knife, which may be murderous in unskilled hands.

I would like to say that the new policy is the Mandates

policy, but I am quite sure that if I did some international lawyer would get hold of the Mandates texts and would go through them as I have done this afternoon and would say there is not a word about that there. What I will say is that it is the policy to which the Mandates System is arriving, if not has arrived, in its practice.

But it will occur to you that you cannot develop these colonial areas without capital. The capital comes from else-where for the main part, at any rate in the beginning. Capital must have its share in the reward, and consequently some at least of the profits of exploitation cannot be devoted to the interests of the local populations. I will agree to all that, but I would point out that under the old policy capital not only had its share in the reward, and the lion's share at that, but it *directed the policy*. It was not in the interests of the inhabitants concerned that capital was invested in this or that area. The capital invested in Congo rubber for example, the capital invested in Liberia at the present time, or being invested, is not in the interests primarily of the populations concerned. Capital goes where profit gleams—sometimes in will o' the wisp fashion, no doubt—not where the best interests of society would choose that it should go. Therefore, under a wiser colonial system, there must be some higher authority than capital to decide whether it shall be invested in this or that line of development, and the 'profit-motive'—a phrase I borrow from a well-known American Bishop—must not be left a free hand. That, it seems to me, is a corollary of the principle laid down by the Mandates Commission in the famous questionnaire to which I referred a minute ago. It says: No, it may be true that you have vast coal-fields in Nigeria, that you have vast copper-mines in the Congo, that you have vast forests in the Cameroons.

It may be true also that some one is willing to invest a million dollars or a million pounds in their exploitation. But have you the labour there? And can you get that labour on conditions satisfactory to this text which speaks about the 'sacred trust of civilization'? Are you sure that this particular kind of labour is one suited to the present capacities of the population? Are you sure that it is the exploitation of this particular form of wealth and not of some other which is at present the most suitable, bearing in mind its effect upon their social progress? Are you sure that of the profits of this exploitation, an adequate proportion will be devoted to furthering their social progress?

If not, then wait. These resources must remain undeveloped until conditions change, because it is the development of the *people* rather than of the *resources* of the country at which the new policy aims. It puts people first and resources second, a new orientation much more difficult to follow out than the other. Has it ever struck you how much easier it is to exploit men than to exploit mines? A great deal easier, especially when the men are a few hundred years behind you in development.

Perhaps I could spend a few minutes in telling you what else I think the new policy implies. Land I have mentioned. It implies that the land shall be guaranteed to the workers. It shall not be wrenched from them. In the Mandates System another principle insisted upon is the equality of economic opportunity: it is laid down that all the fifty-five nations of the League should have equal rights of trading in areas under mandate. Unfortunately the framers of the system were not equally insistent on the rights of trade of the native who lives in some of those areas. There are plenty of cases in colonial experience where the right of trade is something of this kind: the native produces, we will say, copra or collects forest rubber. Under existing law in many areas he is obliged to sell that copra or forest rubber to one monopolistic organization at a fixed price. He is also frequently enough obliged, either by law or by circumstances, to buy what he needs from the same organization. You can see what chances there are to become rich, not for the native, but for other people. I am told that there is an area in Africa now where palm oil is sold to one monopolistic corporation at exactly 25 per cent. of what is paid for it in the colony next door, where there is an open market. With regard to trade, then, the new policy means no forced selling, and no forced buying. It means no big concessions of the old type which exist still in some colonial empires, where a company is given a concession of land for certain purposes with the implication, sometimes put down in black and white, sometimes not, that it has the right to call for labour on the local population. Under the new policy, capital coming into colonial areas must accept the same risks as capital coming into a European area; that is to say, if it can get labour by offering good conditions then let it do so; if it cannot, then let it do without. As the British Under-Secretary of State for the Colonies said in regard to a case of that kind quite recently, the obtaining of labour is one of the risks of the undertaking. If the undertaking is not well-conducted and cannot get labour voluntarily no Administration should use its power in order to force labour.

Freedom of employment and honest recruiting is another indispensable element in the new policy. On the history of trickery and fraud and force in obtaining labour we could spend the whole afternoon, from the 'blackbirding' in the Pacific, which still goes on a little, to the pretended contracts which natives who cannot read and, if they could, cannot understand, are persuaded to sign, to find themselves tied up for three years under severe penalties for breach. All that must go entirely.

I mentioned a minute ago that we must have an education policy. Perhaps I could dilate on that for a moment. What I mean is this. All the best colonial experience now agrees that the native who won't work is a very rare bird indeed, provided that you give him conditions which he likes. With the native it is not always the question of wages which is the deciding factor in persuading him into employment. It is rather conditions and treatment. Instead then of forcing labour upon them, with all in the way of suffering and resentment which that means, let us adopt the policy—successful wherever it has been tried—of education to labour. The only objection to it that I can conceive is that it is slower in producing immediate results, and that objection only holds if we admit that our policy is a mere 'get-rich-quick' one! There is plenty of evidence that the labourers we are here discussing do not differ in essence from the rest of mankind, and that they will put themselves to work willingly enough when they see some good for themselves coming from it. Put an end to the trickery and corruption and force, none of which ever educated any native to be a workman, in spite of what has been said on the point. I could quote you passages from company reports, for example, some time ago, in which they say that the great difficulty is to get over the initial laziness of the native, and you get over this initial laziness by making him practically a slave, making him work under the whip for a couple of years, after which he becomes quite a good worker. It is not true that he becomes quite a good worker: he does not. If you can conceive any policy of educating a native or any one else to labour by such methods successfully, I shall be very much astonished. The very fact that supplies of labour obtained under that method —and still obtained under that method in some areas, though not in areas under mandate—have to be constantly recruited from further and further and further afield shows that as a policy of education in labour it is a dead failure.

One more point and I have finished. These policies of land, of education, of honest trading, of honest recruiting, must be accompanied *pari passu* by social policies in regard to the improvement of conditions, of food, housing, village conditions, of sanitation conditions, and so on. Social progress must not be outdistanced by the Industrial Revolution which is going on all the time. It was outdistanced in our own England, and you know the results. It is being outdistanced in Central Africa, and there the results are infinitely worse.

Now let me indicate what I think may be the role of the Mandates System in all this. At present there is a great stirring of the dry bones of colonial offices—and some of the bones were very dry, very dry indeed—but in Belgium, in England, in France, there is a stirring. I think sometimes that the stirring in some of the colonial offices has been brought about by the fact that there is a great shortage of labour, that populations have been disappearing in Central Africa. But whether for that reason or not, there is a stirring for which we may be thankful. There is a definite attempt now to conserve population by methods not quite so good as those by which an ordinary American farmer or an English farmer would conserve his stock, but still it is a move in the right direction. The problem of the conservation of populations, it has been found, implies the further problem of making them prosperous and happy.

Under the Mandates System we have, I think, the best central point at which these new tendencies are likely to be gathered together and co-ordinated in the light of the fundamental basis of the System, namely, the idea of the 'sacred trust', for two reasons.

The first is that the fundamental idea is there—the sacred trust; and the second is that the Mandates Commission works in the light of day. I know it does not meet in public. It closes its doors. But its documents and its observations, as it calls them, are completely public, and what goes on in the areas under mandate also reaches the public in a sense which is not true of other colonial areas. Under the Mandates System we have then the possibility of evolving the new policy and building upon it, developing it, adding to it, as the knowledge of colonial areas and colonial peoples increases, and we have the second possibility that the experience there gained may be extended to other similar areas which are not at present under mandate.

I have no time to expand my dream, if it be a dream. I think there is a possibility that with these various factors at work, these new ideas, this new publicity in colonial affairs, we may succeed eventually in producing among as yet undeveloped peoples a kind of society which will avoid some of the mistakes of our own, which will not inevitably go through the long and painful history of our upward struggle, and which in two words may be a new type of civilization resting on a different economic basis.

CHAPTER VII

THE LEAGUE AND THE PROTECTION OF LINGUISTIC, RACIAL, AND RELIGIOUS MINORITIES

i. *The Limits of the Activities of the League.*

Mr. KERSHAW:

MY remarks to you to-day must be prefaced by a reservation of a very necessary, but none the less depressing, character. I cannot, for obvious reasons, undertake to discuss the situation of any particular minority in any particular country. You will find, therefore, in what I have to say, no cheerful indiscretions regarding the present situation of such minorities nor any expression of opinion as to whether they are better off to-day than they were five years ago.

Moreover, the process of removing the gilt from the otherwise unattractive gingerbread I have to offer you cannot end even at this point. You will note that the title I have given to my remarks is 'The League and the Protection of Minorities'—not simply 'The Protection of Minorities', and still less 'Minorities in Europe'. I chose that title because it sets out clearly the limits within which I must confine my discourse, and enables me to place in their proper proportion the activities of the League in the matter of the protection of minorities. The authoritative and permissible action of the League in concrete cases of the protection of minorities is confined to those countries which have assumed international obligations in that respect, and have placed those obligations under League guarantee. It is a matter of common knowledge that there are minorities not protected by the League. Some of these minorities are actively self-conscious; others might be called minorities in a latent or potential state. I am not concerned, in my remarks to-day, with the position of such minorities. Their situation and aspirations may be a perfectly legitimate subject for debate in other quarters, but would be out of place in an exposition of the existing rights and duties of the League in protecting minorities.

There is a further point to be borne in mind when comparing the activity of the League in minorities questions with what I might call the minorities problem as a whole. I have said that the League guarantee applies only to certain States. It is true that these comprise the greater number of States having minorities, but still not all are included under the guarantee. It is equally true that the guarantee *within* the States bound by international minorities obligations does not include all the rights or privileges that minorities might desire. In saying this I merely wish to bring out the fact that the action of the League is based on specific treaty stipulations. What is outside those stipulations may, or may not, be a morally legitimate subject for claims on the part of minorities. The point of practical importance is that the League acts within the limits of the present treaties. The treaties make no mention of the moon. It is therefore no use a minority asking the League to procure it the moon on the basis of the existing treaties. One way to secure at least a claim to the moon would be to revise or extend the treaties. But that, as you will realize, is a matter into which I cannot enter here.

I hope that in these introductory remarks I have made clear the relation of the actual activity of the League in minorities protection to the minorities problem as a whole.

I might perhaps sum up the position as follows: The minorities problem as a whole concerns all the aspirations of all minorities that recognize themselves as such; the League guarantees to minorities certain definite rights in certain countries. There is one qualification to be made to the latter statement: if a minorities question became so serious as really to threaten a breach of the peace between two States members of the League, it would always be possible for a State member to invoke Article 11 of the Covenant. That, however, would be an act of a political character which is outside the province of minorities protection strictly so-called.

It may perhaps be most convenient to consider in the first place the origin of the minorities treaties, then to pass to an examination of their nature and scope, and finally to indicate the procedure that has been adopted by the League with a view to ensuring their efficacy.

ii. *The Origin of the Minorities Treaties.*

The origin of the treaties is to be found primarily in the war of 1914–18, and in the nature of the peace which followed. The war emphasized once more the constant danger to peace arising from the presence in Europe of discontented and unprotected minorities, and the peace, by creating new States and greatly enlarging others out of territories containing large elements of population of a different race or language or religion from the dominant element in the State, changed the incidence and extent of the danger without suppressing it. Even more, the rise to independence of lately subject peoples, coupled with the passions unchained during the war, made it probable that the minorities problem would be far more acute after than before the war. It therefore seemed desirable and necessary to the organizers of peace that some sure guarantee of certain elementary rights should be given to the minority populations in the new States, or in those which had received large increases of territory. This desire was further reinforced from the moral point of view by a fact of prime significance in minorities questions, namely that the minorities now enclosed in a new State, with a perhaps hostile majority of different race or language, were not, in general, newcomers to the lands on which they lived. They were not to be regarded as immigrants in the sense of persons who leave their own land to settle voluntarily in a foreign country. The minorities of Europe have in most cases been settled for generations, even for centuries, in the lands they occupy at present. The transfer of their citizenship, and their inclusion in a foreign State, were in general made without their consent. It was therefore a gesture both morally commendable and practically necessary to ensure that in their new State they should not be obliged to forgo entirely all remembrance of, or links with, their ancient language and culture, and should further be protected against any unfavourable treatment based solely on their membership of a minority.

iii. *Their Nature and Scope.*

How was this protection to be granted and rendered effective? The idea of minorities protection was not new in European diplomacy. A number of earlier treaties, in particular several made during the nineteenth century and relating to the Balkans, contained provisions regarding the protection of religious minorities. But these treaties in general gave the right of intervention to the Great Powers, thereby creating a danger either of the protection remaining ineffective, through the failure of the Great Powers to intervene, or if intervention took place, of allowing a Great Power to interfere in the internal affairs of another country. To avoid these drawbacks it was necessary to find as protecting agency a body which had both a permanent and an international character, ensuring on the one hand that the execution of minorities treaties would be the subject of constant scrutiny, and on the other hand that any form of intervention would be entirely neutral and international. The League of Nations offered both these advantages, and it was to the League of Nations that the Principal Allied and Associated Powers entrusted the task of protection laid down in the various minorities treaties. These treaties began with that signed between the Principal Allied and Associated Powers and Poland at Versailles on 28 June 1919. Similar treaties were subsequently signed relating to the Kingdom of the Serbs, Croats and Slovenes, Czechoslovakia, Roumania, and Greece. Further, the general treaties of peace with Austria, Bulgaria, Hungary, and Turkey contain special chapters relating to the protection of minorities. Moreover, in response to a resolution of the First Assembly of the League of Nations, certain States, on their admission to the League, made a declaration before the Council, to the general effect that they would apply to such minorities as inhabited their territory the same principles as appeared in the minorities treaties already in force. Such declarations were made by Albania in 1921, Finland (in respect of the Aaland Islands) in 1921, Lithuania in 1922, Estonia in 1923, and Latvia in 1923. Finally, to complete the list of these obligations, mention should be made of the minorities provisions of the Germano-Polish Convention relating to Upper Silesia (1922), and of the Convention concerning the Memel Territory, concluded in 1924. It will thus be seen that from the Northern Baltic to the Aegean

Sea there is in the east of Europe no country which has not undertaken certain international obligations to its racial, linguistic, or religious minorities. The number of persons to whom this protection applies may be placed at roughly thirty millions.

The rights guaranteed to minorities, allowing for greater or less detail and for the special situation of certain minorities, are the same in all the treaties or declarations. Examined analytically, and not according to the order in which the articles are placed, the first of the rights guaranteed to minorities may be considered to be the right to nationality. This right is of prime importance in the application of the minorities treaties, owing to the fact that in general the protection given by these treaties is granted only to nationals of the State concerned. It is evident, therefore, that the establishment of the right to nationality is an indispensable preliminary condition for the effective application of the treaties.

Nationality according to the minorities treaties is established either by birth in the territory of the State concerned, or, subject to certain detailed conditions, by permanent domicile at the date of coming into force of the treaty. These provisions apply, in the case of States not newly created but receiving large increases of territory, both to the older portion of the national territory and to the portions newly added. The acquisition of nationality in virtue of these clauses is granted *ipso facto*, and without the requirement of any formality. It is therefore to be presumed that members of a minority, referring by that term to persons long settled in the lands on which they live, have in general acquired without hindrance the nationality of their new State, and thereby qualified for the protection granted by the remaining

M

clauses of the treaty. Should it appear, however, that the right to nationality is contested or unduly withheld, thereby preventing the application of the fuller protection, then it may be assumed, generally speaking, that the withholding of the nationality may constitute a sufficient reason for setting in motion the machinery devised by the League for dealing with concrete cases of minorities protection.

From this starting-point the treaties proceed to build up a series of guarantees both of principle and of fact. The central principle is that which lays down that all citizens of the country shall be equal before the law, and shall enjoy the same civil and political rights without distinction as to race, language, or religion. This principle is further developed in another article, which specifies that citizens who belong to racial, religious, or linguistic minorities shall enjoy the same treatment and security in law and in fact as other citizens of the country. This is the basis of all the minorities treaties. It is further worked out in other articles of the treaties which provide for the full and complete protection of life and liberty, for the free exercise, whether public or private, of any creed, religion, or belief whose practices are not inconsistent with public order and public morals, and for the right freely to use any language in private intercourse, in commerce, in religion, in the press, or in publications of any kind, or at public meetings. Of a similar character is the guarantee that differences of religion, creed, or confession shall not prejudice any citizen in matters relating to the enjoyment of civil or political rights, as, for instance, admission to public employments, functions, and honours, or the exercise of professions and industries. There are, further, certain positive rights, such as that to adequate facilities for the use of a language other than the State language, either

orally or in writing, before the Courts, and the several provisions relating to education. In the latter respect, the
minorities are given the right equally with other citizens
of the State to establish, manage, and control at their own
expense charitable, religious, and social institutions, schools,
and other educational establishments, with the right to use
their own language and to exercise their religion freely
therein. Provision is also made that in towns and districts
in which a considerable proportion of citizens of a speech
other than that of the majority are resident, adequate facilities will be given for ensuring that in the primary schools
the instruction shall be given to the children of the minority
through the medium of their own language, the Government being authorized, however, to make the teaching of the
State language compulsory in such schools. Equally, in districts inhabited by a considerable proportion of a minority,
they are guaranteed an equitable share in the enjoyment and
application of the sums which may be provided out of public
funds for educational, religious, or charitable purposes.

It will be seen from this brief outline of the contents of the
treaties why I referred earlier in the present lecture to possible aspirations of the minorities which are not met by the
terms of the treaties. The rights granted by the treaties are
extensive and important, but they obviously do not cover
such questions as the so-called 'cultural autonomy', which
frequently figures among the claims made by organized
minorities. It is an equally obvious but still important fact
that the treaties refer only to minorities of race, language,
or religion, and not to political or social minorities. On the
other hand, with the exception of the right to public elementary schools and to a share in State funds for educational,
religious, or charitable purposes, all the rights in favour of

minorities are granted to every individual member of a minority in the sense of the treaties. Naturally, the minorities in most cases possess a certain organization, and the most important complaints will be those regarding measures which affect a minority as a whole. But the treaties do not require that a complaint should concern a minority as a whole.

iv. *Procedure.*

We now come to the most important provision in the treaties, namely, that which gives them their efficacy as international instruments, and lays down the method of intervention in the case of an infraction or danger of infraction of any of their stipulations. The first point to be noted in this article is that the Principal Allied and Associated Powers, who concluded the treaty with each of the States concerned, in fact passed their rights and duties under the treaty to the Council of the League of Nations and to its individual members. Thus, there is a provision that the treaty shall not be modified without the assent of a majority of the Council of the League of Nations, and the Principal Allied and Associated Powers agree that they will not withhold their assent from any modification which is in due form assented to by a majority of the Council. These stipulations are the natural corollary of that by which the State concerned agrees that the stipulations in the treaty, so far as they affect persons belonging to racial, religious, or linguistic minorities, constitute obligations of international concern and are to be placed under the guarantee of the League of Nations. By this clause, the protection of the minorities concerned is removed from the domain of action by single States as such, and is placed in an international atmosphere with an international body as the effective means of protection. An alternative is offered to the old method of direct intervention by one State in the affairs of another where minorities are concerned. Even if a State derives rights of intervention from its capacity as a member of the Council of the League of Nations, that intervention is an entirely different thing from direct intervention without the authorization conferred by membership of the Council and by the international character of the minorities obligations.

The same article of the treaties goes on to specify the manner and extent of the action that may be taken by the Council in application of the minorities treaties. The State bound by the treaty agrees that any member of the Council shall have the right to bring to the attention of the Council any infraction or any danger of infraction of any of these obligations. It is further agreed that the Council may thereupon take such action and give such direction as it may deem proper and effective in the circumstances. This is the basis on which the procedure established by the League of Nations for the protection of minorities has been built up. There are certain important features to be noted, both of a positive and of a negative character. As regards the action of the Council when actually seized of a minorities question, the provision of the treaty already quoted allows the Council the widest limits of action. On the other hand, the right of calling attention to an infraction or a danger of infraction is reserved to members of the Council alone. It follows that even a State which is a member of the League but is not a member of the Council cannot seize the Council of a concrete question relating to an infraction or danger of infraction of the minorities treaties, unless, as indicated above, quite exceptionally under Article 11 of the Covenant. Still less have the minorities themselves the right—except in one special case, Upper Silesia—actually to seize the Council of a question relating to the treaties.

Why is it that the right of seizing the Council is conferred on members of the Council alone? We touch here on one of the most delicate questions in the execution of the minorities treaties, namely, the fact of national sovereignty. It is quite clear that the minorities treaties are a limitation of the national sovereignty of the States they bind. The State is limited in certain respects in its power over a number of its citizens. When it is remembered that the guarantee of this limitation is an international guarantee, it is, I think, clear that the central question of the administration of the minorities treaties is that of conciliating as far as possible the effective exercise of an international guarantee with current conceptions of national sovereignty. Would the theory and the actual fact of national sovereignty admit, for instance, that certain of the citizens of a State should have the right, as a party in a legal procedure, to cite their State before an international body? I think there is no doubt that this would not be admitted by any modern State except in very special areas and in very special circumstances. But was it possible, or desirable even, that a very large number of States, say all the members of the League of Nations, should have the right of intervention in the internal affairs of a particular country, even though that right be exercised through an international body? There were difficulties in the way of giving even this extension to the right of intervention. On the other hand, once the treaty specified that it is the Council which is competent to deal with an infraction or danger of infraction of the treaties, it seemed natural, and it seemed further an adequate guarantee, that the individual members of the Council, as such, should alone be legally capable of calling the Council's attention to a concrete minorities case.

v. *Petitions.*

It was evident, however, that complaints or petitions regarding any infraction or danger of infraction of the treaties, either from States not represented on the Council, or from the minorities themselves, could not be neglected merely because the actual right of seizing the Council was reserved to Council members. The method adopted to conciliate this situation of fact with the legal position created by the guarantee clause of the treaty was clearly to admit the right of States not members of the Council or of the minorities themselves to send in petitions to the League of Nations, but to indicate equally clearly that such petitions could not have the effect of validly seizing the Council, but must be treated as sources of information for its members. It followed as a natural consequence that petitions of this nature might be addressed to the League on behalf of a minority by individuals or institutions not actually belonging to the minority, and in fact this has happened in a number of cases. It is important to grasp this conception of minorities petitions (other than cases brought forward by members of the Council) as mere sources of information if the procedure adopted by the Council is to be fully understood. One might call that procedure an attempt to conciliate the strict limitations imposed by the treaties in the matter of intervention with a due recognition of the fact that the minorities themselves, or States members of the League, might reasonably expect to have their complaints considered. The Council faced this problem as early as 1920, and adopted further resolutions on procedure at various dates up to 1926. It would be tedious for me to enter into this procedure in all its details, and I shall therefore confine myself to tracing the course of a petition sent in by a minority to the Secretariat. The first point to be noted is that the Secretariat is not authorized to treat members of a minority who send in a complaint as parties to a legal dispute with their own Government. It necessarily follows that unless a case reaches the full Council, when it may be presumed that the documents relating to it are made public, the petitioner will receive from the Secretariat only an acknowledgement of the receipt of his complaint, and no further information regarding the development of the procedure. This absence of information has been the subject of numerous complaints on the part of minorities or their representatives, but I think it will appear from what I have just said regarding the nature of the guarantee clause of the treaties and the facts of national sovereignty, that it is very difficult in the present circumstances to give more information to petitioners than is actually done. If you are interested in the matter of communication between the Secretariat and minorities petitioners, you will find the present practice fully described in a memorandum of the Secretary-General approved by the Council on 10 June 1926 (Official Journal, July 1926, pp. 878 and 986).

As soon as a petition regarding the protection of minorities is received by the Secretariat, it is submitted to a preliminary examination by the competent section. The object of this examination is to decide whether the petition can be accepted for submission to the regular procedure, or whether it should be declared inadmissible, and accordingly rejected. The preliminary and superficial tests to be applied by the Secretariat relate to the origin, the form, and the content of petitions. As regards origin, the only condition required is that the petition must not emanate from an anonymous or unauthenticated source, and as regards form, that the petition must not be worded in violent language. As regards their content, petitions (*a*) must have in view the protection of minorities in accordance with the treaties; (*b*) in particular, must not be submitted in the form of a request for the severance of political relations between the minority in question and the State of which it forms a part; and (*c*) must contain information or refer to facts which have not recently been the subject of a petition submitted to the ordinary procedure. Apart from the elementary safeguards against anonymity and abusive language, and against the violation of the principle *non bis in idem*, these conditions amount to saying that petitions must relate to qualified persons, and must ask for rights that are granted by the treaty.

Once a petition has been accepted as regular by the Secretary-General, he is obliged to forward it for possible observations to the Government concerned. That Government is allowed three weeks in which to inform the Secretariat whether it proposes to present observations, and a total period of two months in which to submit its comments. There are provisions for the extension by the President of the Council of this period of two months, and in urgent cases, or when petitions come from a State member of the League, for the immediate communication of petitions to the members of the Council without waiting for the observations of the interested Government. On receiving a petition from the Secretariat, the Government has the right to dispute its receivability. This preliminary question must then be submitted to the President of the Council, who if he so desires may consult two other members of the Council before giving his decision. It is further possible for the Government to lay a question of receivability before the full Council itself.

vi. *The Committees of Three.*

On the receipt of the Government's observations on a minorities petition, the two documents are communicated together by the Secretary-General, without comment, to the members of the Council for their information. The Secretariat then draws the attention of the President of the Council to the document containing the petition and observations, with a view to his appointing two other members of the Council to act with him in the so-called Committee of Three. Every receivable minorities petition comes before such a Committee. The examination by the Committee is undertaken with a view to determining whether one or more members of the Council should bring the subject of the petition to the Council's notice as constituting an infraction or danger of infraction of the treaties. Obviously, since all the members of the Council have the right to bring a question to the notice of the Council, and since they all have received communication of the documents concerned, any member outside the Committee retains the right to seize the full Council. But the constitution of the Committee of Three has several clear advantages. In the first place, it ensures that every receivable petition, without any exception, will be submitted to a detailed and serious examination by at least three members of the Council. Further, the existence of a Committee of Three removes one difficulty in the way of individual action on the part of members of the Council, namely, that such action might be considered an unfriendly act by the Government incriminated. No

Government can consider that a Committee composed of the President of the Council and two other members is actuated by unfriendly motives in bringing a complaint to the notice of the Council. Finally, the Committee itself, composed as it is of responsible representatives of the Governments on the Council, is often able to use its influence to make friendly suggestions to the Government concerned. In this connexion I cannot do better than quote to you certain passages regarding the activities of the Committees of Three contained in a report approved by the Sixth Assembly, and subsequently taken note of by the Council itself:

'The meetings of the Minorities Committee, or more correctly of the various minorities committees, which are simultaneously at work, generally take place during the sessions of the Council. Of late, some meetings have also taken place between the sessions of the Council owing to the difficulty of finding in all cases during the sessions of the Council the time necessary for the discussion of these matters, which are sometimes extremely detailed and prolonged, and which always have a delicate side to them and require the most conscientious preparation both by the Secretariat and by the members of the Council.

'The examination of a case by the Minorities Committee is not, of course, restricted to the formal meetings of the Committee. It is the duty of each member of the Committee, as well as of the Secretariat, to proceed to this examination without delay after the communication to the Council of the document relating to the case. The Secretariat begins an examination of the case without waiting for the distribution of this document. The discussion is accordingly from the first meeting of the three members of the Committee, except perhaps in cases of extreme urgency, based on a very considerable amount of preparatory work.

'The meetings of the Committee are held in private, and no formal Minutes are kept. Each Committee is free to adopt its own procedure.

'It results from the object of the work undertaken by a Minorities Committee that its members are free to form the best opinion they can of all the factors in the case which they are asked to examine. They may take into consideration the greater or less importance of the case, and its more or less general significance. They may take into account the attitude more or less conciliatory of the interested Government towards the requests of the minority as well as the attitude more or less loyal of the persons belonging to the minority. They may form the opinion, in a particular case, that the petitioner should have resorted to the administrative or judicial authorities of the country before addressing the League of Nations. In the Minorities Committees all these factors are continually discussed and taken into consideration.

'The members of the Committee may, moreover, enter into correspondence with the interested Government with a view to removing doubts or misunderstandings or making friendly suggestions to the Government to induce it to modify its attitude on a point which, failing such a solution, would appear to the members of the Committee to be a case which should be brought to the attention of the Council. Before deciding whether it should or should not draw the attention of the Council to a matter which is the subject of a petition the members of a Committee have in many cases asked the interested Government for supplementary information either in general terms or by putting definite questions. In some cases, such requests have been accompanied by other suggestions, as for example, that the interested Government should postpone taking any steps which might have the effect of creating a *fait accompli* before the Committee was in a position to take a decision on the question of substance.

'The members of the Committee have, in certain cases, made personal representations to the representative of the interested Government, with the object of drawing friendly attention to the advisability of putting an end to the difficulties with which the minority is concerned. In the majority of cases the Committee addresses the Government in question through the Director of the

Minorities Section of the Secretariat, either by writing or verbally, either formally or informally.

'The Committee often does not reach a final decision, even after having received all the supplementary information which it may desire. The case may be regarded rather as a link in a long chain than as an independent affair, and the members of the Committee sometimes consider that such a case, although of secondary importance in itself, may be of a character to be brought before the Council, if other similar cases should arise. The Committee, in these circumstances, invites the Minorities Section to follow the case for a certain period of time, and to notify it if there should arise any fact which would appear to justify a further discussion between its members.'

The passages I have just read will show, I think, how important a function the Committees of Three perform in the operation of the system of minorities protection elaborated by the League. It is no doubt possible to conceive other ways of attacking the problem. Without entering into alternative suggestions, I should like to call your attention to several difficulties which stand in the way of adopting a system other than that of Council Committees for the consideration of concrete minorities questions. In the first place, the Covenant itself is silent as regards the question of minorities. We have nothing equivalent to the provisions regarding mandates in Article 22 as a basis for building up the minorities procedure. In the second place, the treaties themselves, by the very nature of their guarantee clause, impose certain legal limitations on any procedure that could be established. The significant feature of the Committee of Three procedure, from a legal point of view, is that it keeps within the limits permissible under the treaties. In other words, it is the members of the Council alone who have the right to bring to the notice of the Council any infraction or danger of infraction

of the treaties, and the Committees of Three are composed
of members of the Council.

vii. *The Permanent Court.*

As I have already indicated, the Council when actually
seized of a minorities question is free to determine its own
procedure in each case. That procedure may well include,
as it has done in several cases, an application by the Council
to the Permanent Court of International Justice for an advisory opinion. The Council, of course, is not bound by the
terms of such an advisory opinion, but it naturally carries
with it great moral and legal authority. There is, however,
a possibility of referring a minorities question to the Permanent Court in a manner which should not be confused
with an application by the Council for an advisory opinion.
The guarantee clause of the treaties in its final paragraph
lays down that any difference of opinion as to questions of
law or fact arising out of the treaty between the Government concerned and any one of the Principal Allied and
Associated Powers or any other Power, a member of the
Council of the League of Nations, shall be held to be a
dispute of an international character under Article 14 of the
Covenant. The Government concerned agrees that any such
dispute shall, if the other party thereto demands, be referred
to the Permanent Court of International Justice. The decision of the Permanent Court shall be final, and shall have
the same force and effect as an award under Article 13 of the
Covenant. This provision in effect means that an individual
member of the Council may, apart altogether from the Council procedure, obtain from the Permanent Court a judgement binding on a State bound by a minorities treaty. Up
to the present, there has been only one case in which this

provision has been used, namely, that in which Germany
cited Poland before the Permanent Court in January
1928 on a matter relating to minority schools in Upper
Silesia.

viii. *The Assembly.*

I have made no reference so far to the action of the Assembly in regard to minorities questions, although I need scarcely
recall that the Assembly on a number of occasions has dealt
at some length with general questions relating to minorities
protection. What is the relation between the action of the
Council and of the Assembly in minorities questions? It
would seem to follow from the treaties that the Council
alone is competent to deal with actual cases of infraction or
danger of infraction of the treaties. In practice also it is the
Council which has laid down the main lines of the procedure.
The Assembly, however, clearly retains the right firstly to
discuss any question of procedure and even to make regulations thereon, and secondly to review and discuss the actual
work of the Council in minorities protection, as summarized
every year in the annual report on the work of the Council
and of the Secretariat. You will in fact remember that during
the Second, Third, Fourth, and Sixth Assemblies, there were
lengthy discussions on minorities procedure. As a result of
those discussions, the Assembly adopted several resolutions
of which perhaps the most important, as an expression of
principle, were those of 21 September 1922. Of the five
resolutions then adopted, I would draw your attention in
particular to that in which the Assembly, while recognizing
the primary right of the minorities to be protected by the
League from oppression, also emphasized the duty incumbent
on persons belonging to racial, religious, or linguistic minor-

ities to co-operate as loyal fellow citizens with the nations to which they now belong. In a further resolution, the Assembly expressed the hope that the States which are not bound by any legal obligations to the League with respect to minorities would nevertheless observe in the treatment of their own racial, religious, or linguistic minorities at least as high a standard of justice and toleration as is required by any of the treaties and by the regular action of the Council. It is apparent from these resolutions and from the recognition that 'in ordinary circumstances the League can best promote good relations between the various signatory Governments and persons belonging to racial, religious, or linguistic minorities placed under their sovereignty by benevolent and informal communications with those Governments' that the Assembly, whilst duly concerned that the situation not only of the minorities protected by the treaties, but of all other minorities, should be properly safeguarded, was in no way unmindful of the peculiar difficulties, both legal and practical, involved in the protection of minorities by the League.

ix. *Conclusion.*

If my remarks to you to-day have done nothing else, they will, I believe, have shown you that the protection of minorities is one of the most delicate questions with which the League has to deal. It is delicate alike from the legal and from the practical point of view. It involves not only complicated questions of international law and the due consideration of the theory and fact of national sovereignty, but also the difficulties involved in devising a practical means for giving expression to the possible grievances of some eighteen or twenty different minorities of greatly varying degrees of culture and organization in almost as many different Europeanpean countries.

You will doubtless have observed that the task I have set myself has been purely one of exposition. I have not attempted either to criticize or to defend the existing procedure in the matter of minorities protection by the League. It would be idle to contend that the system adopted has given universal satisfaction. But that system has at least been the result of a sober and mature consideration of the terms of the Treaties themselves and of the facts of international life as it is at present organized. Call it, if you will— as indeed, you might call the League of Nations itself—the somewhat surprising offspring of Justice and Diplomacy. Divine Justice may be inclined to suspect a changeling in the child. But I should not be surprised if Diplomacy, for quite different reasons, were a little aghast at the infant's appearance. In any case, it is well to remember that there are two parents, and the present anatomy of society offers very little support for the assumption that there should be only one.

SOME SPECIAL PROBLEMS

CHAPTER VIII

AMERICA'S RELATION TO WORLD PEACE

Professor MANLEY O. HUDSON:

I MUST confess that I feel some difficulty in addressing myself to the subject 'America's Relation to World Peace'. My chief difficulty in speaking on this subject before such an international audience arises from the fact that I am an American national, and I have probably as many prejudices of nationality as the nationals of other countries. I do not want to appear in the guise of a special pleader for the role which the United States of America has played in international relations during the course of the last ten years; it would discount anything I might say if I appeared to do so. On the other hand, I have no desire to criticize, outside of my own country, the foreign policy of my own Government. Perhaps the only way of escape from my dilemma is to proceed to a temporary denationalization of myself; but, if I were to do that with any degree of success, I should also have to ask you to denationalize yourselves as listeners. There is some prejudice, moreover, against any person who speaks on behalf of what he considers to be the interests of a world community. I wish it were possible for us, in a modern world, to discuss such problems as come before this Institute as citizens of a world community, attached to and zealous to serve the interests of a whole world community. If, however, any of you has a prejudice against internationalizing himself in that way, I would suggest that in our process of denationalization you and I, for the purposes of our discussion this evening, call ourselves citizens of a great republic, a very old republic, whose nationality has not carried for very many generations any special commitment in the consideration of international policy. I invite you to become with me, for the course of an hour, citizens of the Republic of Geneva. Let us ask ourselves how America's relation to world peace might appear to a citizen of this great Republic of Geneva. I realize, of course, that here again we may be committing ourselves to a particular point of view. Switzerland has no navy; Switzerland has no colonies; Switzerland has no neighbours who can possibly dream of any Swiss imperialism. Even in the course of this past year, when the little Duchy of Liechtenstein found it necessary to bring to an end a commercial treaty with Switzerland, the Swiss Federal Council bade the Liechtenstein people 'Bon voyage' and told them they were very glad to end the treaty. Let us see how the policy of a great country, with a great navy, with colonies, with interests in every part of the world, and its contribution to the peace of the world, must appear to the citizens of a republic situated as is this Republic of Geneva.

i. *America's Advantages and Disadvantages.*

In the beginning, I think we must recognize that there have been certain difficulties in the American position during these last years with which we, as citizens of the Republic of Geneva, ought to have full sympathy. First of all, I think we ought to sympathize with the United States of America because it is in the unenviable position of occupying a place of predominance among the twenty-one nations of the Western hemisphere. A country with as much power and as much predominance among its neighbours as has the United States in the Western hemisphere, is bound to feel the disadvantage of having no rival, of not being compelled to consult other countries and other Governments, of not being in a position where it must of necessity shape its policy with respect to the opinions of the peoples who are around it. That is, it seems to me, a distinct disadvantage from which the United States of America suffers. You may find it a second disadvantage, looking at the situation from the point of view of the Republic of Geneva, that the United States has come, in the course of the past few years, into the position of having too great an influence in world affairs, even outside the Western hemisphere. It played a very great role in the war; the war left it a creditor of most of the nations of the world, and of course that brings in its train a good many disagreeable circumstances; and the experience in the war has put the people of the United States into a position where they do not, perhaps, always give other peoples full credit for the efforts that they are making—they may even be at times a bit disdainful of the efforts in which other peoples are engaged. Then there is a third difficulty from which the United States suffers—its very great and growing dependence on foreign trade. The standard of living of the people of the United States has come to be such that no American can live his ordinary daily life without drawing upon very distant peoples whom he does not know for his daily fare. That creates a position of dependence in which a people must of necessity, perhaps, take a strong line, where they must be very careful about their sources of supply, where they must assert themselves in distant parts of the world as they would not do if their standard of living were otherwise.

Those, then, seem to be three disadvantages from which

America has suffered during the course of these last years. Let me repeat them: first, the predominance of the United States in the Western hemisphere; second, the large influence of the United States in Europe; and third, the growing dependence of the United States on foreign trade.

Perhaps you will think, however, that those difficulties are entirely offset by the special advantages which the United States has in its relations with other peoples. Let us see what some of the advantages are. In the first place, I think America is very fortunately situated (and with our Geneva eyes we shall envy her this) in that she has no neighbours who are potential enemies and whom she need fear. The territory of the United States stretches from the Atlantic to the Pacific. Her people occupy a larger area than is occupied by any other people in the world, with two or three exceptions. They have to the north a neighbour, the Dominion of Canada, with whom their relations have for a hundred years been exemplary. Unless it be on the borders of Switzerland, I do not know any other place in the world where two peoples during the course of a whole century have carried on better or more neighbourly relations than have the peoples of North America north of the Rio Grande. There are no fortifications on the long Canadian frontier; there are no ships of war to defend the one people against the other. The two peoples have, in fact, put it outside of their ken that there should be a war between them. To the south, however, the United States has a neighbour with whom I am afraid the record is not quite so exemplary. Relations between the United States and Mexico have been distinctly bad during the course of the last twenty years, and I am afraid that those two peoples have not set a good example to others in the conduct of their current relations.

Then there is a second advantage which America has in her tradition of disinterestedness in the affairs of other peoples. Somehow in the early history of the country it came to be a settled principle of American foreign policy that there should be no interference in the affairs of other continents. If that principle is only of geographical application by the United States, if in fact America does intervene in the South American continent and in Asia, still, the tradition itself—the fact that people believe in it—is a very great advantage in America's position with reference to world peace.

In the third place, the American people have had a very great advantage during this past decade and more, because the United States has been the greatest dispenser of bounties that the world has ever seen. It was the privilege of the people of the United States, during the course of these last years, to relieve a great deal of suffering in Europe and in Asia. Their record in feeding the Russians, in feeding the Germans, and in sending supplies of all sorts in times of famine, is a record of which I think we in Geneva might well be envious. Moreover, there are various groups of people in the United States, such as, I believe, do not exist in other countries, who make it their business to attempt to assist peoples in other countries. In that connexion we might mention the great Zionist movement in the United States, for the Zionists get a large part of their financial support from the people of the United States. One of the most glorious examples of bountiful action that is to be found anywhere in history, is the record during the past two decades of the Rockefeller Foundation of the United States —a great Foundation, devoted to an improvement in the world's health, working in every part of the world without any considerations of nationality to limit its action, and always working in a most intelligent and far-seeing manner. Now, actions of that kind—the sending of help wherever it is required, the support which the American people give to such movements as Zionism, the interest taken by the Rockefeller Foundation in the health of the world—cannot fail, I think, to react on the political thought of a people, and I believe they have had a great effect on the policy of the United States.

In the fourth place, I think the American people have a certain advantage because of the idealistic strain in which they are supposed abroad, and perhaps justly supposed, to attack the solution of public problems. I am one of those who think there is a good deal of danger in idealism. I find principles very difficult things to manage. I believe one can have bad ideals and serve them just as loyally and just as unselfishly as good ideals. In the long run, however, I think it is a great asset of the American people that they do have this idealistic approach to public questions. At no time was this more apparent than in 1919, when America refrained from asking any kind of territorial advantage for herself at the close of the World War.

I shall not attempt to weigh the advantages against the disadvantages that I have mentioned. I shall ask you to weigh them, however, in the course of the review that we shall make of America's relation to world peace. That review I propose to arrange under five headings. I propose to examine the record of the United States during the past decade with reference to international arbitration; its record with reference to inter-American organization; its record with reference to the League of Nations; its record with reference to the Permanent Court of International Justice; and its efforts to encourage agreements between States that they will not go to war. There are thus five headings under which we shall examine America's relation to World Peace: arbitration, inter-American relations, the League of Nations, the Permanent Court, and the renunciation of war.

ii. *Progress in Arbitration Treaties.*

I take first the subject of arbitration, because its roots go back beyond the decade we are considering. There has been a great tradition in the United States of America, ever since the successful Geneva arbitration more than half a century ago, favouring a broad policy of advancing international arbitration. The United States played, I think, a very creditable role at the Hague Peace Conference of 1899 and again at the Hague Peace Conference of 1907. On both of those occasions the representatives of the United States spoke in favour of the largest possible extension of international arbitration. They supported the creation of the Permanent Court of Arbitration in 1899, and it was they who put forward a scheme in 1907 for the creation of a new Permanent Court of Arbitral Justice. Then, following the Second Peace Conference at The Hague in 1907, the Government of the United States made a very notable series of arbitration treaties with a number of other Governments. Those treaties are generally known in the United States as the Root Arbitration Treaties. They followed a model in its actual wording offered to them by Great Britain and France in the Franco-British Arbitration Treaty of 1904. The American arbitration treaties of 1908 served a very useful purpose, and in the course of the years that have since passed they have on several occasions served as the basis for a recourse to arbitration. In 1913, however, the Government of the United States, under the leadership of Secretary Bryan, thought it necessary that a more inclusive network of treaties should be made, and Secretary Bryan concluded some thirty conciliation treaties with other Governments, of which more than twenty were ratified. Those treaties provided for the reference of all disputes to a Permanent Conciliation Commission, and the Governments entering into them agreed that they would not go to war until such a Commission had been given an opportunity to make a report. The Root Treaties of 1908 have recently begun to expire. The first of them expired less than a year ago, and a Root Treaty on the 1908 model between the United States and France expired on 6 February last. At that time the Government of the United States entered into a new treaty with the Government of the French Republic, a treaty going beyond the Root Treaty in some measure, improving upon it in some ways, but a treaty which I think you and I ought now to examine in the light of what has happened during these latter years.

The Root Treaty of 1908, which followed the Franco-British model, excluded from arbitration questions affecting the national honour or the vital interests of the contracting countries. Now, of course, if you make an agreement to arbitrate everything except those things that may affect your national honour or your vital interests, you have not agreed to arbitrate anything that you do not want to arbitrate when the question arises. That, I think, has been seen for a long time, and many Governments have said in the course of the last few years that a formula of that kind does not correspond to the needs of the modern world. That formula, as I say, appeared in the Root Treaty of 1908, but fortunately it was dropped in the treaty which was signed on behalf of the United States and France in February of this year, and instead the two Governments have agreed to submit to arbitration differences relating to legal questions, either by the use of the Permanent Court of Arbitration at The Hague or by the use of any other competent tribunal. But in the exceptions which were made in the treaty of 6 February there are certain expressions which you may think go quite as far by way of exclusion as the formula concerning national honour and vital interests. For instance, the two Governments say that the provisions of the treaty 'do not cover any matter which is within the domestic jurisdiction of either of the High Contracting Parties'. It is one thing for the Covenant of the League of Nations to say that the jurisdiction of the Council does not cover matters of domestic jurisdiction, for it is left to the Council to say what is a matter of domestic jurisdiction; it is quite another thing for an arbitration treaty, entered into in this year 1928, to say that questions within the domestic jurisdiction of either of the parties do not come under the treaty, leaving it open to either of the parties to say what is or is not a domestic question. The exceptions in the treaty exclude from its provisions, also, any matter which depends on or involves the maintenance of the traditional attitude of the United States concerning American questions, commonly described as the Monroe Doctrine. On the whole, the exceptions in the treaty are such that in my judgement it does not mark much advance on the arbitration treaties of 1908. Yet at the present time it is being made a basis of negotiations with various other Governments, and in the course of the last few months the United States has signed other arbitration treaties on that model, notably with Germany. Perhaps one would not expect a country with the disadvantages of the United States to make quite the same kind of arbitration treaty that could be made, for example, by Switzerland. The treaties concluded in the course of the past ten years by the Swiss Federal Council at Berne are excellent models. The treaty between the United States and France is behind the styles as they are exemplified in the treaties recently made by many European Governments.

In the course of the last few months the Government of the United States has begun to implement the Bryan Treaties of 1913, and it is now in process of concluding similar treaties with various other Governments. Since 1913 no case has ever been referred to the Permanent Conciliation Commissions provided for in the Bryan Treaties, and in fact I think few of us have thought about who were the individuals composing these Commissions. During the course of the last few months, however, the Government of the United States has assiduously been trying to complete their membership. It is now definitely a part of its policy to implement the Bryan Treaties already signed and to conclude similar treaties with various other Governments. If you want to see where that leaves the United States, I suggest you take a Bryan Treaty providing for a Permanent Conciliation Commission and an arbitration treaty providing for the arbitration of legal questions and combine them, and then compare the combined result with the model treaties of arbitration and conciliation which are to be discussed at the Assembly of the League of Nations next month. (You will find the latter in a League document numbered C. 342. M. 100, published on 5 July, 1928.)

iii. *Inter-American Relations.*

So much then for the role of the United States with regard to arbitration during the course of these last years. Let us now look at a very important part of America's foreign relations, having to do with inter-American relations, or the relations between the various States of the Western hemisphere. In the first place, I think one cannot understand the problems of the Western hemisphere without an attempt to understand what is meant by the Monroe doctrine. That doctrine has been referred to by Costa Rica in the course of the last week. I say that it is necessary to attempt to understand the Monroe doctrine, yet the Monroe doctrine is not something to be defined. It is rather something that is felt. The original Monroe doctrine was that the Government of the United States would not tolerate any aggression by any European Power in the Western hemisphere. I think that doctrine must have served in its time a most useful purpose, and it has doubtless contributed to the setting up of the twenty republics to the south of the United States. But to-day it is very difficult to know just what is meant by the Monroe doctrine, and just how far its penumbra extends. It has not prevented the establishment of a working system of conferences between the Governments of the various American Republics. In the course of the last thirty years six international conferences of American States have been held, and those conferences now promise to recur in the future at stated intervals. There is to be a conference of American States in the future at least once in every five years. They are, I think, an excellent means of increasing understanding. It is a wholesome thing for Governments to have their politicians meeting the politicians of other Governments, and such conferences are worth while even if they reach no definite agreements.

In the course of these thirty years a number of multilateral international treaties have been made by the American conferences. But even more significant, perhaps, is the technical and special co-operation which they encourage. You may be interested to know of some of the conferences that are now in prospect, for in addition to the political conference, held once in five years, the cultural and scientific and commercial representatives of the American peoples meet more often. The last conference which met at Havana in February envisaged, for example, a Pan-American Congress of Journalists, a series of Pan-American Commercial Conferences, a Commission of Bibliographic Experts, American Conferences on Trade Marks and on the establishment of Steamship Lines, a Pan-American Commission of Importers and Exporters, a Commission on Communications Statistics, a Commission on Agricultural Co-operation, an International Commission of Jurists, and many others. All these meetings, envisaged at the sixth Conference of American States held at Havana this year, measure the growing co-operation among the American Republics. Indeed most of the co-operation is along lines which are usually referred to as not political. When the Havana Conference met last year, the great political problem of Nicaragua was hardly mentioned.

The American Republics are served by a permanent body known as the Pan-American Union. This Secretariat operates under certain limitations which the Secretariat of the League of Nations does not feel. In the first place, it is controlled by a governing board which consists always of the diplomats of the various American countries stationed at Washington. After a long contest it has now been decided that the representatives need not be diplomats at Washington. In the second place the Chairman of the Governing Board of the Pan-American Union, who has a powerful influence, has always been the Secretary of State of one of the American countries. Now I think it is quite clear that the Council of

the League of Nations would be under a distinct limitation
if a member of the Federal Council at Berne were always the
President of the Council of the League of Nations. The
Pan-American Union has recently undergone some reorganization, and if you will read the latest report on the Pan-
American Union you will see that a very deliberate and obvious
attempt has been made to duplicate many of the activities
of the various organs of the League of Nations. For instance,
there is now to be established some kind of a commission on
intellectual co-operation. Its activities are much greater
to-day than they were a few years ago, and yet the Pan-
American Union is a very small organization and does not
by any means compare in its activity with the Secretariat of
the League of Nations.

There has been in the course of the last few years a good
deal of talk about an American League of Nations. I find
that many people regard the present organization of the
American States as a real League of Nations. But I think
that one cannot study the history of the six conferences of
American States and the history of the Pan-American Union
and feel that there is much similarity to the League of
Nations. The Pan-American Union is serving a most useful
purpose; the conferences of American States are very necessary, and they cannot succeed without it. But I should hesitate to espouse any proposal that there should be created
among the American peoples the kind of League of Nations
that has its centre here in Geneva.

The relations between the various American countries
cannot be considered without giving attention to the occasional instances of intervention by the Government of the
United States in other American countries. Such intervention has taken place in the course of the last few years,

notably in Haiti and in Nicaragua. The Government of the United States is sometimes considered to be an imperialistic Government because of those interventions; but I think one ought to remember the record of the Government of the United States in withdrawing from Cuba, and one must remember also the actual withdrawals from Haiti and Nicaragua. Certainly there is no disposition on the part of the Government of the United States to extend its territory to the south. If there had been such a disposition during the course of the last seventy-five years, many opportunities for the extension have occurred. Without any disposition to extend its territory and without any disposition to do more than to assist in the maintenance of stable government, the Government of the United States has been involved in the affairs both of Haitians and Nicaraguans during the course of the last few years. If the Monroe doctrine is to be interpreted as involving for the United States any obligation to protect the nationals of other countries in Central and South America, then I feel quite sure that the Monroe doctrine needs some kind of internationalization. If the Government of the United States is acting on behalf of any general interest in Nicaragua and in Haiti and in similar instances, it would be much better to have that general interest proclaimed by some international authority. If it is acting solely in its own interest, and incidentally in the interests of other peoples, I think there is still something to be said for the record it has made. Its action has at any rate usually resulted in the long run in making governments more stable and in adding something in the way of law and order to the existing situation. Without attempting to defend that intervention, without attempting to say that there are no cases which would justify it, I think one has to be careful in the balance sheet that one draws, and one ought to say that in the end there have been some general advantages resulting from the intervention.

iv. *America and the League.*

I now come to the relations between the United States and the League of Nations during the course of these last ten years. I shall not dwell on the repudiation of the Covenant by the Government of the United States. I realize that it is difficult for people in other countries to understand the reasons for that repudiation, and I assure them that it is just as difficult for an American to understand the reasons for it. In the first place, it was undoubtedly founded on some desire of the American people to be free from the commitments with which they found themselves in Europe. It was a desire to cut the painter with Europe, as it was so often expressed at the end of the war, but that desire was by no means universal. It became confused with all sorts of issues and the issues finally became so mixed that the American public simply lost its patience with the whole subject. But there is one thing to be mentioned which I think might be borne in mind by a citizen of Geneva. Somehow in North America the written word is an extremely important thing. It seems to have an importance that is not attached to it in other parts of the world. There is a good deal of argument, in connexion with almost any public question in America, about the Constitution of the United States. It has even been suggested to me quite recently that there are certain constitutional difficulties in the way of the full co-operation of the United States with the League of Nations. I believe there are no such constitutional difficulties. The Government of the United States does not differ from many other Governments in various parts of the world in that a popularly elected legislative body shares in the treaty-making function. Most of the work of the League of Nations is carried on from day to day without any formulation of actual treaty agreements, and I see nothing in the structure of the Government of the United States to prevent its co-operating as a Member of the League of Nations.

What has happened in the course of these years since the repudiation of the Covenant? The Government of the United States passed through an era of non-co-operation with other Governments through the use of the League of Nations machinery. At first there was not a very courteous treatment of communications received from the Secretary-General of the League of Nations. But diplomatic amenities were soon established, and in the course of these later years the Government of the United States has been courteous at all times in its dealings with the League of Nations. After the lapse of a few years the Government of the United States found itself in a position where it had to be represented at various conferences of the League of Nations for the purpose of protecting its own interests. In 1925, for example, the Government of the United States was represented at the Opium Conference of the League of Nations. In 1925, also, it was represented by a most able delegation at a conference on the traffic in arms and ammunition. In 1927, the Government of the United States was represented officially at conferences held in this building on no less than four occasions. There was the Economic Conference which was held in May, the Transit Conference which was held in August, the Import and Export Prohibitions Conference which was held in October, and the session of the Preparatory Commission on Disarmament in November. This year—1928—the United States has already been represented at the Conference on

Import and Export Prohibitions held a few days ago, and it will doubtless be represented at the Conference on Economic Statistics to be held in November, at the Conference on Double Taxation to be held in October, and at any meeting of the Preparatory Commission on Disarmament that may be held during the course of the year.

In other words, the United States though not a Member of the League of Nations and, if you care to say so, having repudiated the Covenant of the League, finds it impossible to stay out of the League of Nations with respect to these special phases of its work. Its co-operation has reached a point where it is no longer seriously opposed in the United States. Recently our Secretary of State made a declaration of a policy of co-operation, a declaration so important that I think perhaps I should be justified in reading to you a part of it. In a pamphlet recently published by the Republican National Committee in the United States, Secretary Kellogg said: 'The Government of the United States has continued its policy of friendly and helpful co-operation with the League of Nations on subjects of humanitarian concern.' After referring to the various conferences in which the United States has taken part, he goes on to say: 'The willingness of the United States to co-operate freely, fully, and helpfully with the League in matters of genuine international concern, and our Government's determination to adhere to the policy of non-participation in the League itself, is now well understood at Geneva.' I should like to stress the words 'the willingness of the United States to co-operate freely, fully, and helpfully'. That represents the current feeling of both of the two major political parties in the United States; the Republican platform for the coming presidential election in November expressly proclaims it.

There is only one part of that formula which I as a citizen of Geneva would find in any way unsatisfactory. I should welcome the United States co-operating freely with the League. I should welcome its co-operating fully with the League, but I should be a little hesitant to believe that it was co-operating 'helpfully' for the purpose of being helpful to others. Helpfulness to others is not a thing which is going to determine any continuous line of policy. In the long run Governments are going to pursue the interests of their own peoples as they see them, without attempting to be helpful towards others. They may be helpful to others in times of calamity or special need, but in the long run it is their own interests which they pursue. I think it would be far better if the co-operation of the Government of the United States with the League of Nations could be put on the basis of protecting the interests of the American people. That is what Secretary Hughes did in his speech to the Republican State Convention in New York in 1924 when he said, 'If we find our interests affected we must, of course, take part in conferences called by the League of Nations.'

Let us see how far this formula of free, full, and helpful co-operation actually corresponds with the facts to-day. We will limit it, if you like, to the humanitarian and technical work of the League of Nations. I suppose the health work of the League of Nations would be called humanitarian, and I suppose it would be called technical. I know of no more romantic chapter in human history than that chapter which has been written in the last eight years by the Health Organization of the League of Nations. If you take nothing but the interchanges of public health personnel, of which twenty-eight have been held in the course of the last six years, where is there a more romantic chapter anywhere than in the growth of a world language of public health administration? Those interchanges of public health personnel have been very largely financed by American money. Some 40 per cent. of the money, I think, has come from America—not from the Government of the United States but from the Rockefeller Foundation. Twenty American public health officials have taken part in these interchanges of public health personnel. Yet the Government of the United States has done little or nothing to assist in the health work of the League of Nations. It pays no part of the expense. It is true that the Surgeon-General of the United States sits on the League's Health Committee; but he sits there not as a representative of the Government of the United States but as a representative of the International Public Health Office at Paris. That does not seem to me to be quite 'free and full co-operation'.

Take again the question of opium, where quite clearly the United States must sit in if other Governments are doing so in order to protect its own interests. The United States was represented at an Opium Conference held in Geneva in 1925, but we have not signed the new Opium Treaty which is to be brought into force next month, and our representatives when they attend a meeting of the Permanent Advisory Committee on the Opium Traffic still attend in an 'unofficial capacity'. Or take so small a thing as the registration of treaties here in Geneva. You know that during these last years the Secretariat of the League of Nations has maintained a register of international treaties, and every Member of the League of Nations has agreed that it will register its treaties and that no treaties are to be binding until they are so registered. In the course of the last eight years 1,822 current international engagements have been registered with the Secretariat. The advantage of registration is that if that Article of the Covenant of the League of Nations is carried out there cannot be any secret treaties, and when the texts of those 1,822 international engagements are published, as they are published in the League of Nations Treaty Series, we lawyers who must consult treaties have at hand a single compendium of the world's treaty law. That is a thing with which surely any Government could co-operate without feeling that it is committed in any way. Six years before Germany became a Member of the League, in 1920, the German Government announced that it considered the procedure an excellent one and that it would send its treaties for registration. The Government of Ecuador, though not a Member of the League, for several years past has been registering its treaties. But the United States does not send in its treaties for registration, because our policy of free, full, and helpful co-operation does not seem to go that far.

What is actually happening, of course, is that the United States is more and more coming into this building of the League of Nations at various side-entrances. It may not assist in occupying the whole building; the United States pays none of the expenses of maintaining this Permanent International Civil Service which we call the League Secretariat. It pays none of the running expenses of the League. But it does have a growing part in the different activities that centre here. The policy of free, full, and helpful cooperation by the United States is a policy which still has room in which to grow; it has still a chance for development and expansion, and I think its expansion is inevitable.

v. *America and the World Court.*

I now come to the subject of the attitude of the United States towards the Permanent Court of International Justice. I propose to say very little on this subject. The Permanent Court of International Justice has been a great success. It has succeeded in enlisting the loyal support of peoples throughout the world. In the course of these seven years it has handed down twenty-five Judgements and Opinions. It is now holding its fourteenth session at The Hague. A prominent American has just resigned as judge, and another American has received many nominations to succeed him. Mr. John Bassett Moore may thus be succeeded by Ex-Secretary Charles E. Hughes. Since 1923, however, when the Government of the United States first took some initiative towards giving its support to the Court, nothing has happened to consummate the basis for that support. The Senate of the United States voted a reservation which was not cast in such terms that other Governments thought they could accept it unconditionally, and the consequence is that the matter still hangs fire. The Senate said that if the United States adhered to the Court Protocol, the Court should not entertain any request for an Advisory Opinion relating to any matter in which the United States has or claims an interest without the consent of the United States. It is commonly supposed that the acceptance of that reservation by other countries depends on a solution of the question whether unanimity is required in the Council for a request for an Advisory Opinion. Personally I think a solution of that question has little or nothing to do with the problem raised by the United States reservation. I very much hope that it will not be settled in favour of a requirement of unanimity, but if that solution were adopted it would have little to do with the problem raised by the American fifth reservation, though it might pave the way for further negotiations.

vi. *The Renunciation of War.*

I now come to the fifth subject which I proposed to cover, namely, that of agreements not to resort to war. A very important agreement not to go to war was included in the Peace Treaties of 1919. It is so important, and it is so often forgotten, that I want to read it to you. It is contained in Article 11 of the Covenant of the League of Nations, which says:

'Any war or threat of war, whether immediately affecting any of the Members of the League or not, is hereby declared a matter of concern to the whole League, and the League shall take any action that may be deemed wise and effectual to safeguard the peace of nations.'

There we have a statement that the peace of the world cannot be violated without an invasion of the interests of every nation in the League, and for the purpose of protecting the general peace this part of the Peace Treaties created a continuously functioning machinery, a machinery which in the course of eight years has produced fifty meetings of the Council of the League of Nations and which will produce here next month the ninth meeting of the Assembly of the League. Men were not content at that time to write on paper a statement that a war anywhere was a matter of concern to the whole world. They said that the League should take any action that might be deemed wise and effectual to safeguard peace. They created institutions. They created machinery. They saw the need of agencies to function continuously, to be always on the job, to examine each situation, and to see in case of any war or threat of war what the general interest of peace may demand.

Now other Articles of the Covenant of the League bind the Members of the League not to go to war until after they have submitted to a certain procedure, but I have never considered the other Articles so important as Article 11. I have always thought during the course of these years that Article 11 is the most important of all the Articles. However, my mind is not the mind of an orderly architect. It is not a mind which would think it essential to see every possible crevice stopped up before being willing to proceed another stage further. There are people, however, who want to sew up situations in such a way that neither they nor the people who follow after them can move outside of certain limitations. I have found with regard to my own resolutions that I never keep them. I have found it impossible to sew up myself for the future, and I believe it is quite impossible for any generation to sew up succeeding generations for the future. I believe it is impossible for a single generation to write in black ink on white paper anything that is going to make it impossible for another generation to assert its own freedom of action, and that is why I have always attached such importance to Article 11 of the Covenant of the League of Nations. But my friends, who take a different view, say that a possibility of war has been left open by the Covenant, because the Covenant requires each State only to submit to a certain procedure before going to war. They forget that there is always Article 11, and that under Article 11 any war or threat of war has to be considered by the machinery functioning here in Geneva. It was the views of such people that led for several years here to the drafting of treaties of mutual assistance, and when that effort finally broke down, they led to the drafting of the Protocol of Geneva. After the Protocol was drafted, I welcomed it. I am always willing to accept these things once they have become *faits accomplis*, but I had never seen the necessity for the Protocol, and when it died I was not as disappointed as some of my friends.

When those efforts had failed, a new effort was made here to define aggressive war and to say that under all circumstances aggressive war is a crime. In spite of the failure of this effort, however, the last Assembly of the League of Nations adopted a resolution which is not very much known and which I want to read. This is the text of the resolution adopted by the last Assembly on the proposal of the Polish representative:

'The Assembly declares: that all wars of aggression are and shall always be prohibited; and that every possible means must be employed to settle disputes of every description which may arise between States.'

That was adopted by the representatives of fifty nations last September. I recall that when the Polish delegate offered that resolution at the last Assembly a very prominent man in Geneva said to me, 'This seems to me quite purposeless, for the Covenant of the League is already more useful than any formula of that kind.'

Since the Assembly took that action, however, the situation has been advanced somewhat further. First of all, we had the proposal made by Monsieur Briand to Secretary Kellogg that the Governments of France and of the United States should enter into a treaty for the renunciation of war as an instrument of national policy, and then Secretary

Kellogg countered with a suggestion that such a treaty should be made but that it should be open to the signature of all countries. A treaty is now about to be signed, and I want to read the text of it and ask you to consider the other texts I have read. This is the text of the Briand-Kellogg Pact:

'The High Contracting Parties solemnly declare in the names of their respective peoples that they condemn recourse to war for the solution of international controversies and renounce it as an instrument of national policy in their relations with one another.

'The High Contracting Parties agree that the settlement or solution of all disputes or conflicts, of whatever nature or whatever origin they may be, which may arise among them, shall never be sought except by peaceful means.'

Now that treaty, as I say, is about to be signed. It goes two stages further than the Polish resolution adopted by the last Assembly; firstly because it brings the United States in, as people say, and secondly because it takes the form of an actual treaty which will be submitted to ratification. In considering it, I would have you notice first of all that it is not really a text of legal significance; therefore, I don't want to discuss it as a lawyer. It is, however, a text of great political significance and of great psychological importance. I want to subscribe to everything said here yesterday by Professor Patterson as to the importance of peace by incantation. I think it is most necessary that we should avail ourselves of the advantages of incantation; but as a student of these questions I insist upon trying to know what is incantation when I am engaged in it, and I am interested now to know how far the Briand-Kellogg Treaty is merely a process of peace by incantation.

It is not primarily a legal commitment. It is devised with reference to our present political situation, and that political situation arises from the dissatisfaction of some people with the provisions of the Covenant of the League of Nations and their feeling that the Covenant leaves the situation too open. Now of course I think that the Briand-Kellogg Treaty once it is signed ought to be accepted by all Governments, and personally I should like to see it accepted by the Government of the Union of Socialist Soviet Republics. I think it would be a tragedy, for example, if the Treaty were signed by representatives of the United States and were then repudiated by the Government and the Senate of that country. I am delighted that the various Governments have gone as far as they have. Yet I do not propose to base on this Treaty any hopes for which I cannot find some foundation. In the first place I think the Treaty has already had one unfortunate effect; it seems to have called out of the vague depths of the unphrased a new Monroe doctrine that is going to be in the future a very embarrassing thing for certain people who must discuss the conduct of foreign policy. The United States did not mention its Monroe doctrine in the Treaty. Perhaps Sir Austen Chamberlain was right in saying that the United States would inevitably mention its Monroe doctrine. We cannot even make a treaty with France—the arbitration treaty to which I have already referred—without mentioning the Monroe doctrine; so I suppose it should be mentioned in this connexion. There is one other questionable effect of this Treaty. It renounces war as an instrument of national policy, and that proposal at once directed the minds of certain people to the discussion of aggressive war that had been going on for some time. The United States found it impossible to distinguish between war and aggressive war, but the Government of the United States was able to distinguish between war and wars of self-defence. The Secretary of State of the United States said on 28 April of this year with reference to this Treaty, 'Every nation is free at all times and regardless of treaty provisions to defend its territory from attack and invasion, and it alone is competent to decide whether circumstances require recourse to war in self-defence.' It was with that understanding that the Treaty was signed in Paris in August 1928.

May I now read again, for fear you have forgotten it, Article 11 of the Covenant of the League of Nations:

'Any war or threat of war, whether immediately affecting any of the Members of the League or not . . .'

Nothing is said there about self-defence. Nothing is said there about aggressive war. Nothing is said about each country's determining for itself whether it is acting in self-defence or in defence of its own interests. Have you ever known a country waging war which did not think it was acting in defence of its own interests? In the language of Article 11 of the Covenant, however,

'Any war or threat of war, whether immediately affecting any of the Members of the League or not, is hereby declared a matter of concern to the whole League, and the League shall take any action that may be deemed wise and effectual to safeguard the peace of nations.'

For my part, I have come to wonder whether the discussion of these last years has advanced us very much beyond Article 11 of the Covenant. I have come to wonder whether Article 11 of the Covenant is not a sounder principle than the formulae with which we are now endeavouring to go beyond the Covenant. I cannot believe that a single generation will accomplish by a fiat more than will be accomplished by each generation for itself, by the use of machinery, by the use of continuous processes of peaceful mediation. The great principle to me was that a war anywhere, without distinction as to aggression or self-defence, should be a matter of concern to all peoples, and that all peoples should maintain a machinery for the purpose of protecting their peace.

This Treaty has already taken us away from the Covenant. It does not go so far as the Covenant, if it deals only with those wars that are not defensive and if there is to be read into the record of the forthcoming Conference Secretary Kellogg's statement that every nation is alone competent to decide whether circumstances require recourse to war in self-defence. When Bulgaria thought she was attacked by Greece in 1925, did the authorities of the League of Nations say that Bulgaria alone was competent to say whether she should have recourse to war in self-defence? They did not. They said Bulgaria's obligation under the Covenant of the League of Nations was to come to the Council of the League and discuss the situation with Greece, and that is exactly what Bulgaria did. I cannot believe that any agreement not to go to war will ever take the place of machinery for keeping the world's peace. If that machinery can be operated on the principle that a war anywhere is of concern to the whole world, I would rather pin my faith to that machinery than to what may have been written in a treaty at some time in the past.

There is also another danger, which may not exist in other countries as much as it seems to me to exist in North America. There is a danger that people will feel that when this Treaty has been signed their job is finished and their work is done. The Treaty will say, when it is signed, that the High Contracting Parties agree that the settlement or solution of all disputes or conflicts of whatever origin shall never be sought except by peaceful means. Now what are the peaceful means which are to be used in the settlement of controversies? We know that controversies are going to arise in future. No one supposes that we shall have a dead world where there will not be any controversies. We must have some peaceful means of settlement. But what are they to be? Arbitration treaties, such as the United States made with France on 6 February last? Surely Switzerland would not go back to treaties of that kind. Conciliation commissions such as the United States has set up with other countries which have signed the Bryan Treaties? Those are very useful. The Permanent Court of International Justice? Some forty-eight or fifty countries are supporting that Court, but the United States is not one of them. The Council of the League of Nations, which has met fifty times in eight years? There again is an agency which has proved itself a means of peaceful settlement. I say there is a danger that when this Treaty is signed the false belief will be engendered that the job has been done. It is up to students of international policy such as the people in this Institute to see that such a false belief is not entertained, and to see that the Treaty is used as the means of working for the establishment of new agencies of peaceful settlement. The Treaty which is to be signed may serve as a peg on which men inclined towards peace can in the future hang their insistence. That is going to be its great service. I hope the Treaty will be ratified, and yet I hope that none of us are going to be satisfied when it is ratified, but that all of us are going to use it as a means for insisting on the necessity for establishing new agencies of peaceful settlement.

May I say one closing word to summarize what I have tried to say. The difficulties of the United States during this last period of ten years have grown largely out of the fact that the United States was so powerful. A powerful country has many things to consider which a little country like the Swiss Confederation does not have to bother about. I think the policy of the United States has in general been actuated by right-minded people, but by people who were not always sufficiently careful to make themselves right-minded along with the peoples of other countries. The contribution of the United States has been slow. America has been non-co-operative at times. Yet it has always acted on an idealistic basis, and I think one has to say that with its difficulties the Government of the United States has done a great deal to relate itself to the organization of peace. The new arbitration treaties represent some advance; the new treaties on the Bryan model represent some advance; the new policy of free and full co-operation with the League of Nations represents a great advance; and the Fifth Reservation with reference to the Permanent Court of International Justice will some day be forgotten. The new treaty for the renouncing of war as an instrument of national policy is soon to be signed, and when it is signed it will place in your hands and in mine a new implement for us to use in our struggle with the forces that make against peace.

CHAPTER IX

THE BRITISH COMMONWEALTH AND
THE LEAGUE OF NATIONS

Mr. Delisle Burns:

THE relation between Great Britain and the British Dominions which are Members of the League of Nations is not the same as between any one of these and the other Members of the League; and in the class of Dominions for this purpose must be included India. It may be thought to be detrimental to the League itself that some of its Members should have a special relation among themselves; but that question of principle may be discussed later. All that is now necessary is an acknowledgement of a political fact; for undoubtedly this special relation does exist. The subject for discussion is the nature of this special relationship in so far as it affects the League system.

In what follows here it is suggested that membership in the League does in fact affect beneficially the nature of the relation between Great Britain and the Dominions. It is also to be suggested that the relationship of the Nations of the British Commonwealth has an important influence upon the operation of the League system and that this influence is good. But although both the League system and the British Commonwealth are developing from day to day and the effects of one system on the other are therefore largely matters for speculation, it is possible to analyse the existing situation at least as marking a definite stage in the history of government.

The special relation of the members of the British Commonwealth in the League is often supposed to give rise to a dilemma; for it is said that if the Dominions and Great Britain are separate sovereign States, then there is no single British Commonwealth; but if these nations are not separate sovereign States, then 'Great Britain has seven votes' in the Assembly. There is obviously a contradiction between being one and being many; and in politics one cannot avoid the consequences of a contradiction by calling it a mystery. But it is easy enough to show that there is no mystery at all, nor any contradiction, if the unity of the Commonwealth does not in any way destroy the independence of Members of the League. Clearly, if the Dominion Governments are subordinate in fact to the direction of the Government of Great Britain, then it is unfair to the other Members of the League that the Dominions should be treated as of equal status with them. But it will be shown in what follows here that the unity of the Commonwealth does not in practice involve subordination of one Government to another; and therefore within the League system Great Britain has *not* 'seven votes'.

The air of mystery in which some writers on the British system of government attempt to escape from criticism is objectionable; but even more so is the attitude of superior virtue which is adopted by some British speakers. It has unfortunately been the practice of certain citizens of Great Britain to 'condescend' towards foreigners, and to treat the French as though they were a backward race or the Germans as though they were morally tainted. But this is as objectionable to some of us in Great Britain as it is to those who feel the implied insult to themselves. Not only peoples which speak other tongues have suffered from the bad manners of some Britishers but even those in the United States and in the Dominions have been treated as inferiors. Resentment at the implied criticism of themselves has created even

P

in English-speaking countries some bitter feelings against Great Britain, in spite of the fact that not all Britishers are so obtuse as to ignore the effect on others of their own manners and customs. It is therefore useful to repudiate, in speaking of the British Commonwealth, both the air of mystery and the attitude of condescension. It is not necessary to assume, whatever our power in the world, that we are superior persons specially chosen as a model to others. Nor is it necessary to assert that 'God placed us' in Egypt or that 'the Egyptian people should recognize the conditions which Providence had imposed upon us'.[1] The Suez Canal shares were not bought in heaven. The air of mystery or the claim to special connexions with Deity serves only to obscure the facts of the situation.

i. *New Administrative Practice.*

It is proposed here, therefore, to explain actual practice, not to praise or to blame existing institutions; and perhaps it is better to avoid worship in order that we may see clearly. The fundamental factors in politics are psychological. The feelings or attitudes of actual persons in the Dominions have in fact made it impossible for the Cabinet in Great Britain to treat them as subject races; and these feelings and attitudes, as in ordinary life, can be found expressed in the daily habits and customs of intercourse. The administrative practice, therefore, in the intercourse of the Governments concerned may be taken to indicate the nature of those psychological 'sets' or attitudes in the peoples of the Dominions and Great Britain on which ultimately depends their present relation, one to the other.

[1] The words of Sir Austen Chamberlain in the Official *Papers regarding a Treaty with Egypt.* Cmd. 3050, 1928.

The analysis of constitutional principles does not give so clear an idea of the nature of the relation under discussion as does a statement of administrative practice. It is proposed therefore not to discuss the nature of sovereignty or authority but to give an account of what is actually happening. This is excusable, though it may leave many problems unsolved, for great authorities have recently discussed fully the meaning of the phrases now consecrated by the Imperial Conference of 1926. Professor A. B. Keith's new edition of his *Responsible Government in the Dominions* puts the greatest emphasis upon the predominance of Great Britain or of the Government in Great Britain. His interpretations of constitutional theory underestimate administrative practice. Mr. Zimmern, in his address to this Institute last year, expressed another point of view and seemed to argue that the unity of the Commonwealth was one of tradition and sympathy, not needing organization. Again, a most valuable collection of essays on the subject, by Sir Cecil Hurst and other authorities, has been published under the title of *Great Britain and the Dominions*. All this work, following upon the Report of the Imperial Conference of 1926, provides enough material for the student of constitutional forms and their historical development. It will be assumed to be available to the readers of the following statement of practice.

Administration is three-quarters of government. What a phrase means can more easily be understood by watching its effect upon the practice of official intercourse than by commentary upon the words; and further, administration makes policy in its day-to-day interpretation of the situation. The official who has to find out for the Government of Great Britain what the Government of Canada is going to do, is not concerned to discuss the status of the two Governments, but is compelled to write a letter or send a telegram from some one to some one else. In such acts he makes the actual status of the two Governments what it is. Now since 1926 several changes have been introduced in administrative practice or, as we say, in the 'machinery' for relating the Governments of the Commonwealth among themselves and in relating some of these Governments to certain non-British Governments. The most striking of these new developments are (1) the creation of the Dominions Office under a new Secretary of State, and (2) the appointment of new officials both ambassadorial and intergovernmental. Both these changes are the results of certain changes of feelings and attitude among the peoples of the Dominions and the people of Great Britain. We in Great Britain do not feel inclined to govern our relatives beyond the seas even for their own good; and those relatives seem to have developed a not too complimentary view of their cousins and aunts, the voters of Great Britain. A new situation has been acknowledged to exist, but no one pretends to understand yet all that it implies.

The sacred phrase at the beginning of the Report of the Inter-Imperial Relations Committee 1926 (Cmd. 2768) states the general principle implied in existing practice. Great Britain and the other Dominions of the Crown are 'autonomous communities within the British Empire, equal in status, in no way subordinate one to another in any aspect of their domestic or external affairs, though united by a common allegiance to the Crown and freely associated as members of the British Commonwealth of Nations'. Commentary upon such a creed would perhaps only lead to further obscurities. But the existing practice, which explains that sacred phrase, has recently been changed in two particulars, and these changes indicate the precise meaning both of the unity of

the whole and of the autonomy of the parts. The two particulars of practice introduced are (1) in the relation of
Governors-General to the Governments in the Dominions
and (2) in the signature of Treaties. With regard to other
practical issues in the relation of Great Britain and the
Dominions, Departmental Committees have been set up in
London and in the Dominions to make recommendations on
such subjects as the Judicial Committee of the Privy Council,
methods of legislation, and the scope of the legislation of the
Parliaments concerned. These Committees have already
done much work, but the conclusions have not been sufficiently prepared for the next Imperial Conference. No
change therefore can yet be recorded either in the practice
of legislation in the Dominions, or in the position of the
Judicial Committee of the Privy Council. Omitting these
issues, therefore, the actually accomplished change may be
noted.

ii. 'The Crown.'

In practice, the Governor-General no longer communicates with His Majesty's Government in Great Britain.[1]
He is 'the Crown', not the agent of whatever Cabinet hap-
pens to be elected by the people of Great Britain. But this,
so far from dividing the parts of the Commonwealth, unites
them more intimately in practice; for now the Cabinet in any
Dominion communicates directly with the Cabinet in Great
Britain. Machinery has been set up for improving and in-
creasing this communication, which will be discussed below.
The Governor-General corresponds in some ways to the
King in Great Britain; but it is significant that the first
Governor-General of the Irish Free State was in fact chosen

[1] The change to direct communication of the Government of Great
Britain with the Government in Canada took place on 1 July 1927.

by the Irish Government, the Council of Ministers.[1] It is improbable that any future Governors-General of Dominions will be chosen, as in the old days, solely by the Government of Great Britain. The King no longer acts only by the advice of his Ministers in Great Britain.

The Crown which is, in the person of the Governor-General, present in a Dominion, is the same as the Crown in Great Britain in the person of the King. In a famous case in the Courts it was decided that a soldier who was paid part of his salary by the British Government and part by the Australian had received both parts from the same Crown.[2] Again, in a recent case 'it was intimated that the Crown had been unable to find a witness'.[3] Evidently the Crown is a strange creature. Maitland says that it is very often a 'corporation aggregate'; but he continues 'a better word has recently returned to the Statute book. That word is Commonwealth.' [4]

The unity of the communities in question is found in the allegiance of their members to 'the Crown', which is indeed, in some sense, the Commonwealth itself in one of its aspects. There is a common citizenship. That is to say with regard to the Crown, the citizen in Australia is in the same position as the citizen in Great Britain; and the citizen of France or the United States is in quite a different position. But this does not make the Member of the League called Australia a dependency of the Member of the League called Great Britain. The reason is that common citizenship does not necessarily imply a single instrument of that citizenship. The

1 Dennis Gwynn, *The Irish Free State 1922–1927*, p. 66.
2 See Hurst, in *Great Britain and the Dominions*, p. 52 note.
3 *The Times*, 8 August 1928, on Sydney Contract Scandal.
4 Coll. Papers, iii, p. 259.

citizens of Great Britain who have left Great Britain for the Dominions have lost their right to vote for the Government of Great Britain. If, in leaving Great Britain, they still remain subject to the Parliament and Cabinet in Great Britain, they reduce themselves to the status of a subject people. But the emigrants know their cousins and their aunts in Great Britain too well to consent to leave to their votes the direction of policy in the new lands. They do not feel any more subject or backward than they felt before they left home; indeed they feel less so! Therefore they acquire first the power and now the right to control their own Government, just as they would at home, and to be subject to no other Government than their own in their new country, just as they were subject to none but their own at home. A new and independent Government, that is an elected Cabinet or Executive, has come into existence.

But this is not felt to be a creation of a new political machinery, as for example Czechoslovakia or Estonia was. The Government of a Dominion is therefore in one sense the same Government as that to which those who had votes in Great Britain had been accustomed. Great Britain still remains, in the language of her children beyond the seas, 'home'. But more than sentiment is involved. The Common Law and the traditions of administration have gone beyond the seas in the minds of these pioneers. Therefore the Government they now control is still the Government of 'the Crown'. Some, perhaps the majority, use the more personal word 'King'; some, with legal or administrative ends to serve, prefer a word that seems to refer to an object which has been given a meaning it does not possess of itself. The tiara and the 'red hat' have similar meanings; and for ribaldry a 'brass hat' in the war had some significance. But clearly in

the minds of the citizens of the Commonwealth control of
their separate Cabinets, quite autonomous each with regard
to the other, does not involve repudiation of the common
elements of law and administration for which the word
Crown stands.

Such unity of the British Commonwealth as is expressed
in 'common allegiance to the Crown' must be clearly dis-
tinguished from unity in foreign or international policies.
The sort of separate control over Governments which is
important for our purpose here, is control over foreign policy.
And this is in fact claimed by citizens in the Dominions—
not control over the British Cabinet but control over their
own Cabinets, after the control by the British Cabinet over
theirs has been removed. The actual control exerted depends
upon (1) the creation of a foreign policy where, as in most of
the Dominions, none existed and upon (2) information being
given to the Cabinets of the Dominions with regard to any
acts of the British Cabinet which may affect the fortunes of
British citizens in the Dominions.

But although each Government in the British Commonwealth is separately controlled and is therefore independent
of the others, in contrast with the unity for which the
Crown stands, an entirely different kind of unity exists in
the foreign policies of these Governments. By unity in this
case is meant an *understanding* that the policy of each must
have regard to the policy of the other member 'State' of the
British Commonwealth. It is a confusion to connect the
consultative unity of foreign policy with the administrative
and juridical unity of the Crown, for foreign policy is made
by Cabinets, not by the Crown. The Crown is, in at least
one sense, the supreme executive; and that executive, or that
part of the executive, is identical in all the British Do-

minions and in Great Britain.[1] This unity of the Commonwealth is, therefore, administrative and not merely a unity
of sympathy or general purpose. But even this unity is in
process of development through the daily practice of consultation, which has taken the place of subordination and
instruction given by the Government of Great Britain to the
other Governments. And in any case the unity of allegiance
to the Crown is quite distinct from unity with regard to
foreign policy.

iii. *The new form of Treaty Signature.*

In formal acts, such as the signing of Treaties, the existing
unity is for the future to be expressed by a method introduced
in 1926. All Treaties are to be signed in the name of 'the
Crown', which for this purpose in the Report of 1926 is referred to as 'the Head of the State'. 'Heads of States' is a
peculiar phrase. It harks back to Hobbes's *Leviathan*. But
it may be supposed that the Report intends to make a
'class', of which the British Crown is one specimen and the
other specimens are Presidents or absolute monarchs. It is
regrettable, however, that in Sir Austen Chamberlain's
statement to the Council on this point, the language was
not more carefully considered—shall we say, in the Dominions Office?

The new practice is intended to express that 'the Dominions and India are on a footing of equality with Great
Britain as participants in the Treaties', as the Report of 1926
indicates (p. 22). It does so by uniting each of the Governments directly with the King, in order that the 'plenipoten-

[1] But see Maitland, *Constitutional History*, p. 418: 'The Crown is a
convenient cover for ignorance; it saves us from asking difficult questions
which can only be answered by study of the Statute book.'

tiary' power may clearly belong, for example, to the Canadian
signatory without regard to the Cabinet in Great Britain.
The identification of the British Empire with Great Britain
has ceased to imply that the Government of Great Britain
signs treaties on behalf of any Government in a Dominion

But while releasing the Dominion Cabinets from subordination, the new form of Treaty signature does express the
unity of the Commonwealth through or in the Crown as the
Executive. Does this in fact destroy the 'autonomy' of the
parts, so that one State has many 'votes' in international
relations? The answer must depend upon whose 'will' or
'power' or responsibility is expressed in the signatures. Now
there is no doubt that the signatures indicate quite different
'wills' or powers or responsibilities. The Crown is 'advised'
to sign by quite distinct Cabinets. These Cabinets are instruments of the peoples in the different Dominions; and the
signature in the name of the King therefore is not undemo-
cratic in so far as the King is the chief Executive of the
nations concerned. A further difficulty arises, however, because the Report of 1926 gives another ground, as well as
equality of status, for the new form of signature. It is that
treaties so signed may not bind the members of the British
Commonwealth *inter se*. Not all treaties are of the same
kind. Not all are 'international instruments' making international law; and it may be that in some treaties at present,
for example, economic treaties, the relations of the members
of the Commonwealth are not affected. But clearly there
must be *some* treaties, especially under the League system,
which do bind the members of the Commonwealth *inter se*:
for if they do not, then the Dominions are not full members
of the League. It is useless to call this plain contradiction a
mystery. The Imperial Conference Report clearly goes too

far if it implies that *no* treaties entered into by members of
the League bind the members of the British Commonwealth
inter se.

That the signatures should be grouped under one heading
indicates the unity of the Commonwealth. In this the order
of signature of the Versailles Treaty has been followed; and
not that, for example, in the signature of the Final Act of
the Conference of 1926 on the Permanent Court of International Justice, where 'the British Empire' 'is separated in
the order of signatories from 'Canada' by Bulgaria. No doubt
this second method of signature, separating the units of the
British Commonwealth, follows the practice of seating and
voting at the Assembly and other League meetings. But it
is permissible to suggest that a mistake was made when the
French alphabetical order was applied to the signatories for
the British Commonwealth. There is no reason why even in
seating and in voting Canada and Australia should not be
grouped with Great Britain, unless this would give a false
impression of subordination in regard to the Government of
Great Britain. No one would suggest that their seats should
be so placed as to represent the 'indentation' of their signatures in the Versailles Treaty! But the order of voting is not
important. The order of signature in a treaty is, if that
order includes a reference to the special relationship between
certain signatories.

iv. *The Dominions Office.*

The two formal changes so far discussed are, as was indicated, the results of quite definite political tendencies in the
feelings and attitudes of peoples in the Dominions; but they
are to be understood more easily by reference to the daily
practice of intercourse and administration which maintain

and develop the new situation. This practice is found in the Dominions Office and similar administrative machinery.

The Dominions Office was created, as the Office of the new Secretary of State for the Dominions, by the King's grant of the seals to the Secretary of State and the vote of the Commons on Supply in July 1925.[1] It was then stated that the volume of work and the new kind of work to be done made it necessary to have a special office in Great Britain for Dominion affairs. The Office provides means of communication with regard to foreign policy between the British Foreign Office and the External Affairs department in the Dominions; but it is not merely a 'post office' for forwarding communications, because (1) the general tendency of the opinion or policy in more than one Dominion has to be kept before the British Foreign Office and (2) communications as to British policy need to be explained or discussed with this or that Government in the Dominions. In one sense, however, the Dominions Office is a sort of Foreign Office of the British Government for intercourse with the Dominions.[2] It promotes the direct communication between Cabinets, which is referred to below; and it facilitates direct discussion between the Foreign Secretary in Great Britain and the Ministers dealing with external affairs in the Dominions. A second part of the work of the Dominions Office is concerned with that mysterious entity 'the Crown'. Here the Dominions office has no relation with the Foreign Office, for this is the aspect of the Commonwealth in which 'unity' rather than 'independence' is prominent. Many communica-

[1] *Parl. Debates*, 27 July 1925, vol. 65. Mr. Amery's speech.
[2] Professor Keith (new edition, p. 915) thinks that the Foreign Office and the Prime Minister's Secretariat could do all the work of the Dominions Office; but this does not seem possible.

tions from the Dominions Governors-General come in 'for submission to His Majesty'. The distribution of honours, for example, has nothing to do with the Foreign Office, and the relation of the Dominions Office to other British departments in such matters is rather with the Home Office and the Cabinet Secretariat. Here, however, is one of the most delicate questions in the existing system. The head of the Dominions Office is a Secretary of State who, besides being the King's Secretary, is also a Minister in a Government responsible only to the Parliament in Great Britain. Can the King's Secretary advise 'the Crown' without the responsible Minister of a political party in Great Britain knowing anything about it? Clearly if the Governor-General is the King or the Crown in the Dominions, it cannot be permitted that a Minister in Great Britain shall intervene where no Minister in a Dominion can intervene; but if that is impossible then it would naturally come about that the functions of the Dominions Office for current 'submission' to the King should be dealt with by a Secretariat of the Crown itself independent of the Secretary of State responsible to the British Parliament. In practice even at present all *formal* communications from a Governor-General go, not through the Dominions Office, but direct to the King's Private Secretary.

A third great section of Dominions Office work is concerned with Migration and Trade. The Overseas Settlement Committee has as its chairman the Secretary of State for the Dominions. Its Secretariat is part of the Dominions Office, and it corresponds with such organizations in the Dominions as the Development and Migration Commission in Australia. In this section of the work in Great Britain the connexion is with the British Ministry of Labour. But it should be noted that here also 'autonomy' is complete. The practice of modern States is that their Departments should communicate directly, not through Foreign Offices. The Dominions Office no more directs Australia's policy on Migration than does the British Ministry of Labour or the British Industrial Transference Board. In matters of trade there are two recent additions to the machine, the Imperial Economic Committee and the Empire Marketing Board which provides a Secretariat for this Committee. The I.E.C. consists of representatives of the Dominions and of Great Britain; its function is advisory to all the Governments of the British Commonwealth. The E.M.B. is a small office for the expenditure of the million pounds granted by the British Government in 1925 for promoting the sale of Empire products by advertisement, by advice to traders and to Governments, and by other methods. This office is also under the Secretary of State for the Dominions. It connects in Great Britain with the Board of Trade and the Department of Overseas Trade: and its officials, of course, have no responsibility to any Government but that of Great Britain.

The Dominions Office is still developing its administrative tradition and it is too soon to say whether its work will change. At first one Department dealt with the Dominions of the Northern hemisphere and a second with those of the Southern. A third Department dealt with foreign policy and 'honours'; but the appointment of representatives of the Governments concerned at the different capitals of the British Commonwealth will obviously change in some way the work of the officials in this section of the Dominions Office. In any case the Dominions Secretary of State must inevitably be freed from his existing work with regard to Colonies. The confusion of ancient practice in the

Colonial Office with the new methods of Dominion government is an obstacle to progress.

v. *Dominion Legations.*

Outside the Dominions Office the most interesting new departure is the organization for communication between the Governments of Great Britain and those of some Dominions. For example, there has been for some years now in the Cabinet Office in London a member of the staff of the Australian High Commissioner in London appointed to inform the Commonwealth Prime Minister of the current events in British politics; he also acts as *liaison* for the information of the British Cabinet. This practice followed upon the appointment of a Foreign Office official some years ago to organize, in the Prime Minister's department in Australia, the methods of dealing with foreign or external affairs. By this means the Governments—not through the Crown but diplomatically—are kept in continuous touch. Similarly New Zealand has been lent a Foreign Office official to help in the organizing of the External Affairs Department there. South Africa established a Department of External Affairs on 1 July 1927.

For Great Britain the most significant recent change has been the appointment of a High Commissioner, announced in the King's Speech of 3 August 1928, from the Government of Great Britain to that of Canada. He will be provided with a Secretariat of a diplomatic type. In South Africa the Imperial Secretary, the chief official of the Governor-General in his function as High Commissioner for Basutoland and the other similar territories, has been used for some little time to communicate between the Cabinet in Great Britain and that of the Union of South Africa.

As is well known two Dominions, the Irish Free State and Canada, have diplomatic representatives at Washington, and Canada has another in Paris. Canada is soon to appoint a diplomatic representative in Tokio. It is said that such appointment is made by the Crown on the advice of the Government in Great Britain; but it is more than doubtful whether—even if such advice was given—any constitutional right to give it now exists. The United States Government is represented by Ministers in Ottawa and Dublin. The French and Japanese Governments are appointing Ministers at Ottawa. We have therefore in the case of the Dominions, as new States in international affairs, the growth of machinery similar to that of such newly established States as Estonia or Czechoslovakia. The appointment of Ministers for Canada and the Irish Free State in Washington has not in fact led to any divergence or separation of the policy of those countries from that expressed by the British Ambassador to the United States. Indeed, Lord Bryce remarked long ago that most of the work of a British Ambassador in Washington in his day concerned Canada; and now the British Ambassador is relieved of that, but he is in continual consultation with the two Ministers mentioned. Indeed there is now much less likelihood of ill-feeling in Canada, such as existed in 1887 and earlier, owing to the supposed lack of understanding of the Canadian point of view on the part of a British Minister in Washington.

Similarly, the Union of South Africa, when dealing with the labour supply from the Portuguese Colonies, sends to the British Embassy at Lisbon some one specially competent to express the South African view through the British Ambassador. That is to say, whenever a Dominion has a foreign policy, some machinery is created to express it. But this surely is a better art of government than the appointment of officials for the sake of prestige where there is no work to be done.

In the official machinery which has arisen out of League Membership it may be noted that the presence of two representatives of Dominions, the Irish Free State and Canada, at Geneva is in some ways a provision for diplomatic information such as is derived by the older Governments from ambassadors at many different capitals. But it is also an acknowledgement of the fact that a greater proportion of the foreign policy of certain Governments does flow through the League system than in the case of other Governments. The connexion with the League is valued in Ireland and Canada much more than in Australia or New Zealand; and indeed it was the fact that Dominions had an international status as members of the League that induced the leader of the Sinn Fein Party in 1921 to accept 'Dominion Status' for the Irish Free State.

Again, the Mandates system has created some new practices in government in the Dominions. As Mandatories, Australia, New Zealand, and the Union of South Africa have relations with the League system which are not possessed, for example, by Sweden or Switzerland. The responsibilities of the Dominion Governments with regard to their Mandates are in no way responsibilities of the Government of Great Britain. They are agents of an international trusteeship who demand full power for the exercise of their trust and do not regard themselves as 'on trial'. It must be remembered that New Zealand annexed the Cook Islands in 1898 and Queensland attempted to annex part of New Guinea in 1883. The Union of South Africa conquered German South-West Africa. The Dominion Governments have in fact always regarded themselves as quite competent to rule 'colonial' territories with subject races.

The presence of representatives of the Irish Free State and the Dominions at League meetings has given opportunities for showing the possible divergence of view between the Government of Great Britain and that of some other member of the British Commonwealth. For example, when Sir Cecil Hurst in 1925 in a Commission of the League had said that 'the British Empire' could not accept arbitration, Mr. O'Higgins, speaking for the Irish Free State, said in the same Commission that his Government had not arrived at any decision on the point and that Sir Cecil Hurst's words must be taken to refer to one Government 'not to six'. The presence of Canada on the Council by the side of Great Britain has also shown that the Government of Great Britain does not in fact 'stand for' the peoples of the Dominions. And outside the League system, independence of Great Britain in foreign policy is shown by the Canadian objection to the renewal of the Japanese Treaty in 1921. Thus Dominion status does in practice mean a right to independent policy in foreign affairs, even if, at the moment, the greater part of foreign policy is similar in all the members of the Commonwealth, or even if in some cases the Foreign Office in London guides certain Dominion Governments.

So far the Dominions have been treated as a class; but nothing more obviously proves them to be autonomous nations than the distinction in attitude and policy between one Dominion and another. Perhaps the word Dominion will cease to be used. It was an accident that it was applied to Canada; since, at the time when the word was chosen, many desired 'Kingdom' as the description of Canada. Again, the Irish Free State, although it has 'Dominion Status' is not really a Dominion at all. It did not originate in emigration from Great Britain. These, however, are less significant factors than the actually divergent views especially on League matters, which are held in the various countries called Dominions.

New Zealand, at any rate in its majority opinion if not in its Labour Party, is opposed to the theory and practice of equality of status with Great Britain, and is also suspicious or at least unenthusiastic about the League. With regard to equality of status, responsible authorities in New Zealand have denied their right to anything more than consultation when foreign policy is to be decided. The power to disregard the opinion of Dominion Ministers on foreign policy is expressly reserved for the Government in Great Britain by Sir John Salmond, the New Zealand delegate at the Washington Conference of 1921, in his report; as he says: 'If it was considered that the matter was of such general importance that dissent on the part of a Dominion should be disregarded in the interests of the whole Empire, it would have been within the authority of the plenipotentiaries of Great Britain to assent to the treaty on behalf of the Empire as a whole, without regard to such dissent.'[1]   Again, it is common in New Zealand to speak of the British Empire and not of the British Commonwealth; and to use the title 'Imperial Government' to indicate the Government in Great Britain.[2]

With regard to the League of Nations Mr. Massey in 1922 said in the New Zealand Parliament: 'I have never liked the

[1] Quoted in *Great Britain and the Dominions*, p. 375.
[2] Under the Act of 12 April 1927. 'Parliament shall hereafter be known as the Parliament of the United Kingdom of Great Britain and Northern Ireland.' There is no such thing as 'the Imperial Parliament'.

arrangement which was made in connexion with the League
of Nations. There was one dangerous feature in it. I did
not agree that in signing the Peace Treaty we became independent nations.' Again in 1924 Mr. Massey, replying to
the British Labour Government's letter on the Singapore
base, said: 'You say that your "Government stands for international co-operation through a strengthened and enlarged
League of Nations". In reply to that I must say that if the
defence of the Empire is to depend upon the League of
Nations only, then it may turn out to be a pity that the
League was ever brought into being. The very existence of
the Empire depends upon the Imperial Navy."[1]   This is
certainly independence with regard to the policy of the
Cabinet then in office in Great Britain.

No doubt similar sentiments exist in other Dominions.
They are sentiments connected with a certain political outlook and not necessarily dominant in a particular place; but
the distance of New Zealand from the points of irritation in
international life and the absence of any special relation to
any non-British group or Government make it easy for New
Zealand to have no foreign policy at all. Nevertheless, the
currents of international life reach even those shores. It
has been found useful for the New Zealand Government to
hear what is going on, even if it hesitates to assume any
responsibility for it: and therefore an official of the British
Foreign Office has been lent to the New Zealand Government to inform them of manners and customs in diplomatic
practice and to assist in organizing an External Affairs Department in Wellington.

At the opposite extreme in the scale of claims and in their
attitudes to the League are the Irish Free State and Canada.

[1] *Idem*, p. 377.

For them the status of 'autonomous communities' is much more like complete independence. The Irish Free State is said to have the status of a Dominion without being in fact a Dominion at all.[1] It is held by many to be an independent nation in a treaty relation, since 6 December 1921, with Great Britain. In practice the High Commissioner for the Irish Free State in London frequently acts as a diplomatic official and is therefore unlike the High Commissioners for the other Dominions. But the fact that Dublin is near London makes personal consultation of Cabinet Ministers easier; and the interest of the Government and people of the Irish Free State in the Irish population in Great Britain, Australia, Canada, and the United States, together with the fact that 98 per cent. of Irish exports go to Great Britain, makes it impossible for the Irish Free State to sever its connexion with the Commonwealth.

The Irish connexion with the United States led to the appointment of a diplomatic representative in Washington. In the League Assembly the Irish Free State in 1926 stood for election to a seat on the Council, quite independently of the advice or support of Great Britain. Thus with regard to the Government of Great Britain the Government of the Irish Free State acts as an independent Government and with regard to the League it seeks to put forward a definite international point of view of its own.

But the Irish Free State is comparatively new in its membership of the British Commonwealth and the League. Its position has been largely modelled upon that of Canada, which, as the oldest of the Dominions, has perhaps the greatest influence at present in the development of the rela-

[1] Professor Smiddy, speaking for the Irish Free State, *Great Britain and the Dominions*, p. 109.

tion of the other sections of the Commonwealth to Great Britain. An attempt to describe in a summary form the influence of Canada is inevitably open to criticism because of omissions which must be made; but with due allowance for the necessary limit of the subject under discussion here, it may be said that (1) Canada is working out in practice the fullest and clearest expression of 'autonomy', and (2) is also giving a new turn to the meaning of 'the Crown' as the unifying element in the British Commonwealth.

The practice of autonomy involves the creation of new organs for expressing a distinctive point of view in foreign policy. This Canada is doing. It is an American nation. It has for many years had to play a part in the development of a civilization which in fact is common to the whole of North America and is as different from the European as the European is different from the Russian. Canada *must* have a foreign policy; although for New Zealand or South Africa a foreign policy is still perhaps somewhat of a luxury. And as an American nation Canada knows very well the alternative to retaining 'the Crown' as part of her system of Government. But 'the Crown' to-day is by no means what 'the Crown' was when the United States came into existence; and the Parliament and Cabinet of Great Britain are no longer uncertain of their power to control 'the Crown' in Great Britain. In Benjamin Franklin's day 'the Crown' had a foreign policy of its own; and the effort of the British Cabinet to control 'the Crown' involved an attempt to control British citizens outside Great Britain. Now the policy of 'the Crown' is controlled by different groups of citizens in different communities of the Commonwealth. Canada, therefore, is united in allegiance to 'the Crown' of the twentieth century and, while completely independent in her foreign policy, co-operates in the same general purposes for which Great Britain stands.

vi. *The Special Position of India.*

In the discussion so far India has been omitted: but India is a Member of the League and is certainly within the British Empire, if not the British Commonwealth. India stands in a very peculiar position. That it is 'one' with the Government of Great Britain is clear: and its unity with that Government is in fact at present a unity of subordination, as the daily practice of the Secretary of State for India and the Viceroy indicates. But the India which is a Member of the League is not only British India, directly governed by the British executive, but also the Indian States which are in treaty relations with Great Britain and are certainly not subordinate to the Government of Great Britain in the same sense as British India is subordinate. Even the Indian States, however, are by treaties bound to leave their foreign relations in the control of the British Government, and therefore they lack that independence of policy which has been taken by or granted to the British Dominions. In all foreign policy, therefore, India quite clearly forms a unity with Great Britain but has no 'equality of status'. It is impossible to apply to India the phrase 'autonomous in all aspects of domestic or external affairs'. The relation of India to Great Britain is inconsistent with India's membership of the League; and in view of the implied promise on the admission of India as a Member of the League, Great Britain is morally bound to make the change required. How this inconsistency has occurred is quite well known. In 1917 the Government of Great Britain evidently contemplated a self-governing British India. In 1919 the Government of India Act granted to

British India the first elements of self-government in Provincial matters, while leaving the central government still under direct control of Great Britain. But in 1920, when 'India' became a Member of the League, the current had already set in another direction. The new system began to operate in Indian government; but whether it was in fact successful or not, the advance towards self-government proceeded no farther. If the ideals of 1917 and 1919 had been realized, there would be no inconsistency in India's Membership in the League; and the only way of removing that inconsistency is the grant of self-government or 'equality of status', so that India should be 'in no way subordinate in any aspect of her domestic or internal affairs'. No doubt the granting of this power in the future remains the policy of the British Government; and therefore India may be a Member of the League in view of her future status, but present powers in view of future responsibilities are difficult to reconcile with the spirit, if not with the text, of the Covenant. And if it is said that the requirement of autonomy in the case of new Members of the League does not hold with respect to 'original' Members, then it is confessed that Great Britain has at least two votes in the Assembly and a passive instrument of her policy covered by an alien name.

Some autonomy is already possessed by India. With regard to the International Labour Organization India has in practice much greater independence than in other League matters, although even in these the Secretary of State is formally in control. The Government of India communicates directly with the I.L.O. An Indian sits on the Governing Body. The India Office in London does not interfere in the ratification of Conventions, perhaps because 'labour' reform in India is regarded as unlikely to affect British predominance. But

the *League of Nations* 233

whatever the reason, the Government of India in this respect has some autonomy.

Again, even in diplomatic or political issues, the position is not the same now as it was in 1919; for some autonomy has been granted. The Government of India has no control over Provincial 'transferred' subjects; that is to say, British India is autonomous in the 'internal affairs', education, roads, agriculture, and land revenues. Again, it is a publicly acknowledged convention that if the Government of India and the Legislative Assembly are agreed on any measure the Secretary of State will not oppose it. An example is the tariff on steel. Thirdly, the preference granted to British manufacturers has now ceased to exist, since the High Commissioner in London is no longer under the Secretary of State but under the Government of India. Before the reforms 94 per cent. of India's requirements of this kind was supplied by British firms; but now only 76 per cent. is so supplied and India is freer therefore to buy in France or Germany. Trade Commissioners for India may be appointed to posts on the European continent.

Another sign of a new status for India is the presence of an Indian as Agent for the Government of India in South Africa, following upon negotiations between the two Governments. Again, in practice, the representatives of India on League Committees often do oppose the policy of Great Britain; and although their appointment is controlled, their policy is not controlled in all details by the India Office. It remains, however, unsatisfactory not only from the Indian point of view but for the validity of the League system that further steps are not taken to decrease such subordination of the Government of India to the Government of Great Britain as still exists. For example, why should all communications between the Government of India and the League pass through the India Office in London? Why should there not be an Indian as chief delegate for India at the Assembly—as indeed the Government of India would desire.[1] It is ominous that the official statement made on behalf of the Secretary of State in the Council of State in India should imply that only an Englishman can be trusted to understand the diplomatic issues involved or the British view of them. This is plainly at variance with the principle of separate Membership of the League; for it implies subordination. Again, on the League Health organization India is represented by an Englishman, who may indeed be the most competent person available but whose presence does give the impression of the subordination of India to Great Britain. Finally, Indian Princes follow one another in the delegations to the Assembly; but surely this position is one for a Minister, not a Prince, and for a man who can acquire experience by continuous service. The truth is that the British Government is not giving proper consideration to India's status in the League system. India provides funds for the League and is sixth on the list of States in order of amount provided—far above any Dominion; but the India Office so far opposes the suggestion made in a Commission of the Assembly that a League Office should be established in India. The obviously dependent position of India in the League has a pernicious effect upon the status of the Dominions, with which India is often classed; and it is therefore of importance to the Dominions that India should have a status due to every League Member. The issue is not one of autocracy against democracy. There are autocracies, unfortunately for the League system, among the League Mem-

[1] See *Council of State Debates*, 13 March 1928.

bers: but whatever the Government of India may be, it certainly should not, at least in League matters, be subordinate to the Secretary of State.

vii. *Conclusions.*

Certain general conclusions may be suggested for discussion rather than as final statements. The unity of the Commonwealth does not prevent independence in the policy of the Governments composing it, even if these independent Governments co-operate. The autonomy of the Dominions, but not of India, is undeniable; and the machinery for giving each Dominion Government the ability to play its own part in the affairs of the world and particularly in the League system is being rapidly developed by the Dominions Governments themselves and with the assistance of the Government of Great Britain. The consultation at League meetings between representatives of the Governments of the Commonwealth increases rather than decreases the ability of the Dominions Governments to exercise their influence in the League system. The Governments of the South American States similarly hold informal consultations. It is only in an atmosphere of war or of rivalries, not in an atmosphere of co-operation for common purposes, that consultations appear to be dangerous.

The effect of the League system on the character of the British Commonwealth is shown, first, in the opportunities provided by the Assembly, the Council, the General Conference and Governing Body of the International Labour Office for frequent contact between the Dominions Governments and the British Government. The writers of the Imperial Conference Report of 1926, who stated that more frequent consultation was desirable, did not even refer to the meetings of representatives at Geneva. But the advantage to the Dominion Governments of meeting the British Government *not in London* is obvious: for it gives them in a 'neutral' atmosphere more real equality. There is, however, so much misunderstanding among foreign nations with regard to the nature of the autonomy of the Dominions that it was hardly possible to suggest in an official Report that the League system gave an opportunity for consultation to the members of the British Commonwealth.

A second effect of the League system on the Commonwealth is the 'speeding up' of the contacts of the Dominions with foreign States. The Departments of External Affairs which have grown up in the Dominions are partly the results of continuous communication on League matters. Indeed it is through the League that the Dominions have made their influence felt in many aspects of international affairs; and it is felt in Canada and the Irish Free State that the League system provides some opportunities for their development as States in the world of diplomacy and economic intercourse.

The effect upon the League system of the influence of the British Dominions is, first, a reinforcement of the non-European point of view. The South American States and Japan have some influence in preventing the concentration of the League system upon European quarrels and European problems of transport, commerce, and finance. Whatever importance, however, the European continent may have, there are other parts of the world which are more important for the international intercourse of the future. It would be regrettable if the League were obsessed with local European rivalries. But for the Dominions and for Great Britain in relation to the Dominions, the chief problems of international intercourse are not European; these countries therefore save

the League from European provincialism. They supply
something in the League system which would have been
present even more powerfully if the United States had been
a member during the nine years of the League's work. Again,
especially in I.L.O. and economic matters, the influence of
the newer civilization of Canada and Australia provides a
corrective to European standards in the status of 'labour'
and the organization of employment. Secondly, the Dominions and Great Britain in the League form a unit which
is not a military alliance and is not formed in view of any
military rivalries. It would be impolitic, not to say impolite,
to make comparisons with any other groupings within the
League. In any case war is definitely 'ruled out' in the relation of Great Britain and the Dominions. This does not
mean that war is logically inconceivable. In the old days,
before self-government, any forces raised in Canada or Australia which were used against Great Britain would be rebel
forces, and war, other than civil war, was therefore logically
inconceivable; but now, any forces raised by His Majesty's
Ministers in Canada or Australia are just as truly the King's
forces as are the forces raised in Great Britain, and it is therefore logically conceivable that the King in Great Britain
should be at war with the King in Australia. But war is
'ruled out' by the assumptions on which rests the relation of
Great Britain and the Dominions. These assumptions are,
if the phrase can be used with this reference, conventions
of the constitution as binding as any formal code. They are
not sentiments or emotions but actual principles of practice.
That is to say, the Dominions and Great Britain, having in
fact the power to wage war severally, have renounced that
power and 'outlawed war' as between themselves. No provision is made in preparation for 'defence' against Great

Britain by any Dominion nor by Great Britain against any Dominion, nor by any Dominion against the others. *And there is no sanction provided* to meet the case of any one of the members of the Commonwealth which might infringe the principle that such war is outlawed. It would not be reasonable even to imply that the British Commonwealth can be a model or lesson to the other Members of the League; for their positions are radically different and other nations are not 'backward' in their mutual relations. Nor is it reasonable to suggest that the League should be improved by adopting a system of relations like those in the British Commonwealth. It is pharisaical to claim superiority. But it is an advantage for the League system to have within it at least one grouping of its Members which definitely rules out all war between them; and it is an advantage to have within the League system a large-scale co-operation of certain Governments for purposes even of mutual assistance in war, where no one of the group ever dreams of the possibility of being attacked by any other. The Committee of Imperial Defence which still represents, in its 'advice' and its other activities, an older régime, will itself feel the change of atmosphere which real autonomy of the Dominions involves.

Thirdly, the British Dominions and the Irish Free State belong to a class of States whose populations are concentrated upon economic development and are not agitated about defence or prestige. The United States is of the same type. To press the comparison by naming States of another type would perhaps be unwise; but clearly in some States the peoples and their Governments are obsessed with rivalries beyond their frontiers. They think in military terms. It may be a necessity of their position in a continent of diverse languages and traditions; but on the other hand the Dominions are not in a position nor in a mood to concentrate upon foreign dangers. Their peoples are aware of the vast resources of new territories and their Governments are in the main organizations for economic development. It strengthens the tendencies in the League system which point towards peaceful development rather than military security to have among the Members of the League such new and growing countries. The League may exist a century hence, when European rivalries will be as obsolete as the quarrels of kings a century ago now are. And the Dominions of which we are now thinking may soon be not populations of three to seven millions—like Scandinavian States—but populations of fifty or a hundred millions in highly civilized democracies. The future of the League as a system of co-operation in the development of resources may come to depend more and more upon the support of the Dominions.

Finally, it is through the relation of such governmental units as the Dominions and Great Britain that the new conceptions of independence or of 'sovereignty', if that word can still be used, are being worked out. Mr. Hertzog's Party in South Africa, according to Article 4 of its old programme, aimed at 'sovereign independence'; and yet Mr. Hertzog professed his satisfaction at the Report of 1926, which uses the word 'autonomy'. The situation is even further developed since the Congress of the same Party on 9 August 1928 has accepted a motion agreeing that the declaration of the Imperial Conference is 'tantamount to our attainment of sovereign independence and of power to exercise our functions as a State at our own discretion'. This is an extreme case of interpretation and the constitutional terms are not in question here. The point is that 'sovereignty', whatever it means in modern life, certainly does not mean isolation or absence of all relations with other States.[1]

If sovereignty in the modern world meant isolation or lack of all responsibility towards other States, not even France or Italy could be called sovereign. But so far as the old word can be used in reference to international relations it does not mean more than autonomy within a community of States; and in that sense the Dominions are sovereign. The absurd idea that any Government or people is 'free' to disregard moral obligations and such legal obligations as are expressed in treaties, even for the sake of self-defence, is only preserved in the mausoleums of juristic controversy. All peoples are responsible morally for such acts as affect other peoples and all Governments are responsible legally in certain definite cases although, as Professor Brierly shows in his new book, international law has not yet advanced the limits of legal responsibility even so far as the generally admitted moral responsibility of States now extends. In the new world of international relations, the daily administrative acts connecting Great Britain and the Dominions show how co-operation can secure autonomy.

The contribution which the British Commonwealth may make to the organization of peace is not merely sentimental. The friendliness of the nations in allegiance to the same Crown is an important political fact; but a far more significant fact is the growing experience of organization for the intercourse of Governments which follow the same lines of policy without sacrificing the responsibility or the distinctiveness of each. By such means peace will be established and war become obsolete, for peace is not the mere cessation of

[1] See Phelan, 'Sovereignty of the Irish Free State,' *Review of Nations*, March 1927.

war, nor a preparation for new war; nor is it a mere organization for a new kind of 'war to end war'. The obsession with the danger of future war is probably an atavism, like the attempt to decide who is an 'aggressor'. But whatever the present need for soothing the fears of peoples unnerved by recent explosions, real peace is positive—not a prevention of war but a co-operation in common purposes for the development of civilized life. Such co-operation is a problem of administrative organization, not of emotional rhetoric, and the organization which is being worked out by the Governments and peoples of the British Commonwealth is therefore of the greatest importance internationally. By the experience of such co-operation all nations may yet contrive to develop an intercourse which will rest upon the assumption that war between them is impossible.

CHAPTER X

ASIA AND THE LEAGUE

Lord OLIVIER:

I SPEAK here this morning with extreme diffidence for two principal reasons. One of them is that I was born in Essex and brought up to believe that the sun rose over Walton-on-the-Naze and set over Penzance with a passing glance at the Scilly Isles. On the other hand, I recognize that many of my audience here to-day are citizens of the United States of America who have doubtless been brought up to believe that the sun rises somewhere over Long Island and sets over San Francisco. Naturally the field of world affairs presents to persons raised under those different conditions, not only a different set of circumstances, but also a very different perspective. Moreover, I am not an Asiatic, and it is an enterprise of great assurance on my part to attempt to deal with the views and feelings of Asiatics, more especially in the presence of the Chairman, who himself has striven on the spot to make himself acquainted with those feelings and with those points of view. I speak, as most of our speakers here have done no doubt, simply as a contributor to a general understanding of what the world means, and with the complete belief that, on the whole, human nature is very much the same all over the world, and that one of the objects and purposes of the League of Nations is to establish and turn that fact to account.

I am conscious the lecture I am about to give will appear to many of you confused and ill-arranged. I feel that myself. The fact is that the relations of the League with Asiatic nations are as multiple as the relations of the League with

European nations. There are three main departments of those relations. First of all we have the League as existing in its primary purpose for mutual co-operation, especially with regard to questions of peace and war and international hostilities and antagonisms. Secondly, we have it operating in what may be called an authoritatively regulative function in connexion with Mandates, and in that department also it touches certain Asiatic or semi-Asiatic peoples. Thirdly, we have its very great function—a function which I may call an auxiliatory administrative function—whereby it organizes mutual assistance, means of consultation and joint action resulting in conventions and so on.

Finally, I want to deal in my concluding observations with the general confrontation of what is called the East with the West, with what are our feelings or impressions about it at the present day, and how that confrontation is likely, in my opinion, to raise in the future questions for the League.

i. *General Relations of the Asiatic Powers with the League.*

The Asiatic nations which are members of the League are the following. First, Japan, which is a permament member of the Council of the League. Secondly, China, which was on the Council in 1921 to 1923, and 1926 to 1928. I must say it appears to be rather regrettable that just at this moment, when the affairs of China are becoming of extreme world-wide importance, by the normal action of the constitution, China would not be likely to be represented immediately upon the Council of the League. Siam is a member of the League, Persia is a member of the League, and India is a member of the League.

Affiliated to the League in the position of mandated terri-

tories are the Near Eastern countries of Syria, Palestine, and
Iraq. I do not myself think of those countries as really
Asiatic. They are Mediterranean countries. They belong
to the Near East, and the civilizations of Syria and Palestine
and Arabia are part of our own European civilization, and
have contributed immensely to it. Those lie really, therefore,
in the nursery of our own European civilization, and are not
in the sense in which we generally think of them Asiatic
peoples or typically Asiatic communities. Japan, on behalf
of the League, holds the mandate for the administration of
certain islands in the Pacific.

The activities of the League touch and intercur with the
affairs of Asiatic communities in respect of diverse matters
of world-wide interest, especially in connexion with the
improvement of health conditions and with the prevention
and abatement of disease, of the traffic in women and children, the traffic in drugs, and such special questions as the
settlement of Armenian and other refugees displaced from
Turkish territories by the operations of the great war and
its sequels. But the organization of the League of Nations
having come into being chiefly as a device for finding remedies for tensions arising out of the relations between European States, the Asiatic countries not unnaturally appear less
prominently as active participators in those pacificatory conferences and conversations. Japan, however, as one of the
principal military and naval powers of the East, and as an
associate of the Allies in the Great War, necessarily took in
this connexion a prominent place in the League constitution.
But the Asiatic world in general has reasons, the discussion
of which will form part of the theme of this lecture, for
standing in a particular attitude towards the Western nations
in general, including in that term the United States of

America, and towards the great commercial imperialistic States of Britain, France, Germany, Holland, and the United States in particular.

The entry of Japan into an association with such antecedents was a very significant and important event, but important and weighty as is the position of Japan in the League, her attitude, as it impresses an outside observer, remains, not unnaturally, under the circumstances of the historical relations between West and East, somewhat reserved, and certainly by no means effusive; very correct and judicial, and it might be said, predominantly of a watchful character. But perhaps the most impressive feature of the policy of Japan in connexion with the League is the continuous goodwill shown by that Power to agree to and accommodate her plans to any scheme of naval limitation in which the protagonists among her associates may find it possible to agree among themselves. This goodwill has been a very conspicuous feature both in the Washington Conference on the Limitation of Armaments and in the inconclusive Geneva Conference convened by President Coolidge in 1927.

I should like to have the pleasure of quoting to you the words of Viscount Ishii, the Japanese Ambassador to France and first Delegate of Japan to the Assembly, in the debate with reference to the Protocol. Every one who has followed the affairs of the League will recall the immense amount of valuable co-operation and able contribution that has been given by Viscount Ishii towards the actual practical business of the League. This is what he said in the debate on the Protocol:

'Mr. Chairman, Ladies and Gentlemen,

'For a month past the Japanese Delegation has co-operated with you loyally and sincerely in preparing the Protocol. The task which we have undertaken is undoubtedly one of unparalleled importance. We have therefore stated our point of view with a complete frankness which at times has unavoidably given rise to somewhat critical discussions, but we have been inspired throughout by a spirit of conciliation and a sincere desire for agreement. The only point which we were anxious to press was a purely legal one, and in so doing we were inspired solely by a genuine desire to arrive at a logical and consistent result. In a programme so complex and difficult nothing but the sincerest candour and goodwill can lead to final and lasting success. Thanks to the splendid efforts of all concerned we have succeeded in laying the foundations of our great project for the pacification of the world by arbitration and security and for the liberation of mankind from the heavy burden of armaments. We also congratulate ourselves on the judicious manner in which the First and Third Committees have worded the draft resolution. It is so formulated that all the delegations can accept it unreservedly and it therefore represents a great advance on the road towards general agreement. The Japanese Delegation has great satisfaction in declaring that it is prepared to give its full approval to the draft resolution.'

I should also like to read what Mr. Tch'enne Lin, the Minister Plenipotentiary at Stockholm, said when speaking on behalf of China:

'Mr. President, Ladies and Gentlemen,

'Upon receiving the final draft of the Protocol, the Chinese Delegation immediately communicated it to its Government for an opinion. Unfortunately, however, owing to our country's remote position and to lack of time, we have been unable to consult our Government as fully as we could have wished. I desire, however, to state that the Chinese Delegation is prepared to vote without any reservation for the draft resolution submitted to the Assembly. It hopes that the vote will be unanimous so that public opinion may fully appreciate the value of the work of the First and Third Committees which has been admirably expounded by the two distin-

guished Rapporteurs. We rejoice that we are able to take part in
this great and universal manifestation of the sentiments of solidarity,
peace and justice, sentiments which have never before received
such solemn and moving expression.'

As in the negotiations with regard to naval disarmament,
so also in the scheme of the Protocol, Japan has taken a
prominent and salutary part in the furtherance of negotiations for the prevention of international conflicts. The attitude displayed by Japan in this connexion renders it a source
of great satisfaction for those who hope for good to the
world from the League of Nations proceedings that this
great Power should have been an original Member and remains continuously prominent and influential in its counsels.

I may mention here that though Turkey is not a Member
of the League she has had a good deal to do with it in various
particulars, as for instance, with regard to the Treaty of
Lausanne, the frontier with Iraq, and the continuous negotiations with which many of you are familiar with regard to
the Straits Commission, and other cases. That is to say, the
League has had direct negotiations with Turkey which could
not have been carried on on behalf of the other European
Powers in such a satisfactory manner unless the League had
existed.

With regard to India, I understand my friend Mr. DeLisle
Burns discussed yesterday the topic of the actual constitutional position of India in the League, and I do not propose
to touch on that question myself to-day.

With reference to the association of India in the actual
work of the League, it is interesting to observe that at the
last Assembly there were two Indian delegates on the Committee on Constitutional and Legal Questions; there were
three Indian delegates on the Committee on Technical

Organizations, and three on that dealing with the Reduction of Armaments; there were two on the Committee on Budgetary and Financial Questions; three on the Committee on Social and Humanitarian Questions, and two on the Committee on Political Questions, Mandates, Slavery, &c., and no one who has read these debates can fail to recognize the extreme ability and value of the contributions made by Indian statesmen to these discussions. Sir C. P. Ayyar was the Rapporteur on the general work of the Health Organization. The Report states that in the resolution which he submitted to the Committee and which was in turn submitted to the Second Committee and approved, the Indian point of view was explicitly recognized. Note was made of the tendency towards universality in the work of the Health Organization and of the circumstance that the activity of the Singapore branch formed the chief physical link between the Eastern countries and the League Organization. (Personally, I cannot but regard this Singapore Institution as being of better augury for the world than the project of the British Government to make Singapore the head-quarters of Imperial naval power.) 'Largely in consequence of the recommendations of the Committee', says the report from which I am quoting, 'it has been decided that the League's Malaria Commission should visit India in the course of the present year.' Reading this report and the other reports on the work of the Assembly, I think no one can fail to be impressed by the value of the Indian contributions.

Since the civil wars have become serious, the position of China in the League has become somewhat anomalous. The Chinese representatives on the Council, the Assembly, and the Opium Commission have represented the increasingly impotent Government of Pekin, and consequently have been unable to commit any part of China to any line of policy. At the same time the League has felt it essential to maintain any link, however frail, with China, and it was this sentiment which caused the election of China to the Council in 1926. Chinese Governments, for their part, have not ceased to recognize the existence of the League, even on one or two occasions in a manner which was not altogether welcomed by the authorities of the League as entirely proper. On various occasions when disturbances have occurred between the Chinese and other nationals, the Chinese have immediately called the attention of the League to it, but have been very politely informed that the particular commission or conclave of the League concerned could not take any notice of their observations. Nevertheless, I think it shows quite a welcome spirit that so long as China is in the League of Nations she should recognize the existence of the League as being an institution which must be interested in and ought to take cognisance of, and be officially informed of, any cases of dispute that may arise, such as those which occurred at Tsinanfu and Nanking or elsewhere.

Similarly the Japanese deposited with the League a copy of their memorandum to China with reference to the difficulty at Tsinanfu.

Persia also is a member of the League, and in regard to the primary purposes of the League Persia has succeeded in exercising an influence of considerable importance in one particular. There was a debate in 1923 proposing an amendment of Article 10 of the Covenant, which runs as follows: 'The Members of the League undertake to respect and preserve as against external aggression the territorial integrity and existing political independence of all Members of the League.' An amendment was proposed to add at the end of the Article the words 'taking into account the political and geographical circumstances of each State'. That is the kind of proviso which oriental nations—and some other people—are accustomed to regard with a good deal of suspicion, and although the delegates on that occasion were almost unanimous in their desire to adopt that amendment (the effect of which, I take it, would have been to make each State itself the judge of those circumstances—a position arising also in connexion with the Kellogg Pact), the Persian delegate stubbornly and obstinately opposed his vote, and that rather laxative amendment was not on that occasion adopted.

That disposes, so far as I think I can go into them, of the superficial aspects of the general relations of Asiatic Powers with the League for its primary purpose.

ii. *Mandates in Asia.*

I do not think I could profitably spend the time at our disposal by discussing at any length the administration of the Mandates for Iraq, Syria, and Palestine. Each of these territories has been the subject of some acute political controversies, arising out of special local circumstances and not entirely characteristic of the general relation between European and Asiatic communities. Palestine has been the sphere of a peculiar policy of special and individual interest, and what the League is chiefly concerned with there is to safeguard the rights of the minorities during the gradual growth of a united community as a result of that experiment. Syria has been the scene of troubles with regard to the handling of which it is impossible to say anything agreeable, any more than it is possible to do so with regard to the circumstances under which it became a mandated rather than a self-determining territory. I observe that the latest development in the history of the Syrian mandate is that the High Commissioner has suspended the labours of the Constituent Assembly for three months in consequence of a manifestation savouring of a desire to obtain self-determination, by the inclusion in a draft convention adopted by it of articles deemed by him inconsistent with the terms of the mandate. The Constituent Assembly, after affirming its wish to maintain its good relations with the representatives of France, has indicated its desire to adhere to the articles disapproved of, and the High Commissioner has explained his attitude on the ground that certain time was required to find an issue from this situation.

Such incidents afford to the psychology of Asiatic peoples test cases of the good faith of the principles on which the mandates system and the Covenant are ostensibly founded. They are somewhat disposed to suspect that the question whether any mandated people may be regarded as having arrived at a stage when it is capable of managing its own affairs is liable to be affected rather excessively by regard to the economic and political interests of the Mandatory Power. It is to be hoped that the further consideration which is to be given will successfully dispose of any grounds for such a suspicion, and it is unfortunate that the early character of the history of this mandate was such as to provoke it. Such suspicion is an active element in the attitude in which Asiatic peoples judge of European intentions and policy towards them, whether operating through the institutions of the League or in more direct relations.

With regard to Iraq, while it would be unfair to ignore the extent to which the political interests of the Iraq Government conduced to the recent settlement of the terms of the mandate under the auspices of the League of Nations, it has been obvious and unquestioned that the real question of European interest in the settlement of the boundary between Iraq and Turkey was the location of valuable mineral wealth. This brings Iraq into line with all those undeveloped countries, the resources of which European enterprise has so long been eager, and is daily becoming increasingly eager, to exploit for the profit of Europeans, while it might be in the interests of the less enterprising nationals of those territories that those resources should remain undeveloped a little longer, until they are in a position to take greater advantage of them themselves. You have heard what Mr. Grimshaw said very pertinently on that topic yesterday.

iii. *Asia and the Technical Organizations of the League.*

No one who observes what the League of Nations is doing, even in that superficial degree which alone is possible to members of the general public who have not the opportunity or the time to acquaint themselves intimately with all the ramifications of its activities, can fail to be impressed with the volume and value of the work that is being done, subsidiary to the purposes of the ideas which inspired those most active in the League's creation, by its associated bodies for special purposes, of which the most conspicuous, perhaps, is the International Labour Organization, but of which the World Economic Conference and its Economic Consultative Committee and the Health Organization with its various commissions are also highly important.

The operations of these subsidiary institutions of the League are establishing contacts with Asiatic peoples properly so-called which are in my opinion of immense importance and value for the reinforcement of the more popularly imagined purposes of the League. Our European diplomatists are still largely governed by the axioms, the criteria of value and the scales of social and national importance which governed European diplomacy before the War. These scales have regard to balance of military power and to the protection of what are broadly known as commercial interests and which behind the scenes are essentially financial interests and the veiled mysteries of banking and money power. The prole tariats of the European world, and with them the international scientific world and the trained economists, have long been impatient of these scales of value, and one result of the Great War was the exposure and the upheaval of immense consciousness of these subordinate interests.

That was the reason why the International Labour Organization was founded, which the publicists of our syndicated Presses often treat as an impertinent excrescence on the idea of the League. The World Economic Conference and the International Health Organization have a similar significance. Industrial relations and industrial systems differing in various countries, the superficial and plausible propaganda of nationalists and protectionists against which the World Economic Conference has borne such vigorous witness, which are a product of and which thrive on ignorance, the different standards of living and the vital conditions which are so much affected by hygienic and sanitary conditions—all these are among the fundamental creative causes of war.

Reading the report of the meeting of the Economic and Consultative Committee held in May last, I was surprised and somewhat amused to notice the statement that the Committee had become aware in the course of its discussions of the initiative taken by the Italian Government with the object of bringing about closer relations between the International Institute of Agriculture and the League. The International Institute of Agriculture is an institution practically entirely unknown to the general public of Europe, and, according to my experience, completely ignored by its statesmen. Having been privileged to take some part in its operations, I have no hesitation in saying that it ought to be recognized as one of the most potentially important institutions in the world. The ideas and purposes for which it was founded, and which have been most ably pursued, are of fundamental importance to the handling of the great questions of supply and nutrition, which lie so largely at the root of industrial and economic antagonisms. The Indian delegates on the Committee were foremost in laying particular stress on the fact that the nutritive and agricultural conditions of the great oriental peoples were the fundamental problem with them, and it is precisely with such problems that the International Institute of Agriculture should deal and can deal, and that Institute ought to be intimately associated with and itself become an organ of the League. It is to the credit of the Indian delegates that they insisted on that so strongly in the World Economic Conference.

The League provides a central clearing house for the results of the researches and for the conclusions of all such international bodies, in which the representatives of all nations meet on equal terms. The judgements and policies of all these international bodies are, as all who are acquainted with them will confirm, far more liberal than those of our national governments.

The application of these observations to the topic of my paper is that through the organizations of the League we are able to obtain, and we do obtain, on a footing of international republicanism, the interest and co-operation of the most intelligent Asiatics in a manner which brings it to bear upon European political judgements. Conversely, it is already perceptible that this increased contact is enabling Asiatics to make fuller and more confident use of whatever has been learnt by Western science and economics in connexion with industry. They find in these institutions and conferences a much more liberal and enlightened atmosphere than they find in the Press, the political utterances, the bureaucratic attitude, and the national policies of the States from which their colleagues are drawn. The reports and recommendations of all these League institutions consequently form an accelerating force in the rationalization of international affairs, and also of the internal affairs of Eastern communities.

The great advantage of these institutions is that they do get at and give us the rationalized facts. Such of us as have given lifelong attention to the facts of our relations with alien peoples, African or Asiatic, have mostly long been agreed as to their significance. The proceedings under the auspices of the League in regard to opium, in regard to slavery, in regard to forced labour and in regard to labour conditions generally in Africa, in India, and in other Eastern communities which have been drawn under European influence, and the plain common sense of such findings as those of the World Economic Conference, are all of them assets of a weight and cogency we might well have despaired to see brought to bear on the intelligence of the world by any other method in clearing up the world's understanding of the fundamental causes of war, with the symptoms of which, in armaments, and international jealousies, and exclusivenesses, aggressions, and hostilities, the League of Nations is in popular conception chiefly established to deal. They have this

salient value in connexion with these front-rank purposes of
the League quite as truly as they have value in their direct
reactions upon the internal welfare of peoples.

I could dilate at great length on the work of the Health
Organization, which has been immensely assisted by the
enthusiasm of Japan and of India, and which is in process of
doing for the world what colonial administrators like myself
have continually despaired of seeing done in our British
colonial empire. Piecemeal we have continually tried to deal
with the idiotic arrangements connected with Quarantine
and public health, often founded on the grossest superstition
with regard to the causes of such diseases as malaria, which
have been prevalent. When, as a Colonial Governor, I tried
to introduce the ordinary rational anti-malaria measures, I
found the whole medical profession in my colony, with perhaps one or two exceptions, resolutely sceptical on the subject. They said: 'It is all nonsense; every one knows that
malaria is propagated by climatic conditions, through the
air,' and so on. It was not until we had got our experts to
go on a popular campaign of elementary lectures that we
could convince our medical officers that the modern theory
of malaria was sound. Now it has been established and can
be brought home to the new countries, and any intelligent
statesman or politician in these new countries is at once prepared to do what he can to abate disease in his own community by putting into operation measures which now have
behind them the authority of the whole scientific world.

The East, with its cholera, dysentery, typhoid, plague,
small-pox, and so on has constantly been a terror to the
European world, because we had not analysed the causes of
these things or been able to make the Governments of
Eastern countries understand them. Now we have an or-

ganization which enables us to do that. The Health Organization is proving of great assistance in regard to those Asiatic and African countries which in the past have been sources of danger and difficulty to the world in the matter of disease, and in the course of a generation I hope it will entirely change the whole of the sanitary conditions of the civilized and uncivilized world. Those are things which could not be done except with the authority of the League of Nations.

In relation to Asiatic peoples the International Labour Organization which was set up under the Versailles Treaty to endeavour to secure and maintain fair and humane conditions of labour for men, women, and children in the countries of the members of the League and in all countries to which their commercial and industrial relations extend, is an institution of very substantial importance and influence. The Capitalist or European system of industry in the course of its development in European countries since the onset of the industrial revolution has stimulated in the chief industrial countries, notably in Britain, which led the way in that industrial revolution, an enormous development of self-protective social tissue in the form of industrial legislation and wage-workers' organization. The extension of the European industrial system, full grown, to Asiatic countries found their wage-earning populations unorganized and helpless, whilst even the stimulus of increased trade enhanced the pressure upon the workers in industries already established by native development in those communities. All the worst horrors produced by the industrial revolution in England among the new industrial proletariat were reproduced and still persist in virulent and accentuated forms among the workers in Indian cotton and jute mills, in Japan, and among the Persian carpet makers. The European industrial system took these oriental workers by surprise and at a disadvantage.

Most of the workers of Europe had grown, like the eels, accustomed to being skinned alive, but the Asiatic workers were not, and any one who has investigated even superficially the victims of the conditions of the factory system in those countries knows the terrible reaction these conditions have had upon the various sections of the population. Democratic industrial and trade union organization were alike unknown to them. Now the International Labour Office gives them the schemes which they should apply in their own countries, and in that it is doing most valuable service to the world.

We are accustomed, and in many respects with obvious justification, to speak and think of the labouring classes of Oriental countries as very ignorant and inefficient people, very unskilled in the technique of Western industrial civilization. These populations, moreover, have not evolved democratic systems of government, except in regard to parochial and minor local affairs. They have had no incentive to elaborate organizations of wage-workers or any approaches towards industrial democracy such as have been developed and are still being developed in European communities. But they are not, whenever their daily life is brought into contact with the operations of capitalism, found incapable of apprehending the idea of combination, still less so that of the State regulation of industry for the protection of workers. Their weakness lies in the fact that they have no training in the technique of combination or co-operation and have not acquired by generations of painful experience appreciation of the loyalties and self-sacrifices on the part of the individual and necessary for their working. The development of the tissue of industrial democracy in Japan has been extraordinarily rapid. In India, partly because India has not been a self-governing country, it has been comparatively fragmentary and feeble, yet the Indian Government and the provincial Governments show steady and during recent years a distinctly notable progress in the public regulation of industry, and the opportunity of obtaining representation in the Councils of the International Labour Office has stimulated and encouraged the progress of workers' organization in India.

I have here a document issued by the League of Nations Union on India, and I will just give you the headings of the matters in which improvements have been made in India, as in Japan and elsewhere, through the reactions of the League of Nations: Hours of employment and holidays; the protection of women; the protection of children and young persons in industry; the protection of seamen; assistance of agricultural workers; industrial hygiene; unemployment and migration; reciprocity of treatment for foreign workers; principles of inspection; social insurance; freedom of association; wages and general inquiries. With regard to all these subjects you may say that before the institution of the League of Nations the State organization or the social organization of Indian industry was practically non-existent. The British Government in India had never regarded it as its duty to interfere in industrial matters any more than it had regarded it as its duty to interfere in religious matters. As you know, the general aim of the British Government was to maintain peace and order, to provide for the development of the country by railways and to avoid famine, to create works of irrigation, and so on, and to deal with the larger matters which the State could efficiently deal with and which it did deal with with considerable efficiency; but no more than Mr. Baldwin's Government has now did it ever have any disposition to interfere in the relations between capital and labour, and it is only owing to the influence of the International Labour Office and the League of Nations that any great stir has been made during recent years in those directions. I might mention, as examples, the action that has been taken in Japan, and the action that has been taken in Persia with regard to the child carpet-weavers, and I might also mention the very interesting progress of the International Conventions with regard to opium.

With regard to opium we have had two matters to deal with; first of all the question of internal consumption of opium in certain countries, which has been held to be a matter of concern in regard to these particular Governments, and in connexion with that the League of Nations Organization was invited by Persia to send out—and did send out—a very able commissioner for the Government of China on the whole question of opium growing in the economy of Persia. With regard to international matters we have had two things to deal with, first of all the export of opium itself, chiefly the question of the trade in noxious drugs, derivatives of opium, which are prohibited from being used except under medical advice in the European or civilized countries of the world. The sale of these drugs is ostensibly prohibited in the United States and in England and elsewhere, except under defined conditions; that is to say, the great question is how to bridle the commercial interests in this deleterious traffic in drugs. If it was presumed that these drugs were only allowed to be introduced into civilized European countries for medical purposes, and to be dispensed only under medical certificate, then it was perfectly obvious that great quantities of opium were being absorbed in those countries which had by no means passed through those channels, and the chief activities and the various discussions arising out of the League of Nations organization have been directed to regulating that international trade. At the special session on the illicit traffic, held in October 1927, the Committee considered very many suggestions. The American member said it was evident that the production of derivative drugs could not be checked in those factories which are not under direct Government control. Therefore he proposed the nationalization of factories. It is interesting to know that this is the solution which has been adopted in India already; and it is now proposed by the American delegate to be adopted in all countries. The German member added the further suggestion that the drug factories should be internationalized—a still farther-reaching proposal. Here you have this dreadful socialist virus cropping up in the League of Nations. You have an American saying you should have national factories, and now you have a German proposing that the manufacture should be internationalized and placed under the League of Nations. Well, I do not know, but I daresay some people would object to the placing of drug manufacture under the League of Nations on the same principle that some of our stalwarts in England have objected to the placing of betting under the system of the totalisator, and taxing betting. I myself regard it as one of the best methods of controlling betting. However, a good many people have opposite notions. I think that this problem of the traffic in opium is soluble because the extent of the drug traffic is determined not so much by the avidity of the addicts as by the profits of the traffickers. If public opinion was aroused and the Government determined that the life of the trafficker should become very hard for him, the traffic would cease soon enough.

Siam has signed and ratified the Opium Conventions; it is the only Oriental State not under European domination to do so.

iv. *General Relations between East and West.*

Now I come to the more general aspect of the relations between West and East.

The history of the last two years in China has made it evident that an adjustment of the controversies arising out of the application to her economic resources of the European system must immediately and for some time to come engage the determined consideration of the principal Powers between whom and China these controversies have arisen. It is to be expected that however disposed some of those Powers may be to maintain the attitude that these controversies concern themselves and China alone, they may be a matter of interest, and I greatly hope of effectual discussion to the League of Nations Assembly, and especially to the representatives of those nations whose situation in regard to European activities has analogies with that of China.

China, Japan, her nearest neighbour principally concerned in those controversies, and India, in so far as her representatives can speak with an Asiatic voice, who are all loyal adherents to the principles and ideas of the League, have good reason to demand that these controversies should be handled from the point of view of the common interests of the world of which the League was intended to be an expressive organ. Japan, like America, Britain, and France, has capitalistic interests in China and neighbouring regions. She has also direct imperial interests, as has France, in territories of the Chinese connexion and as has Britain in India and Indo-China. But Japan has also what I may call a proletarian interest in questions of colonization outside of China and of her own islands, just as India has in Natal and East Africa, and as China has in other parts of the East. And her proletarian interests are essentially similar to the proletarian interests of the native peoples of Africa, and indeed in regard to these proletarian interests the interests of these Asiatic and African nationalities are identical with those of European proletarianism in its relations with European capitalism. This fact is perfectly clearly discerned by the educated representatives of the proletariat and of the proletarian interests in all countries, European, African, or Asiatic.

In a contribution to the *Nineteenth Century Review* of March 1924, Mr. Chao Hsin Chu, Chinese Chargé d'Affaires in London, bears witness to the good will which the idea of the League of Nations enjoys in his country. He says:

'I have dealt with the exact position of my country because the public should understand Chinese aspirations and keenness—I might almost say enthusiasm—for the principles of the League of Nations. I am well aware that it is most important to arouse public opinion, and we shall do that in China by convincing the people that the League will ensure fair play for their country and will give them a guarantee that their rights and privileges will not be overlooked. Perhaps, indeed, the League now seems to pay much more attention to Europe than to any other part of the world. This is unfortunate. Its scope should not be narrow, nor its activities limited to local affairs in Europe. Its very title shows this. It is, in short, a world-wide concern. If it ever ceases so to be, there can be but one outcome—the nations situated in the American continent will establish a League of their own and those in Asia will follow suit. In that case, such action would have a demoralizing effect on the very principle of the League's establishment, namely, that it was to cover the whole world with its activities and busy itself with the interests of the family of nations. All the problems of first-class importance germinated in the Far East. You are face to face with many issues of magnitude which spring from the meeting of world civilizations and mark the dawn of new and sometimes conflicting ideals. Such germination is a slow process. It may extend over centuries. The League should be sufficiently authoritative, sufficiently catholic, and sufficiently world-wide to deal adequately with all of them. But this can only be accomplished by the recognition of the special position of China and of Asia in general. There must be no recurrence of the procedure in 1923, when, to use a well-known Chinese literary expression, our critics threw stones into the well when we were already falling down inside. The victim is in sound health, but objects on principle to the treatment then received. In the interests of the League itself there should be no repetition of it. Surely in this great modern crusade the Powers should remember that they can count on the unqualified support of China if they allow her scope and opportunity, and such support may well be invaluable. Registering my impressions of the important facts of the present world situation, it seems to me that the increasing prospect of a consolidation of China is perhaps the most important. The earnest desire of all well-wishers of China for that consolidation may perhaps dispose us to be too sanguine upon the subject, but when I consider the enormous discouragement and misrepresentation on the part of the Governments, and still more the public Press, of the other great Powers concerned in her affairs, against which the progress of the Nationalist Government has been accomplished, I do not think we need be despondent.'

I have referred to the quality of distrust and reticence and reserve which transpires in the attitude of Oriental nations towards the Western world, and which in certain strata of their populations matures into a profound, and, in some cases, an openly expressed and manifested hostility. Such elements of dissension between the peoples of the world it is the idea and the purpose of the League of Nations to mitigate and to exorcise. It is notable that this disaffected attitude has,

during recent times, increasingly identified itself with that of
the Socialist and Labour movements in European countries
towards the capitalist system, or, as Mr. H. G. Wells considers that it should preferably be called, the European economic system. The commonest and most concise charge
brought by the Asiatic world against the European is that
of exploitation and of militarist and imperialistic policy backing exploitation. At the risk of making myself tedious to an
audience no doubt quite familiar with the history and the
justification of the critique which finds expression in this
protesting attitude, I venture to endeavour to set forth in
elementary terms what has appeared to myself, as an ad-
herent now for forty-five years of the European Socialist
movement, to be the root of the opposition.

The characteristic operations of what we now call generally Capital originate in that very early stage of human
development when pastoralism began to supersede or to
compete with agriculture. When I was at school I was taught,
very likely quite fancifully, that the word Capital was identical with the word Cattle. Abel was, according to Hebrew
scriptures, the earliest capitalist. He was a keeper of flocks
and herds. Cain tilled the ground. Whether or not the
legend is true that the odour of Abel's roast veal was more
pleasing to Jehovah than that of Cain's burnt onions, it has
been rationalistically conjectured that the true economic
reason why Cain killed Abel was that Abel's cattle trespassed
upon and devoured his crops. The pastoral hordes from the
earliest beginnings of civilization until the present day have
formed the earliest typical Capitalist class. They did not
live by the work of their hands; they had domesticated sub-
missive animals to sustain them by biting and predigesting
the uncultivated exfoliation of the earth. All that the cattle

capitalist or capitalist people require is land and water; but land and water they must have, and as their flocks increase they must drive them into lands preoccupied by other populations, whether tillers of the ground, or themselves also cattle-owners. This incentive, quite independently of the desire to appropriate the wealth of the unwarlike, agricultural peoples, as the Hyksos herdsmen people did that of Egypt, has continuously been the cause of international war. The history of South Africa furnishes copious modern examples. Cattle-owning peoples, of course, especially in Europe, have developed an improved agriculture of their own, carried on with the aid of the muscular labour of cattle; but wherever they extended their occupation of the lands of more primitive producers, they enslaved those peoples and pressed them as bondsmen into the service of their industry. The character of the subjection of labour to capital has, of course, been extensively modified by the industrial revolution of the machine age, which produced a proletariat acutely conscious of its subjection to the land and capital-owning classes. European populations, notwithstanding the constant disclaimers of the spokesmen of the Capitalist system that there is any antagonism of interest between the two classes, continue with increasing persistence to accept the Socialist critique of the situation. When I joined the Socialist movement in England there were, I suppose, five hundred men and women in that country who recognized the cogency of its analysis. There are now at least five million, comprising all the best educated and intelligent members of the wage-earning class and those most conversant with and experienced in public affairs. They are of opinion that organized modern capital exploits the wage worker.

Now the relations of European and Asiatic peoples originate in what appears to the capitalist class of Europe to be an entirely innocent, natural, and beneficent extension of their productive efficiency. When the British commercial class began to extend its operations of trade it was pursuing a process essentially similar to that of the pastoral capitalist who desired that his cattle should feed on other people's land. They wanted the produce of outland countries, and by what is called the investment of capital they were enabled to get it. The process in its elementary stages may be palpably not only innocent but advantageous to both. Similarly it might have been argued that the colonization of a primitive agricultural country by European ranchers and by farmers employing European capitalist methods was ostensibly innocent and palpably beneficial.

But the complaint of Asiatic peoples in the more modern stages of their contact with Europeans has been, first of all, that the European proceeds from the offer of voluntary trade to the insistence upon a right for his nationals to enter the country and settle for trading purposes. That development is conspicuous all over the modern history of European relations with Orientals. You must, the former say, allow our people to trade with those of yours who desire it, and you must keep in order that large, stupid mass of your population who unreasonably object to your doing so. Europe established trading-stations in Africa, India, the East Indies, China, Japan, and compelled the authorities of those countries to allow those privileged establishments. But the desire to depasture European capital upon productive foreign territories did not limit itself to the employment of trading capital. The great and efficient capitalism of Europe perceived that its productive operations could be applied in these territories with as much advantage as the Saxon invaders perceived that their system of cattle agriculture could be applied to the fertile lowlands and river valleys of England with which the more primitive British populations had been unable or had failed to cope. Europeans therefore introduced into Oriental countries their systems of railways and their machine industry. The banks of Europe financed these undertakings, thus depasturing their shareholding cattle upon the fields of Asia. It was easy for their agents often to demonstrate to individuals in power in Asiatic Governments that this would be to the economic advantage of their countries. They made it of great personal advantage, at any rate, to many such individuals to accept their reasoning. In this process of permeation it continually became necessary either to restrain the fractiousness of untutored barbarian populations by strengthening the police and military force of the country, or more simply, and especially where the rulers failed to prevent molestation, to supersede the incompetent native Government either by nominees of its own or by its own European agents. In India this process went very far, so far that, when the administrative responsibilities of Britain became so important as to be a matter of national political interest, it began to be protested that Europeans had a duty, not only of exploitation and commerce, but also of good government of the inhabitants. The process, of course, did not go so far in Japan and China. In both these countries European Powers or the United States of America insisted on establishing their treaty ports, their foreign concessions, enforcing the rights of the concessionaires of their nations in their own Courts of Justice and in some instances on controlling the finance of the country in order to secure the interest on loans of European capital. Now from the point of view of what Mr. Wells calls the European System and what Socialists call Capitalist Imperialism, all this is, of course, quite beneficial and normal. If foreign Governments do not insist that their subjects shall honour the contracts they have made on their behalf, they must be made to do so. If their Courts of Justice are unreliable, they must be ousted. If their subjects commit atrocities the country must receive punishment. Now in all these countries there have been many capable statesmen who have admired and welcomed much in the European system. Japan being a patriotic and manageable nation, whose educated classes were endowed with an extremely adaptive intelligence, was able at a comparatively early stage of the process of the depasturing of European capital to revolt against and to repel the practical encroachments of power with which European Governments maintained it in India, China, and other Eastern countries. I take the most familiar instances: I might have spoken of Persia, or half a dozen less familiar examples. But the net result of this depasturing system, which capitalist mentality is convinced is an essential advantage not only to capitalist Europe but to the world, is that the Asiatic peoples find themselves in the position that European nations have in fact acquired a supremacy over them: a threefold supremacy— a supremacy over the natural resources of much of their territories, which have become the monopolized property of foreign capitalist syndicates, a supremacy over great numbers of their labouring population who have become proletarian wage-workers, and most irritatingly an usurped supremacy over some of the most essential departments of their national Government. I have referred to Japan as having, by an astonishing and most energetic effort, repelled these European encroachments; but the watchful and perhaps the somewhat austere attitude of Japan in connexion with the League of

Nations reflects, I think, her profound understanding of what
it is she has had to contend with and might still have to contend with in the characteristics of the European development.

I should like to quote some very simple language from a
memorandum which was sent to Dame Adelaide Anderson
by some Chinese workers in 1924, when she was investigating
industrial conditions in China. It expresses in the simplest
possible words what the reaction upon the new proletariat
of China is of the industrial system introduced by Europeans:

'We saw in the newspapers that you came to investigate conditions regarding Chinese workers, so we wish to say to you a few
words in frankness. . . . Ever since we came here to work we have
not enjoyed the happiness of having holidays on Sundays, National
Anniversary Day, Dragon Boat Festival Day, Harvest Moon Festival Day or Labour Day . . . we work 12-hour shifts, day and night:
but including the time coming and going to and from the factory,
we spend 14 hours a day . . . when we change over from day to
night shift 16 hours a day. . . . Because of earning a few mouthfuls
of rice we are unable to obey the holy commands . . . we have no
time to do anything that is beneficial to the public. . . . During
the night shift, especially during the hours between two and half-
past five, we feel very tired . . . in fine, we are treated as prisoners,
animals, and machines . . . we are peaceful workers, we do not wish
to do anything that is beyond us. But we are forced by circumstances, so we plead to you to say a word of justice for us.'

That is the statement made by people who, I think, you will
recognize are a people of real civilization, as you know the
Chinese to be, of civilization in the small matters of life,
encountered with a powerful machine which entirely destroys
the habits and simplicities of that civilization. China is
organized on a philosophy of the recognition that most of
the human world must, and always will be, poor, and in the

process of centuries of that recognition it has, as the peoples of India in similar circumstances also have done, evolved an enormous complex of beautiful social manners and aesthetic art, so that when you go to India or to China and take up an ordinary cooking-pot or feeding-vessel of the poorest classes, you recognize a thing of beauty, and you wonder how it is that such an outlandish and barbarous people can possibly have made it. They make it and they use it because they like it, and they keep their harvest-moon festivals and they have their pleasant ceremonies with lanterns and flags because they are a people of simple civilized tastes, and not of the heavy civilized tastes of beer-drinking and cinema-going, and other violent delights which are congenial to our proletariats. But that is their civilization, and no one can come into contact with the Asiatic peoples without seeing that a general civilization, not a European civilization, has permeated the whole of the people to a greater extent than it permeates, at the present time, almost any European community, or than it ever has permeated any European community since those possibly fabulous times in the Middle Ages in England and in Italy, when the people were really producers of artistic things for themselves. Now, that exists in China, and that is what we are destroying in China, and that destruction is what the Chinese people, from the lowest to the highest, complain of.

Now, every European nation, for the sake of its self-respect, maintains in the traditions taught in its schools (so far as any instruction in modern political history is given in them) a certain consistent account of its dealings with Oriental communities. These traditions and this historical account inevitably follow the accepted ideas of the dominant economic theory of those European countries. The dominant economic theory among the classes influential in imperialist and commercial extension being that the operations of capitalist commerce and industry are admirable and beneficial, and any criticism of or opposition to them, whether among its own subordinate classes, or among the populations of foreign nations, irrational, perverse, and unpatriotic, it is not difficult for the successive generations that pass through our elementary and public schools, and even our universities, to accept it as axiomatic that the attitude of Oriental nations towards European imperialism, industrialism, and large-scale commercialism, as exhibited formerly in Japan, consistently in China, and during the last forty or fifty years increasingly in India, is an unreasonable and ungrateful sentiment, the vigorous recent development and increase of which is attributable to the perverse activities of those wicked people the Socialists, and in particular to the active propaganda of Communist theories by that cosmopolitan bogey the Russian Bolshevist. But the truth of the matter is this, that whereas what we ourselves tell them about our economic system, and about its benefits, does not coincide with their experiences, as manifested in that short extract I gave you from the manifesto of those Chinese workers, yet when the Communist Bolshevist goes to South African workers suffering under the colour bar and anti-Indian legislation and so on, when he goes to Chinese workers suffering under the conditions quoted and tells them: 'If you accept the capitalist system, this and that will happen to you,' they say: 'These people tell us truly what it is that is happening to us: we see that they tell us the truth about what happens to us from the incursion of foreigners into our countries and from the introduction of the foreign systems of industry into our land. These people tell us the truth. The people who come from England and other European countries do not tell us the truth of the results of their system. We know the truth as we feel it. These Bolshevists, these Russian Communists, tell us what we recognize, what happens to us; therefore they must be good counsellors.' I do not myself consider that they are good counsellors; but in South Africa in present conditions, and in China, and everywhere in the East where you have the European system of control of industry producing the results which it does upon the workers, you have no antidote to give to the Communist propaganda which tells those workers that that is the inevitable result of the European system. That is why Bolshevism is always attractive and powerful among the depressed classes of the Asiatic communities.

v. *Conclusion.*

The League of Nations, as I have said, was conceived as a remedy for antagonisms arising out of the developments of European civilization, and so far as I have observed the immediate interests of Asiatic countries in its operations might reasonably appear to them as remote, as such interests appear to the Government of the United States in regard to that country. Japan became, with obvious propriety, a member of the League, and a leading member, because she has elected to adopt and acquire the position of a modern capitalist industrial and imperialist State, and has addressed the remarkable energy and intelligence of her people to achieving the essentials of that position with great rapidity and success. She is now a militarized, industrialized, and commercialized nation of the first rank, and is one of that precise order of nations for the adjustment of the international contacts of which the idea of the League was conceived, and its constitution framed.

T

But of the other great Asiatic countries of which the principal contain the Chinese group and the Indian group, the same cannot be said. Looking at these communities from Europe, we discern, very inadequately indeed for the most part, that they have had ancient civilizations of their own, and some definite conceptions of communal national life, but so far as what we ourselves speak of as civilization is concerned, that seems to us to fade out into the Asiatic atmosphere, and to reach its remotest and most attenuated manifestations in what we call the Far East. On the other hand, that Western civilization of ours has passed over the Atlantic to North America. North America, the United States and Canada, are disposed to regard those complications of European civilization which have rendered the League desirable for the old European nations, with their latest accession Japan, as separated from them by the Atlantic; and they exhibit a very natural desire to leave them, and all things connected with them, on the other side of that cleansing flood. At the same time, the peculiar efficiencies of Western European civilization, as distinct from those humanities which it inherited from the Mediterranean and from the Semitic and Eastern worlds, is most highly developed on the North American continent, so that, in a sense, characteristic Western civilization culminates not in Europe but in North America, and drops plumb on the western coast into the Pacific Ocean, from the shores of which, if you keep Japan out of focus, you look upon what is to us the back end of Asiatic civilization; and I often wonder how, to a philosophical American student who interests himself in those lands and who is already exploring them by scientific and sociological expeditions, the Asiatic perspective appears. I cannot help thinking that to a study conducted in the scientific temper, that is to say, casting aside the preconceptions and common formulas which European, and especially British, politicians have acquired or absorbed in the light of history of our relations with the East, viewed from our side of the contact, the premises of the significance of Asiatic civilization might appear very different. America has a good deal of money and scientific energy to expend, and spends a good deal, and I hope will be spending more, on the indulgence of scientific, artistic, and sociological inquiry. What I say, therefore, about the fundamentals of the relations between Asia proper, in the sense of her own civilization, and those affairs of the Western world which fall within the scope of the League, I say with great diffidence from the point of view of an Englishman who has only formed his impressions about the facts from looking at them in a direction in which they are habitually sifted and generalized through the medium of European history and tradition, whereas from the American side the scene presents itself the other way round, and in the right perspective, China, Japan, and India offering themselves to consideration as national complexes the characteristics of which can be judged on their own merits and on their own value, except in so far as America has developed colonial and commercial relations with those communities. In so far as she has yet done so or attempted to do so, I venture to think that, however sound her theory may be that the Atlantic absolves her from any necessity of associating herself with the League at Geneva, the argument is less reliable with regard to the Pacific. Japan was the first Oriental nation that indicated effectually to America that she would not tolerate interference in her affairs, and from that starting-point Japan has developed her independence and power until it is difficult to see why, if Europe has affairs with America and Japan on the one side, and Japan, on an equal status, similar affairs with America on the other, these affairs are not likely to be most reasonably and conveniently dealt with through the mechanism of the League. To speak perfectly frankly, it appears to us, and I should not wonder if it appeared to Japan, a little difficult to imagine that the international world will be content to continue to maintain a duplicate set of conferences, one to discuss affairs which concern America and another to discuss those which the United States consider do not concern them. From such particular conferences, if any, the United States can reasonably and economically keep away.

We have been waiting for many years for the stabilization of the internal affairs of China, so that she could acquire a government of her own. In the face of all these obstacles, and at the cost of desperate expedients and uncontrollable excesses, the nationalist republican movement inspired by Sun Yat Sen is steadily making good. China is a member of the League, and her representative has always shown her a loyal and whole-hearted member. I am not aware of any reason at all for supposing that the nationalist Government now recognized or about to be recognized by the European and American Powers will be less thorough in its confidence and co-operation, or that it will not desire to make the utmost use of its right as an important member of the League of Nations. All of us here will, I am sure, desire that it should.

I think it is obvious that during the next few years the League of Nations, either directly through those procedures which its constitution guarantees to its members, or indirectly through the operations of other conferences inspired by its fundamental ideas or even instituted and promoted through its administration, ought to have a great deal to

say, and ought to be able to exercise a very important influence, towards the rectification of the position of China among
the great nationalities of the world. Indeed, I think that
prospect or possibility is the most important point of contact
of the idea of the League of Nations with the interests of
Asia proper to-day.

THE GENERAL PROBLEM

CHAPTER XI

THE FUNCTION OF LAW IN INTERNATIONAL RELATIONS

Professor BRIERLY:

THE title of this lecture: 'The Function of Law in International Relations,' suggests two different though related lines of thought. It suggests in the first place a question of fact, the question what part law is actually playing in international relations as things are, and it suggests in the second place a question of principle, namely, what are the potentialities of law and what are its limitations, law being the specialized instrument of social welfare that it is. No one can profitably plan or prophesy an improved international order, unless he has given the best thought of which he is capable to these two subjects, and that must be my excuse, if an excuse is needed, for attempting to speak within the limits of a single lecture on two subjects each of which is so far-reaching as the two I have indicated.

My first task, then, will be to attempt to give as concisely as possible some idea of what the existing system of international law is, and what it is doing for us at present in the sphere of international relations. International law comes to us in two different forms. It is either what we call the *customary* law of nations, or what we have come to call in recent times the *conventional* law. All the older part of the system, including the foundation upon which the conventional law itself rests, is simply customary law, but in quite recent times a growing mass of new rules has been created by treaties or conventions between States. Each of these forms of international law calls for a short explanation.

i. *Customary Law.*

Lawyers mean by a *custom* something more than a mere habit or practice. They mean by it a habit or practice which is not only observed in fact, but which has also come to be regarded as an obligatory habit or practice by those who observe it. By what process that feeling of obligation comes to be attached to certain practices and not to others is a question for sociologists to explain; it is not a process peculiar to the relations of States towards one another, but one through which, as the history of law shows us, every system of law passes in the course of its development. It has been said that nobody was ever present to see the beginning of a custom, and at any rate we may be sure that any one who was present was not aware at the time what he was witnessing. It is more important for our present purpose to note some of the features that are characteristic of customary law in general, and therefore of international law in particular.

Let me take first a negative characteristic. Customary law is very rarely broken, and contrary to a popular superstition about international law that is true of international law as well as of every other species of customary law. If such a statement sounds paradoxical, it is because of our inveterate habit of thinking of international law as though it were simply or solely a law relating to the conduct of war. The so-called laws of war are frequently broken, but the far more important international law of peace, with which alone we are here concerned, is broken exceedingly seldom. That is not the unconsidered view of an optimist, and I am prepared to admit at once that international law has defects quite as serious as would be the frequent violation of it. But if it is true, it does contain this moral. It means that the prime requisite of reform in international law is not, as some people would have us believe, the devising of more effective means of enforcing the law as we have it, of more effective 'sanctions' as they are called. That prescription rests upon a mistaken diagnosis of what is wrong with international law; it is the favourite prescription of the amateur, who is impressed by the conspicuous difference between international and other law, arising from the fact that the latter generally has behind it a system of pains and penalties which work with fair regularity against the law-breaker, and jumps too hastily to the conclusion that this system is what makes law, other than international, efficient. That is not to say that the question of how to provide better means of enforcing international law may not, in certain eventualities, become urgent; but merely that this is not the question most immediately urgent, nor one on which the possibility of other reforms is waiting.

The real defects of customary international law are that it grows exceedingly slowly, and that consequently its range is extremely limited. All customary law grows slowly, because not only has a habit to grow up of doing a particular thing or of doing a thing in a particular way, but there has also to be the growth of the feeling that the habit is binding, the feeling that it is not merely a more convenient course, but that it is a more right course than any other in the circumstances in which we are called upon to act. Further not only is this process of growth necessarily very slow; it is also exceedingly indefinite, and exceedingly haphazard. It is always difficult to say at any particular moment whether the process of growth has gone so far that there has emerged a fully-grown binding custom; it is haphazard because it is not always on those matters on which a binding rule seems most desirable that a rule grows up. It is a process which goes on, in our national systems of law as well as in the international system, but with the difference that in our national systems it has now come to occupy a very minor place in the general development of law, simply because our national systems have advanced beyond this customary stage of development in which international law for the most part still remains. None the less, if we look for a moment at the same process as it can be traced in a national system, we may derive some notion of the magnitude of the handicap under which international law is still suffering.

Our Anglo-American system of the common law was, in its origin, as international law still is, simply a system of customary law, but for centuries now we have had courts of law applying the common law, and by applying developing it, until it has ceased to be, except to a very minor extent, a customary system at all, and has become a judge-made system of law. What has happened in the course of the centuries of development of the common law is simply that the courts by decision after decision have made explicit in rules of law, always capable of being further developed and of being modified, corrected, and so on, the sentiments of our communities about what the law ought to be; they have stimulated a process which, without their aid, would have gone on exceedingly slowly, so slowly that it is quite inconceivable that the common law, without their assistance, could have developed so as to fit it to be a law capable of meeting the needs of our communities in modern times. Doubtless the courts never have performed and do not perform to-day a function such as that with anything like mathematical accuracy, and there are other factors, such as professional tradition, which have a part in the formation of their decisions; but they perform it with sufficient accuracy to make their results acceptable on the whole to the communities of England and America. The sentiments that the judges weave into the law in this way are themselves in a constant state of development, and the judges are constantly developing the law more or less in unison with the growth of the sentiments. They are able to do that because judges are not supermen; they are in general just men of intellect and of character who are representative of their times and countries. They share the prevailing opinions, and they instinctively weave them into their decisions.

Now this priceless aid to the development of a customary law has hitherto been almost non-existent in the international sphere, and it will be a long time yet before the International Court of Justice is able to do for international law anything at all comparable to what the vast number of English and American courts sitting day by day for centuries have been able to do for the common law. But the process has begun. An international court has to-day been established on foundations that are well and truly laid, so that at long last the customary law of nations has set its course in the only right direction for its development.

Let me take a second handicap from which this part of international law suffers as contrasted with a national system of customary law. A customary law develops more rapidly at a period of history when men have not yet begun to think of law in general as something which it is within their own power to control and to create. In all early societies we know that the idea of legislation, of the process of creating new rules of law by deliberate action, is hardly known; it is an idea which, as the history of law teaches us, develops relatively late in the progress of civilization. In primitive societies men do not have a notion of the law as something which they have made and which they can alter; it is something which is there, and of which they have to take account, almost as they have to take account of natural forces. But when at a later stage of civilization the notion of legislation has come into existence, it tends to supersede the unconscious development of law. Since new law can be so easily made, men come to feel that if new law is wanted it ought to be made by a conscious, deliberate process. They look, and look reasonably, for something more formal in the promulgation of law than the mere instinctive growth of a custom. They look for an act of legislation, or at the very least for a decision of the courts, with the result that the capacity for the instinctive development of law becomes atrophied. But internationally that leads to this rather curious position. We do not change our mentality when we turn from the national to the international sphere. We carry over into the international sphere the legal self-consciousness that we have developed in thinking about our national systems of law, and thus create a psychological difficulty in the way of the recognition of new international customs, which people living under a customary law have, so to speak, no right to feel at all. We have in fact attained to a degree of legal sophistication, if I may call it so, which makes a system of customary law for any relations, international or national, hopelessly anachronistic.

Let me suggest one further point of contrast between a national and an international customary system. It is fairly obvious that a customary law will grow more quickly, and that it will bring within its ambit more of the relations of life, when the society with which it deals is closely knit together, and especially when it is a homogeneous society. Mere convenience, the fact that one course of conduct is slightly more convenient than another, has much to do with the acceptance and the observance of a custom. Sometimes the mere fact that it is necessary to have a rule of some sort, though it may not matter very much what the rule is, seems to be the operative cause of the growth of a customary rule. An obvious illustration is the rule of the road. Englishmen drive to the left, and Americans drive to the right. It does not matter which rule is adopted, but it does matter very much that every one should drive to the same side on the same road, and it matters more in proportion to the density of the traffic.

Such a rule—and it is true of any customary rule—does not succeed in establishing itself unless its non-observance would produce a considerable degree of inconvenience, as may be seen from the futility of all attempts to establish a rule of the road for pedestrians in England; it has always to contend for recognition against apathy, against conservatism, against our natural and healthy distaste for discipline. Only the inconvenience of unregulated contacts, which increases as a society is more numerous, and a dislike of collisions, which grows up more easily when it is homogeneous, can prevail against forces such as these. And unfortunately, if we consider the character of the international society, it is clear at once that though it is a society incomparably more compact than it was a hundred years ago, it is still, compared with any national society, one very loosely knit together. It is a society in which the members are not in constant, but only in relatively occasional, contact with one another. It is a society, too, in which the members differ from one another in innumerable ways. They differ in race, in colour, in language, in culture, in traditions, in numbers, in strength, in economic development, and so on, and although all these differences are, of course, commonplaces, we do not always consider them in the light of their effect upon the development of international law, which is immensely important. The texture of international society offers almost every conceivable obstacle towards the growth—the unconscious growth—of a customary law of nations.

In view of such considerations as these it may seem curious that the utter inadequacy of a purely customary system, obvious as it may seem to us, was not generally realized until comparatively recent times. Only on quite rare occasions have States in the past set themselves to do what individuals everywhere know must be done if law and order are to prevail within their own countries; only occasionally have they set themselves to *create* law by their deliberate action.

ii. *Conventional Law.*

That brings me to the second element in the existing system, the so-called conventional law. The first occasion upon which States, so far as I know, ever set themselves to make new law by convention was at the Congress of Vienna in 1815, when they made a rather half-hearted attempt to secure freedom of navigation on international rivers, and also legislated against the slave-trade. It was not until the second half of the nineteenth century that the work of creating international law began to be taken up at all seriously, but from the Treaty of Paris in 1856 onwards it is possible to discern two separate movements, both leading in that direction. To call them movements perhaps gives an idea of system which was as a matter of fact almost entirely absent;

rather there were two series of events, almost disconnected, which happened, however, to be leading in the same direction.

One of these series of events had its impulse in the desire to mitigate the brutalities of war. It started with the Declaration of Paris itself in 1856, and it was carried down through the Geneva Conventions, the Hague Conventions, and so on, to the Washington Resolutions of 1921, and there have even been some later attempts. But without denying that some results were achieved by that movement, it may well be doubted whether they were at all commensurate with the enthusiastic efforts which were devoted to it; and since there are still some who desire to see those efforts renewed, it is right that those who believe that they were directed towards a false and unattainable ideal, namely, the debarbarization of something essentially barbarous, should speak out their minds. One of their chief effects, as it seems to me, has been to justify out of the mouths of international lawyers themselves the popular superstition that international law is mainly interested in the conduct of hostilities, and that it regards war as a normal and permanent incident of international relations. Mr. L. F. Woolf, in his admirable little book on *International Government*, makes this comment: 'What', he says, 'should we think of a State in which there were no laws to prevent riot, and murder, and violence, but very detailed and complicated laws governing the conduct of persons engaged in riots, and murder, and violence?'

Fortunately, however, there began about the same time a second movement, less conspicuous and arousing no popular enthusiasm, but one in which we can trace the true beginning of the conscious foundation of an international legal order. With the increasing complication of our civilization it became more and more obvious that the whole business of governing the world simply could no longer be carried on efficiently in purely national compartments, with the result that one subject after another was taken out of the sphere of purely national government and put on an international footing. Mr. Woolf has described the successive steps of the process in the book just referred to with an admirable combination of scholarship and humour. To a certain extent the impulse behind the process has been the same as that which has led to the growth of the federal power at the expense of the States in the American Constitution. In both cases it lay not in deliberate policy, but in the sheer pressure of circumstance. Sometimes in the international field it took the form of the actual setting up of an international organ of Government, such, for instance, as the Universal Postal Union. At other times it simply led to agreements between the States to co-ordinate the uses that they would make of their own national governing powers. The latter method was adopted in such matters as extradition and health and a great many others. Some of the experiments have been very successful, some have been less so, but cumulatively they are of the utmost importance. In a recent article in the *American Journal of International Law* on the 'Development of International Law since the War' Mr. Manley O. Hudson has printed a list of 228 instruments of international legislation of this kind entered into between 1864 and 1914, and another list of 166 which have been entered into between 1919 and 1927, and he points out how immensely 'the system of conference and co-operation which we know as the League of Nations' has facilitated this beneficial process by creating a habit and a technique of international legislation. There can be no doubt at all that it must be mainly to the carrying on of this movement, and to the improvement, if possible, of its methods, that we must look for the future extension of international law.

Even this very summary account of what international law consists of at the present time may perhaps serve to suggest what its difficulties are. Most of them may be summed up in the term, lack of organization. International law lacks an organization for enforcement, although, for the reasons I touched on earlier, that is not the immediately urgent need. It needs also more organs of interpretation, that is to say, more courts, and more use of those that it already possesses. But above all it needs more facility of adaptation to international conditions, more responsiveness to international needs, something that will do for it that which legislation does for law within a State, and that which nothing but legislation can do. This last need is incomparably the most important, and unfortunately it is also the most difficult to provide for. Something would be achieved if we could secure a greater readiness to use the legislative machinery that we already possess, for so long as nations are unwilling to allow new laws to be made by majority vote—and any important departure from the unanimity principle is probably neither practicable nor desirable for a long time to come—it is difficult, perhaps, to see that the existing machinery, especially the League machinery, can be improved in any important respect. The problem is rather to get it used more freely, and to get it used in the right spirit.

iii. *The Limitations of Law.*

But the practical result of these defects, and particularly of the slow working of the processes of development, is that far the greater part of the activities of any State are not at present regulated by international law at all; they remain, in the phrase which was introduced by paragraph 8 of Article 15 of the Covenant, matters within a State's 'domestic jurisdiction'. That phrase should not lead us to imagine that such matters are necessarily 'domestic' in the sense of being matters of purely internal concern; it is not the 'matters', but the 'jurisdiction' that is described as domestic, and 'domestic jurisdiction' extends to many matters which are not, in the natural sense of the word, purely domestic matters at all, but are matters which concern the interest of more than one State. But while that is so, that is to say, while every State, without any breach of international law, may pursue its own interests within such a wide ambit without regard to the interests of other States, it would be unfair to blame the law for the semi-anarchical state of existing international relations; we should rather blame the States which have hitherto refused to admit the law into the spheres of their activities in which most of their serious disputes arise.

But if the existing condition of international law makes it urgent that we should work for an extension of its sphere, it clearly becomes more necessary than ever that we should at the same time have a correct idea of the part that law, as such, is capable of playing; and that consideration brings me to the second part of my subject. For law is a highly specialized instrument in social life: it simply cannot be cast for any part in a scheme of reform which happens not to be filled by any other instrument. It is an instrument which has its own special capacities and its own special limitations.

Each of the two elements, the customary and the conventional element, in the existing law, as it seems to me, can teach us something about the nature of law in general, which it is important in this context that we should clearly realize. From the existence of the conventional law we may learn that law is something which it is within our power to make and to modify. Until recently, that was the side of the truth which, as I have just been trying to point out, needed emphasizing. To-day we all know that the future of law between nations is in our own power to make or to mar, and therefore we are far more likely to fall into the opposite mistake of thinking that in law we have merely a convenient and malleable instrument. If we do that, however, we shall overlook the lesson that the customary element in the law ought to teach us, for the difficulties that we have seen impeding the growth of customary law are, to a lesser but still to an important degree, difficulties which impede the growth of law as such. Our law-creating efforts can, in a sense, only stimulate the growth of law; they cannot create the ground in which law can flourish and render in our lives the high services of which it is capable, because that ground is not a material thing at all, but a spiritual state of things, and the problem of creating it is not a legal problem but a moral problem. At the present time, a neglect of this vital truth of the spiritual nature of law seems to me to be in danger of stultifying two movements that in themselves hold great promise of good, the movement for the codification of international law, and the movement for the substitution of law for war in international relations; and a short consideration of the aims of those two movements may perhaps help us to a truer appreciation of the function of international law as such.

If, when we speak of 'codifying' international law, we have in mind merely the more rapid creation of conventional international law, so that progressively more and more matters on which át present each State follows its own policy conceived in its own interest, shall be brought within the regulating influence of the law, then we are setting before ourselves an ideal which is both necessary and practicable, although to call such an ideal 'codification' is really an abuse of a term which, to a lawyer, has a perfectly definite meaning, and a different meaning from that. But if we imagine, as much of the language that is used about codification implies, that lawyers can be called upon to produce a comprehensive code of law covering all the important relations of one State with another, then we are harbouring a dangerous delusion. It is true that lawyers could produce such a code; many lawyers have already done so unofficially; but the reform would end with the paper on which such a code was written. Law is not a commodity that can be turned out by methods of standardized large-scale production, nor is it a commodity which it is the business of lawyers to supply; it is something that lawyers can formulate when the law-abiding sentiments of a community supply them with the spiritual stuff out of which law is made; it is never something which lawyers can create out of nothing and impose upon a reluctant community, as hitherto the international community has been reluctant to accept law as the controlling factor in its major concerns. I am not speaking now of technical difficulties in the way of international legislation, but of difficulties that lie much deeper than any question of machinery. Law can no more be reduced to a set of propositions than religion or morality could be; and to attempt to do so is not a short cut to a reformed international order, it is a waste of time. Law is a method of conduct, a way in which persons or States, as the case may be, behave towards one another, by which they govern their relations towards one another, and it exists only in a community which has learnt self-control and consideration for the interests of others. Those who call for a comprehensive code of international law to be devised at once—and some of them are even so ignorant of the nature of law that they refuse to have anything to do with the International Court unless it is provided with a code—seldom seem to have reflected upon the sacrifices of its own particular interests to the general good that is the price that every nation will have to pay for every extension of international law. It is merely childish to talk as though we could have the benefits that law can give us, and yet remain as free as we are at present to carry out separate and conflicting national policies.

iv. *Law not an alternative to War.*

Further it is utterly misleading to speak of law and war as though they were true alternatives. If they were, the problem of peace would be immensely simplified, because even the most bellicose of militarists would hardly persuade a nation to go to war, if going to law were merely another way of achieving the same purpose. Unfortunately that is not so. The aim of war is quite different from the aim of law, and the problem for pacifists is not, as so much current propaganda implies that it is, the relatively easy one of persuading the nations to adopt a new and improved method of carrying out an old purpose: it is the task of persuading them to adopt a changed purpose. The emotional repulsion against war to which such propaganda appeals is valueless as a foundation for law, because it has no roots in any reflection either on the sacrifices that the adoption of law would involve, or on the question how far law is capable of doing for us what war has done as a matter of history. We are tempted to argue, just because war and law both lead to disputes being settled, that therefore they are merely different ways of settling disputes. There is a fallacy in such reasoning, a fallacy of which generally the militarist, whether he is intelligent enough to formulate it or not, is instinctively quite conscious. It is the same fallacy into which the teetotaller falls if he commends water because water is a means of quenching thirst, oblivious of the fact that what the liquor drinker wants is not to quench his thirst *simpliciter*, but to quench it, in a particular way. In the same way, like liquor and water, war and law have simply one function in common; they both lead to the settlement of disputes, but this common function is only incidental to each of them, and not the main function of either.

This is an important point, and it is worth while pausing to consider what relation this function of settling disputes bears to the whole nature of war and law respectively. Why do nations resort to war? They do so not because they want a dispute settled, but because they want it settled in one way and not in any other, because they are determined that their own will in the matter on which they are disputing shall prevail over the will of the other party. The settlement at which war aims may be one that is just or legal or reasonable, but it is not necessarily so. It is, of course, always represented as having all those qualities, but all that we can be quite certain of when a war has broken out is that both sides have preferred to fight rather than not to have their own way. Law, on the other hand, besides being something far more than a means of settling disputes which men or States can resort to in a crisis and forget at other times, is, even when regarded only as a method of settlement, a means by which a State gets, not necessarily the solution that it desires, but the solution that it is held by certain impartial

persons to be entitled to. It leads, therefore, to a result
totally different from that which war leads to; and pacifism
will never make much impression upon national policy until
it is candid enough to admit that difference. So long as it
uses language which implies that law is merely a more sen-
sible way of doing what we have hitherto done by war, the
main stream of national policy will sweep past the puny
barriers that it tries to set up.

What sort of arguments then can we turn to if our object
is to persuade States to accept law instead of war? One possible argument suggests itself at once. We may argue that
while it may be true that a State's object in going to war is
to get, not what it is entitled to, but what it wants, still it
is also true that experience shows that it does not get what
it wants by that means: in other words, we may argue that
war does not pay. Mr. Norman Angell proved that for us
even before the war in *The Great Illusion,* by arguments
which on their own premises have never been refuted, and
the war itself was a practical demonstration of the large
amount of truth that there is in such an argument. We all
know now that the victors in a great war suffer almost as
much as the vanquished, and if intellectual conviction of
its futility could ever banish war, the problem would already
be far on the way towards a solution. But if we are candid
in facing the facts, we shall have to admit that such an argument is only true of major wars. It is not true that a powerful
State which coerces a State much weaker than itself by
action which may or may not be called war, but which really
is either war or the threat of war, does not get what it sets
out to get by that means. And further, even if the argument
were universally true, its psychological foundations are probably unsound, because it attributes a far higher influence to

rational motives of conduct than probably the facts warrant. There is probably more to be hoped for in a less direct method of attacking the problem, and in trying to break it up into its component elements.

For example, if we ask what in the past has been the alternative to war, the answer is that the only alternative has often been submission to the will of the other party, and what is harder for States to bear than mere submission, submission in its most humiliating form. Lack of international organization has often meant that statesmen, with their fingers on the pulse of opinion only in their own country, have been tempted to take up positions into which they would never have allowed themselves to be led if they had had better opportunities of weighing the effects of their actions in other countries, and the same lack has made a position once publicly and definitely taken up exceedingly difficult to withdraw from. Men have been known to play chess supremely well blindfold, but not poker, and foreign affairs are more like poker than chess. A better articulated organization of diplomacy, an organization such as is being built up at Geneva, means in this connexion two things: it means that statesmen are less likely than they were to take up dangerous positions through ignorance of some of the relevant facts, and it means also that even if they do, withdrawal without humiliation is easier than it was. Such an organization can in a very real sense offer an alternative to war, in which law and legal methods will play an important, though not the most important, part. For there is one vitally important limitation of that function of law which consists in the settlement of disputes—a subordinate function of law rightly conceived in any case, as we have already seen—to which we must now turn.

The limitation lies in the simple and obvious fact that a legal settlement is necessarily a settlement on the basis of existing legal rights, and it is not the case that all disputes are disputes about existing rights; they are often, probably generally, disputes in which one party is dissatisfied with its rights. In the past, if that dissatisfaction has been sufficiently keen, and if the State has felt itself sufficiently strong, it has gone to war, knowing that a successful war would have the result of changing its rights. Such a change is often in itself a good and a reasonable thing, and yet, if we could succeed in the task, as it is so often presented to us, of substituting law for war, it would become a thing almost impossible of achievement. The one thing that it is possible to prophesy about the international future is the certainty of change, and any plan for the future which disregards this certainty is worse than useless, it is a positive danger. Nations will wax and wane, new discoveries will be made, new interests will arise, in the future as they always have in the past. A few nations, the English and the Americans in particular, may perhaps say: 'We do not see the necessity of change; we have a place in the sun which is as large as we can comfortably occupy'; but there are others who have less reason to be contented with things as they are, and if we make the acceptance of things as they are the only alternative to war— and that is what the substitution of law for war would mean —we shall merely induce a desperation which no formal repudiation of war will ever safely dam. And although it complicates the problem of peace, it is right and healthy that that should be so. Let us be fair even to the historical mission of war. It has done one great service. Like a great fire, it has often destroyed what deserved to be destroyed, and what, as things were, probably could not have been destroyed by any other means. Somehow or other this beneficial operation of war must be taken over into a regime of peace and performed in a better way, but it cannot be performed by law in the sense in which law is generally commended to us, as a system for the protection of existing rights. To attempt to force all existing national grievances into a legal strait-jacket would be as wrong as it would be futile.

v. *The Present Problem.*

The problem of the peaceful incorporation of changes into an existing order is the supreme problem of statesmanship, national or international. Whenever it is not frankly faced and solved, revolution in the national, and war in the international, field will always in the long run burst the fragile dams of legal formulas by which we vainly try to stabilize a changing world. The paradox of all law is that it cannot keep its vitality unless there exist legal means of overriding legal rights in a proper case, but if we believe that the law exists for men and not men for the law, it is right that this should be so. Within a well-ordered State the pressure for change is more or less successfully canalized by a legislature, which can weigh demands and judge what changes are just, and when. In the international sphere the problem has not yet found its solution.

What, then, does this consideration mean when we translate it into terms of our problem, the function of law in international relations? It means first and foremost that side by side with the development of legal methods of settling disputes, we need a system for the peaceful introduction of changes into the international order, and that without the second of those two reforms an uncompromising insistence on the first would be an actual danger to peace. What form such a machinery might take, and how it is to be created, seem to me to be the paramount questions which should be occupying the attention of those who are interested in peace. The organization of international conciliation under the Covenant, and in many particular treaties, such as Locarno, is one of the most promising advances towards this goal. Another lies in the building up of law by international conventions, for which, again, the League is of supreme importance. Another lies in the direction in which Article 19 of the Covenant—that Article which refers to the consideration of international conditions which are dangerous to the peace —points an as yet hesitating finger. But behind all these lies the need for a new and more spiritual conception of the meaning of law, not as a system of existing rights, but as a great and developing moral force attempting always to formulate what is just and true, and never resting content with its own handiwork. Only if we can come to look upon law in some such spirit as that shall we ever succeed in making of law an alternative to war. Law, as I have already suggested to you, is not a code of rules, but a way of life that has the incidental advantage of making disputes fairly easy to settle when they arise, as they inevitably always will; but this advantage of law is not something which we can have except at a price, and the price is the resolution, on the part of all our States, not invariably to expect to get their own way. A developing international organization can make it possible for States to have their own way, where that way is reasonable and just; and in the end we shall have to rely on a developing international morality to ensure that when a State's own way is neither reasonable nor just, it shall not expect go get it. Law is a part, but it can never be the whole of that process .

CHAPTER XII

THE INFLUENCE OF PUBLIC OPINION ON FOREIGN POLICY

Professor ZIMMERN:

THE subject that has been assigned to me this morning is *yourselves*. You have come to learn at first hand about the League of Nations and about the work that is done here for international co-operation, and the very astute people who have drawn up this programme have at once thrown the ball back to you, so to speak, and asked me to speak about what you can do to help forward the work you are learning about here. The League of Nations is impotent without public opinion. The Governments that co-operate in the Council and Assembly and the technical organizations of the League of Nations, including the Government of the United States, are all of them powerless unless they find some wind in the sails of their respective ships of State; in other words, unless their efforts to improve international relations are backed up by an instructed and idealistic public opinion. The League of Nations is what you make it, and the progress of international relations is at the pace that you set.

i. *Democracy less effective in International than in Domestic affairs.*

Now the problem I want to put before you is this. Public opinion at the present time does not function in foreign affairs. It is not active; it is inert; it is acquiescent; it is largely indifferent. For reasons which I will explain in a moment, public opinion in foreign affairs is something entirely different from public opinion in domestic affairs. The problem we have to discuss together this morning is how we are to remedy that state of things. What can we do to make democracy function as successfully in its handling of foreign affairs as it is functioning in many countries to-day—for instance, the country in which we are speaking, and, on the whole, Britain and the United States—in regard to domestic affairs?

Why does public opinion not function satisfactorily in regard to foreign affairs? For a very simple reason, namely, that they are foreign. They are things outside the range of our own experience. Every one here who has done propaganda work on international relations with popular audiences, knows the difficulty to which I refer. Suppose I ask even members of this audience to go to the map of Europe and at once to put their fingers on, let us say, Czechoslovakia and Jugoslavia, are you all of you quite certain you could do it? I am not sure that even the British present could do it, and I suppose it is less likely that the Americans would be able to do so, dealing as they would be with the geography of a different continent. Take the knowledge which Britishers have of the United States. The other day I heard somebody say: 'What a curious language you have in America; what curious spelling you have; you have a State called OHIO and you spell it I-O-W-A.'

One of the curious paradoxes of this situation is that the very qualities which help democracy to be effective in domestic affairs, hinder it in handling international affairs. Why do we believe in the commonsense of the ordinary voter with regard to a domestic issue? It is not that we think that the ordinary voter will make a very exhaustive study of the technical aspects of this or that question on which he is to vote. We trust his judgement because the common voter has a profound knowledge (which he so to speak inherits, and amid which he grows up; it is part of the air which he breathes) of the temperament, of the institutions, the traditions, and the general atmosphere of the country in which he lives. In other words, he has a background of experience of which he is really unconscious, but which gives him a criterion for judging any particular issue that may arise. He judges a new issue in the light of his knowledge of the main facts. He is like a doctor who diagnoses a given disease or a given situation in a patient against the background of his knowledge of anatomy and biology, and a general knowledge of the patient's condition and constitution. That is to say, the process by which the ordinary voter makes up his mind on this or that particular issue is by supplementing his store of general knowledge by a certain special attention to this or that problem, and on the basis of that, we get what we call the sure judgement of the man-in-the-street, of the plain man, which has so often in the history of democracy revealed itself as more effective than the judgement of this or that clever man or clever school of thinkers.

But in the appreciation of foreign affairs that background is lacking, and consequently the plain man flounders. When you present him with an issue concerning Czechoslovakia, or Europe as a whole, or the world as a whole, or, let us say, China, he has no background. He has no means of judging. He listens, perhaps, to a missionary on China, to a banker on China, and to a government official on China, and he does not know which of the three to believe because he is not living in China; whereas the same three opinions on England or on America could at once be checked by dozens of conversations, sometimes in public houses, sometimes in clubs, sometimes in drawing-rooms and sometimes around the family hearth. It is exactly the element which makes democracy successful at home which prevents it from forming a sure judgement on extra-domestic questions.

There is a second difficulty. The plain man arrives at his decisions, but he arrives at them slowly. He does not sit down at a desk and come to a definite decision at the end of an hour when he has read a paper giving him all the elements of the situation. He is not a business man who has either to give or not to give an order at the end of a morning. The process by which the ordinary voter, and a country consisting of ordinary voters, makes up his and its mind is a process which requires a good deal of time. What the ordinary man thinks in relation to a political problem is generally something like this: 'You have told me about the situation and the other party has done the same. I want a little time to size it up. I want to see how this thing is working and how the march of events confirms or refutes the arguments you are putting before me.' The voter is, therefore, accustomed in a democratic country to spend a good deal of time in dim, inarticulate gestation before coming to a decision. You will find, if you study the history of democracy, that the big decisions have always come about slowly. Questions have been pending for years, and sometimes for generations, before they have come up for final decision.

Now the trouble with the world in which we are living is that decisions have to be made rapidly. Events are moving very rapidly, very much more rapidly than the mind of the ordinary man, and therefore, while the voter in all sincerity is trying to make up his mind about the situation that has been presented to him by the politicians, that situation changes, and when his decision comes, it comes too late, and what he actually does is to sabotage, to use a sort of power of veto rather than to contribute positively to the solution of questions.

Hence, in these post-war years, we have witnessed a constant race between the swiftness of events on the one hand and the swiftness of man's understanding of them on the other, and, on the whole, events have outdistanced the judgements of this or that body of voters. In fact, there are a great many people in the United States of America, as I find every time I go there, who are still judging the League of Nations in the light of the controversy of 1920, and to whom the Geneva League as it is now is absolutely unknown. The League as it is now is something utterly different from what it was in 1920.

It has been said that the mills of God grind slowly, but they grind exceeding sure. I think the same could be said of democracy. The mind of the average man moves slowly, but it moves effectively. But if while the mills are grinding, new ingredients are being put in at every moment, the effectiveness of the grinding process is very much reduced, and the result is not likely to be what the miller expects it to be. There are, therefore, those two great defects—lack of experience and of background, on the one hand, and the increasing swiftness of events on the other.

There is, however, a third difficulty about the working of democracy in foreign affairs, which is far graver than those I have mentioned. The difference between domestic and foreign affairs has ceased to exist. *There are to-day no foreign affairs.* The old frontier by which you could say 'this ministry deals with foreign affairs and all the other ministries deal with home affairs' has disappeared. It has gone the way of another and very similar frontier—that between political questions and industrial questions. Practically all our domestic questions have an international bearing. All of them have some international element entering into them.

Let us take two questions in England and two in the United States. Take coal and unemployment, which are two large and closely related questions in present-day British politics. Can you discuss the coal problem without taking into consideration the big international changes which affect our British coal industry; the utilization of new coal-mines, the changing of frontiers affecting those coal deposits, the substitution of oil for coal, and other matters of the same kind? Can you discuss unemployment without discussing the general economic situation of the world? The effort in England to deal with coal and unemployment by people who have not an international outlook, and by an electorate which has not an international outlook, has led us into very great difficulties. Exactly the same is true in the United States of two issues there, the farm situation and the tariff. Not being an American, I have no right to say more, but these are two issues which obviously can be intelligently understood only by people who have their eyes on the whole world, and not simply on the large but nevertheless limited area of the United States.

The result is that democracy does not to-day function effectively, even in what are still called domestic affairs. An incalculable element has been introduced into the whole of the political field, and that is one of the reasons why democracy has lost a good deal of prestige in recent years, and why it seems to some observers, in Italy and elsewhere, to be less successful than it was in the nineteenth century.

That very international interdependence on which President Wilson laid such stress, and which led him to say that the world should be made safe for democracy, has weakened the working of democratic institutions in the traditional national governments.

ii. *The wrong Remedies.*

Now, what are we to do to try to remedy that situation? Various efforts are being made. I will deal first with some of what I think are the unsatisfactory remedies. There is, in the first place, an attempt by politicians who know the electorate and who rate its possibilities too low, to confine domestic politics to domestic issues. They try to choose issues which exclude so far as possible that incalculable element, and try to give the people something to vote on which they really understand. I suppose that if there is a thoroughly domestic issue in the United States, it is the question of drink. Every country has the right to settle what it will do about alcohol, and that does not very much affect international politics. But if you fight an election on drink, you are taking away from the electorate its power of decision on questions of greater international importance than drink. Similarly, if in England you fight an election on the redistribution of the areas of local government, that may have international repercussions, but they are small. If you fight an election on such an issue, you give the elector an issue which he thoroughly understands and which he enjoys discussing, but which tends to make him forget his larger responsibilities. If that procedure is repeated in numerous elections, if elections continue to be fought on the most domestic issue that can be found, then what must eventually happen will be that the important issues will be settled elsewhere and democracy will be superseded as a real force in government.

It will be merely a puppet show, a sham government, for dealing with issues of lesser importance, the major issues being handed over to two or more bodies of experts or politicians. The voters, in other words, will play at parish politics and world politics will pass into other hands.

The second remedy which is sometimes proposed is what is called the democratic control of foreign affairs. That is to say, an attempt is made to draw a distinction between domestic affairs and foreign affairs, and to introduce special checks in connexion with foreign affairs on the hypothesis that since they are mysterious, since the voter cannot understand them, since there is more chance of foul play and underhand dealing, there ought to be some special means for checking them. It is such considerations as this which have led to proposals for the setting up of special parliamentary committees of the House of Commons and similar Chambers in other countries, to proposals for emphasizing the treaty-making powers of the United States Senate, a popularly-elected body, and for giving parliamentary bodies the power to amend treaties or limit, in this way or that, the powers of plenipotentiaries who are negotiating treaties.

I do not wish to express an opinion one way or the other on the details of these proposals. They may be right in detail while being very unsatisfactory as a complete solution of the problem I am putting before you. It may be that we should be better off in Britain if we had a specially selected committee on foreign affairs in the House of Commons similar to the Committee in the French Chamber. It may be that treaties should be submitted for acceptance or rejection to the House of Commons. All I want to point out is that these suggestions do not solve the problem. In fact they complicate it, because they introduce an element of delay and of further complexity which interferes with the power of Governments to keep up with the rapid movement of events. Sometimes, as we in Europe know only too well, the treaty-making power of the American Senate has played havoc with the plans made in the field of international politics. In fact, all these solutions, whether wise or unwise in detail, involve an element of suspicion as well as an element of delay, and they therefore complicate the problem of evolving satisfactory forms of international co-operation, co-operation between Governments and co-operation between peoples. They involve a survival of the old system of checks and balances which has come down to us to-day as a heritage of the rigid constitutions and the distrust of public opinion which were characteristic of the eighteenth century, of the age before the enlargement of the electorate or the establishment of compulsory systems of general education. Rigid constitutions are not suited to an age of fluid events. Possibly a country like Great Britain, which has never had a rigid constitution, and an organization like the League of Nations, which has not been equipped with one, are better adapted to modern conditions than the other country represented in this room, which has a rigid constitution.

The third suggestion, which is sometimes made, is a suggestion for special education in foreign affairs considered as foreign affairs. The effort has been made to set on foot systems of information and propaganda about the passing issues in international politics. A good deal that is very praiseworthy is being done to educate the American voter in the details of the Tacna-Arica trouble, or the British voter as to the conditions in Upper Silesia. I have seen a good deal of that work, and though I do not want to criticize it, I want to say frankly that I regard that work as the first floor and not the foundation. When you are talking about Tacna and Arica to people who do not know the first thing about Latin-America, or when you talk about Upper Silesia to people who know nothing about Germany and Poland, you are wasting your time and perhaps doing even worse, for you may be teaching people to indulge in idle chatter picked up from a lecture or a leading article which is intensely irritating to those who have studied these and other questions at first hand, and with a full knowledge of their background. Although it is very desirable that the Press and public opinion should be well-informed about this or that happening, and that members of Parliament and of Congress should be able to exercise the requisite criticism on points of detail, nevertheless that process does not solve our real problem, which is the bringing into existence of a large body of opinion that has a sense of the international background and not simply of this or that event which happens to be in the foreground.

iii. *The right Remedy.*

In other words, the only real remedy is a twofold one. First, to go down to the roots of the problem and try to enlarge the vision and the understanding of the citizen, to give him as abiding a sense of the interdependence of the world as he is brought up with of the characteristics and institutions of his own country, and to make him feel, all day long, that he is living in a larger world. That is the first positive remedy.

The second is to make him feel he has to make a contribution that is not merely negative, that he has not simply to stop the Government or the diplomat from doing evil, or to act as a detective, but that he has to give positive service in helping forward the processes of international co-operation and in improving international understanding.

Is this impossible? I believe not. I believe it is possible now to bring into existence in the civilized countries, in those countries that Lord Bryce classed in his great book as 'democracies'; that is to say, not in all countries with democratic constitutions, but in countries where democracy is really a practical reality—and I will not enumerate them— a sufficient body of voters who have that background, who have a sufficient general knowledge of the international situation on which to base a sure judgement of this or that definite issue that is presented to the country.

I believe that to be possible, because we have seen that enlargement of the range of experience and judgement happening in history. No doubt there were many people in 1776 who despaired of ever creating an American public opinion, who said that the inhabitants of the thirteen colonies would never be able to think of themselves as other than Rhode Islanders or New Yorkers or Virginians. But in the process of time, and very quickly, owing to the movement of affairs and owing to the teaching of events—because events do teach us—that American public opinion came into existence. In the same way, an Englishman and a Scotsman have the same background for forming a judgement on any issue presented in Great Britain. You do not find the Scottish elections going one way and the English another. There is a common basis of knowledge and public spirit on which judgement is formed.

I will give you another reason why I believe this enlargement is possible. It has happened in business; it has happened in the economic sphere. What is the process by which a business man, with connexions all over the world, decides whether he will buy or sell, whether he will conclude a given transaction or not? He has to make a political judgement; he has to size up the situation, let us say, in China, and judge whether it is a good thing to invest money in that country, or in Czechoslovakia, or wherever it may be. In other words, any business man who has at all a large range of operations whether for buying or for selling, has to keep his eyes all over the world. He lives in a perpetual sense of the interdependence of the modern world. Stock exchanges may not be very noble institutions, but at any rate they are international institutions, and the people who deal in them have an international outlook. The same is true of banks and large-scale business houses in general.

Moreover, the elements of this wider public opinion are really being formed before our eyes. This public opinion does already exist, as you will see in a minute, in an inchoate way. It exists in embryo, but we have not yet detached it from the other elements of public opinion and seen what it really is and what are its possibilities.

iv. *Some Pitfalls.*

Before I come to that I want to devote a few minutes to the question of the pitfalls, to explain the difficulties into which many of us fall in trying to consider things internationally. I would call this section of my remarks: 'How not to think about foreign affairs.' First of all there is what I would call the pitfall of romanticism. The affairs of the parish pump are solid, real, practical workaday affairs. Outside one's own country everything is apt to be wrapped for many people in an unsubstantial haze, and I think, perhaps, Geneva is the most fairylike of these visions. Some of you may have come here having regarded Geneva as a kind of Paradise inhabited by angels, tireless ministers of grace, immune from every human failing, who are trying in a wicked world to exercise the qualities of celestial beings rather than of ordinary humans. The League of Nations is to many admirers rather like what the Prince of Wales is for some romantic admirers of the British monarchy. It is a hardly human institution made by something more than human hands. I remember very well some years ago standing at the entrance to the Secretariat when a lady—I think she was an American—was concluding a visit to this building, and she came out to an unsympathetic friend who had not gone inside and said: 'You were quite right to stay outside; it is only an office!' I tried to imagine what was in the lady's mind. I think she imagined that if she got inside the building she would see dramatized some great scene of international co-operation. She thought we were play-acting here all day long. That kind of attitude is at the back of many of our minds. We mix up our idealism, which should be a real and permanently active element in our make-up, with our imagination, and our imagination is not based on any real knowledge of the facts. Workers for peace and for international understanding have sometimes, in their efforts to reach the masses, appealed unduly to the imagination, and unduly dramatized the issues. At any rate, that is a temptation into which all of us who work for peace and international understanding may easily fall. It is quite possible that, at the end of this week many of you may be a little disenchanted. This wonderful spot which you so looked forward to visiting may have lost its magic, and become for you very much more solid, workaday, ordinary, and pedestrian. If so, I hope, if you return disenchanted, you will not return disenthused, but will retain the wholesome crusading spirit of which our Chairman spoke in his opening remarks.

The second pitfall is the pitfall of sentimentalism. People sometimes think they can achieve in international politics by rose-water methods, by methods which inflict no pain on any one, results which they would never expect to achieve similarly in national matters. They seem to think that our international doctors can do their job without hurting. Well, sometimes you have to hurt. Sometimes you even have to use force, as a doctor does. I got into trouble through enlarging on that element of my philosophy with some of you last year, so I will not return to it; but I think there are dangers in a too sentimental view of international politics, in thinking that, whilst you retain the policeman at the street corner in the town, you can achieve similar results in the international sphere without any element of police or compulsion.

Thirdly, there is the pitfall of favouritism. For many people, particularly in England, interest in foreign affairs means interest in one particular country. Just as old ladies keep pet dogs and pet parrots, so some elements of our public opinion in England have kept pet countries. It is a traditional British failing. If you study British foreign policy during the nineteenth century, you will find that we have been very kind to some countries—at moments to Greece, at moments to Italy, at moments to Bulgaria, at moments to Armenia— while other countries, such as Poland in its rebellion of 1863, and Denmark in its struggle in 1864, after having been encouraged with vain hopes, were just let drop. We have picked and chosen our temporary favourites, and I am not sure whether our pets have fared any better than those whom we have discarded. There is a sentence of Bernard Shaw which bears on this failing. He remarks, I think in the preface to *John Bull's Other Island*, that 'a Liberal has three duties— a duty to Ireland, a duty to Finland, and a duty to Macedonia'. That attitude of mind is not an intelligent attitude towards foreign affairs, or towards international relations as a whole.

Another pitfall I would mention is what I call the line of least effort, the pursuit of affinities. Englishmen think that if they have made friends with their cousins across the Atlantic (who are not always their cousins, by the way), they have enlarged their tolerance and their charity and their sense of international understanding, and that they can stop there and let the other nations be; and there is a certain danger of that in this gathering of ours. Here we are, two nations, two groups; but there are fifty groups represented in this building. Do not let us regard our gathering as completing the circle. Let us take this fortunate association between Great Britain and the United States in this common venture as a step towards a larger effort at comprehension, a comprehension including those peoples of Latin mind whose intellectual processes are so difficult for us to understand, who always begin with the general when we begin with the particular, who are always logical when we are commonsense. And if we have understood the Latin mind, we have got to go on to the Slav mind, the Far Eastern mind, the Indian mind and all the other varieties of human mind that are summed up in the work of this building. If you stop your internationalism at the point where you have met a foreigner whom it is easy to understand, who has, for instance, the same sense of humour as yourself, you are yielding to a very dangerous temptation, and if too many people yield to that temptation the end will be that we shall divide the world up into a set of groups of people with special psychological affinities, and those groups will be in hostile alinement the one against the other, and the end of that essay in internationalism will be worse than the beginning. We do not want a world of Anglo-Saxons ranged against a world of Slavs or Latins. Our internationalism must aim at the most difficult objective. We must not be satisfied until we have penetrated the mind of the man who is the hardest to understand, even if he is an African, even if he is somebody whom we do not regard as properly adult; because not only is the whole of geography here, but in a sense the whole of history is in the League. All the different stages of development of the mature mind and judgement are in the League, and that process of understanding is very much more difficult than the process of shaking hands with a friend, sitting down and having a drink with him, and discussing how absurd are the mental processes of the other fellow.

There is one last pitfall, and that is what I would call national internationalism. Every nation has its own form of internationalism, as every nation has its own religion. When Christendom broke up at the end of the Middle Ages, it broke up, to a large extent, into national churches, and those national churches adopted their own attitude towards religion. At moments I feel that the League of Nations is in danger of falling into a similar set of national churches. British internationalism is quite different from French internationalism, from Dutch internationalism, or from German internationalism. American internationalism is another very special brand.

In this situation, with all these pitfalls, many clever manipulators of public opinion have succeeded in finding ways of turning this vast Niagara of idealism and goodwill into all sorts of base uses. Very tragic it is to observe how international goodwill may be distorted and misdirected in all kinds of ways. The Press has contributed to it, unscrupulous politicians have contributed to it, all sorts of interests have contributed to it. Into those one cannot enter to-day, but let me suggest to you one or two ways of being on your guard against these people who may try wrongly to utilize your noble impulses. Firstly, read more than one newspaper, and if possible newspapers from more than one country. The Press is not dishonest; it faithfully records not all the conditions, but certain conditions, economic and other, in any given country at any given moment. You can always find out the truth from the Press if you check one interpreter of an opinion or of an interest by another interpreter of an opinion or of an interest. It requires more critical knowledge and judgement to read a modern newspaper and extract the truth as regards the general state of the world at the moment than it requires to read a medieval manuscript, what is called a palimpsest, which has been scribbled over by a second scribe; and the best way to acquire that critical power is to read several papers from several different countries. Secondly, supplement that by reading books and magazines. Do not trust ephemeral judgements; read books by the students of these subjects, and follow them up. There are plenty of good bibliographies, plenty of bodies to tell you what are the good books that are written, and what are the less good books; use your own judgement upon that material, and if possible read books in more than one language. Thirdly, personal contacts. Find out who are the people who best understand and follow what is happening in the world, who hold the threads, whose judgement and knowledge can be relied upon, not only as to events, but even as to personalities, and keep in touch with them. Lastly, travel intelligently. Do not merely get into a train and travel in a group, but get into relation with the people in the countries where you go, and find out from the ordinary man at first hand how things are getting on in France, Germany, Poland, Switzerland, or wherever you happen to be. Do not take your judgements either from the newspapers or from the first porter or waiter with whom you converse, but go to the people who themselves have a well-founded judgement.

v. *The New Public Opinion.*

Now I come to what I promised you, a discussion of the elements of this new public opinion which is, I think, coming into existence. I see two main elements in that public opinion. Firstly, we are beginning to separate out certain general issues, broad general issues of principle, from the immensely complex field of policy. We shall never understand Nicaragua or Upper Silesia, and if we did the situation might change to-morrow; but there are certain general principles upon which we can have a definite opinion, and upon which the American, the Englishman, the German, the Swiss, the Frenchman, can have a common opinion. Two such issues I see. Firstly the issue of peace versus war, the obligation to settle disputes by peaceful means and not by means of violence. If you go to an Englishman or a Canadian and tell him there is a very complicated situation in the east of Europe created by the Treaty of Versailles, and ask him whether he is prepared to fight to defend this or that frontier or to change this or that frontier, he will say that he does not understand it, and will ask why he should give his life for something he does not understand; but if you say to the Englishman, the Canadian, the Dutchman, the Swiss, or any one else in the League: 'Here is an issue: peaceful settlement of this dispute or settlement by violence without due examination,' on that you can mobilize the public opinion of the whole civilized world. The separation of the issue of peace and war from the details of this or that controversy involves an immense advance in international technique; it involves taking away from the Foreign Offices the power to involve us in war by upholding this or that particular national interest in a given controversy. That is why I personally attach very great importance to the movement for the outlawry of war. There is a great deal to discuss about it in detail, but the outlawry of war is a very brave, and I think a very able, attempt to separate the question of the use of violence from all the complicated matters of substance which are involved in this or that dispute; and if you can once establish as a general rule the principle that the nations shall not resort to war, there is no danger in international politics remaining very complicated, there is no danger in the diplomatic system adopting one method for one problem and another method for another problem—upholding the French peasant's desire to get his money back from Russia in French policy towards Russia, upholding British interests with regard to India in British policy towards Russia, and so on. You cannot co-ordinate international policy; it is too complicated, and local public opinion and democracy have made it more complicated; but you can unify public opinion all over the world on the question of the use of peaceful means as against the use of violent means.

There is a second element in international technique on which I think we can unify opinion, and that is the adoption of co-operative methods as against individual methods. The first phrase in the Preamble to the Covenant is 'to promote international co-operation'. We have not yet fully explored the meaning of the words 'international co-operation'. What they mean is that it should be antisocial for a country to take too decided and individual an initiative in regard to a question which affects other countries. Such initiatives may be idealistic or may be interested, but they are in essence discourteous; they create friction because they put aside a co-operative method for an unduly individual method, and a very great deal of friction is caused unknowingly by countries embarking on policies the full repercussion of which they have not studied, and therefore do not realize. The adoption of more co-operative methods in international politics is often simply the adoption of a better etiquette, the adoption among those responsible for public affairs of greater courtesy, similar to that which exists in other great professions, such as the medical profession. That then is one line of advance. You can get a public opinion based on the general acceptance throughout the civilized peoples of certain broad general principles, peace versus war, co-operation versus undue initiative by individual nations.

The next element is the element of what I would call professional public opinion. There is to-day no such thing as the man in the street. Every man in the street is also a man with some special experience; he may be a lawyer, a doctor, a teacher, a banker, an engineer, a workman or a housewife— the woman in the street. In all those capacities he or she has access to some special experience which can be mobilized for international purposes in appropriate professional organizations. Of the women I will not speak; they have their League of Women Voters, their Co-operative Alliances, their National Councils, and so on. I stick to the men. There is a direct line to-day from the workman at the bench to the international organization, through the International Labour Office. It is possible for three or four trade unionists to get together in a club, frame a policy, put it before their national organization, get it taken up, brought to Geneva, and put on the Agenda of the International Labour Conference. In the same way it is possible for doctors, lawyers, and others to organize nationally, and to get the needs of their profession internationally attended to, and not only to attend to the needs of their profession, but to make their particular professional contribution to general international politics. I have not time to develop that now, but you see what I am driving at. I am driving at bringing into existence a judgement in the ordinary voter which is based not on this mysterious X, but on definite practical experience. The workman who wants the Eight Hours' Convention signed by all the countries of the world knows what he wants, and knows why he wants it, and knows what will be the result when the Convention comes into force. He is operating democratically, he is using democracy; he is doing internationally what we said at the beginning was so difficult to do; he has found the sphere in which it can be done. Just in the same way the work of the Health Section for the prevention of disease, which involves an immense amount of detailed work, is of great interest to the medical profession, and the individual doctor has the means of getting the people upstairs here to consider whether this or that new subject shall be put on their agenda, and thus drawn into the field of international politics.

Well, you see my line of advance. I will not develop it. I leave it to you to consider what you, as individuals, can do through your own practical experience to relate the conditions that you understand to the broader problems of this interdependent world. No two of you will operate identically; no two of you will use your democratic citizenship in the same way. You will all vote together on the broad issue of peace versus war, co-operation versus individual initiative, but you will all operate separately with regard to your own professional, practical experience. But in this way I firmly believe that we can find one channel after another for that Niagara of idealism and goodwill which is at present pouring over the rocks unrestrained, unguided, and uncanalized. It is true that we shall never reach a world in which all citizens know everything about every issue, but we can achieve that every one should know something special, and should bring his specialty to bear on the general sphere, and in which every one would have a hold on certain broad principles. We shall have that when we have mobilized the something about everything and the everything about something throughout the whole field of democracy, not only British and American, but French, German, Swiss, Dutch, and so on. When we have that we shall have drawn round the world a girdle of intelligent citizenship, we shall have brought into existence a body of men and women thinking sanely and responsibly about matters within the range of their own enlarged experience. Then I think we shall have laid the foundation of an enduring civilization, because then those men and women will bring into existence the instruments they need for forming that judgement; they will give us those better newspapers, those better means of international intercourse which we all feel to be needed.

So my last words would be: Aim at creating the human agencies for making democracy function better. When you have built up an instructed and responsible public opinion, the material agencies will surely follow.

APPENDIX

CONTENTS OF PROBLEMS OF PEACE
(SECOND SERIES)

SECTION I

THE EVOLUTION OF THE LEAGUE

SECTION II

THE LEAGUE IN ACTION

CONTENTS OF PROBLEMS OF PEACE
(FIRST SERIES)

SECTION III
THE LEAGUE AND THE WORLD TO-DAY

VIII. Germany's International Position since Locarno. By Dr. ARNOLD WOLFERS, Lecturer at the Hochschule für Politik, Berlin.

IX. The Foreign Policy of the United States since the War. By Mr. CHESTER H. ROWELL, formerly Editor of the *Fresno* (California) *Republican*.

X. The Foreign Policy of the Union of Socialist Soviet Republics. By Mr. MICHAEL FARBMAN, Editor of the *Europa Year Book*.

SECTION IV
HISTORICAL PARALLELS AND PRESENT PROBLEMS

XI. The Judicial Settlement of International Disputes. By Dr. JAMES BROWN SCOTT, of the Carnegie Endowment for International Peace.

   (1) Arbitration precedes and culminates in Judicial Settlement.

   (2) The Rôle of the Supreme Court of the United States in the settlement of Inter-state Disputes.

   (3) The Permanent Court of International Justice: its origin and nature.

XII. International Government and National Sovereignty. By Professor H. J. LASKI, of the London School of Economics.

XIII. Public Opinion in Relation to War and Peace.

   (1) The Work of Non-official Organizations. By Dr. JAMES BROWN SCOTT, of the Carnegie Endowment for International Peace.

   (2) The Psychology of Patriotism and the aims of the League of Nations Association. By Dr. J. C. MAXWELL GARNETT, Secretary of the League of Nations Union.